Morrison, Apt. 127
W9-AUI-758

Notes on a Life

ALSO BY ELEANOR COPPOLA

Notes on the Making of Apocalypse Now

Nan A. Talese

Doubleday

New York London Toronto Sydney Auckland

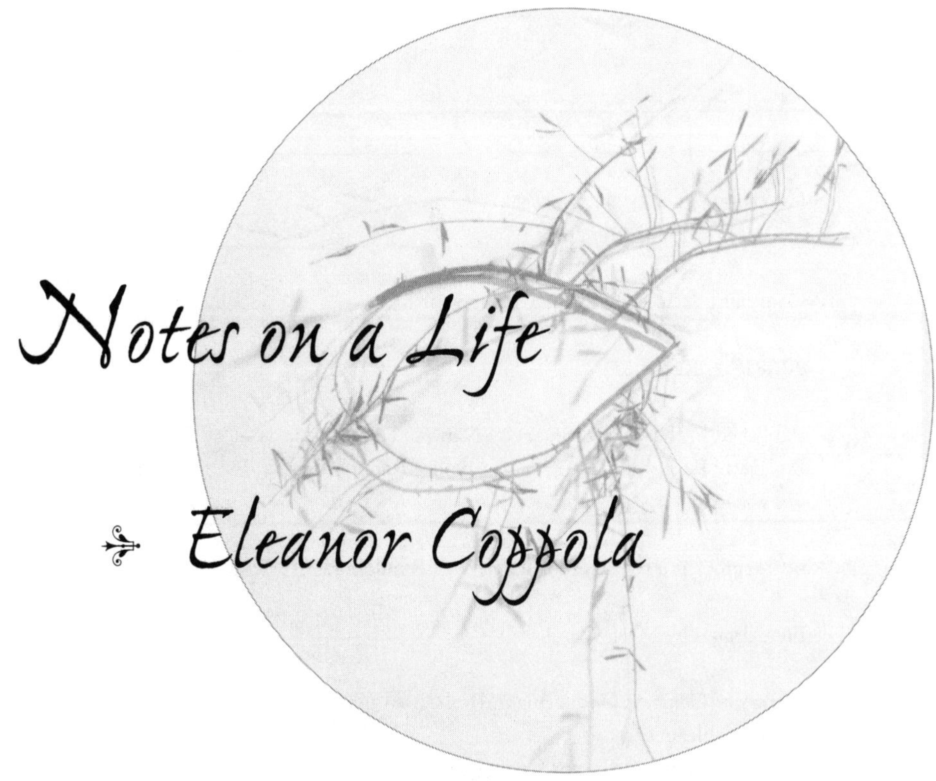

Notes on a Life

Eleanor Coppola

PUBLISHED BY NAN A. TALESE
AN IMPRINT OF DOUBLEDAY

Published in the United States by Nan A. Talese, an imprint of The Doubleday Broadway Publishing Group, a division of Random House, Inc., New York.
www.nanatalese.com

Book design by Maria Carella

Library of Congress Cataloging-in-Publication Data
Coppola, Eleanor.
Notes on a life / Eleanor Coppola. — 1st ed.
p. cm.
1. Coppola, Eleanor. 2. Motion picture producers and directors—United States—Biography. I. Title.
PN1998.3.C6699A3 2007
791.4302'32092—dc22
[B] 2007035628

ISBN 978-0-385-52499-5

PRINTED IN THE UNITED STATES OF AMERICA

10 9 8 7 6 5 4 3 2 1

First Edition

To my family

Notes on a Life

Prologue

I am an observer at heart who has the impulse to record what I see around me, what I experience. I've shot documentary films and videos, but very often what interests me doesn't fit satisfactorily into the frame of a camera or find a way of expression in the artwork I do, so I write. What follows is a selection from my notebooks, both old and recent. In these pages I can see my deep, imponderable love for my husband and our children and the wealth of experiences their extraordinary talents have brought to my life. I also see conflict in my devotion to my remarkable family and a longing to be immersed as a working artist myself. And like every life, mine is formed by the times in which I've lived and by tragedy and triumph.

Perhaps my family members would tell a different story, and maybe they will. I thank them for encouraging me to tell mine.

Part One

May 12, 1986 Washington, D.C.

I am sitting at an old wooden table in this rented apartment in Washington, D.C., our home for Francis's next film, *Gardens of Stone*, a military story involving the honor guard who bury the dead from the Vietnam War in Arlington Cemetery. Francis is doing a final rewrite of the script. Gio is here preparing to shoot video of the rehearsals. During the production they will be working closely together as Gio will be responsible for the video tap to the main camera. He will record what the camera is shooting so that Francis can review the shots immediately rather than wait for film to be developed, and he will be electronically editing sequences. It takes a lot of technical skill. I am reminded of how much Gio has learned from working at Francis's side since the age of sixteen.

On the table top in front of me are note cards with reproductions of Matisse paintings. I am writing thank-you notes for gifts I received on my fiftieth birthday last week. Early this year I began to realize my experiences over the years had stretched me, expanded both my threshold of pain and of exhilaration, pushed me far beyond what I thought were my limits. I felt the family had somehow survived the highs and lows of our lives. The children are well and essentially grown. [Sofia will be fifteen in two days, Roman just turned twenty-one and Gio is twenty-two, soon to be twenty-three.] They are healthy, loving and creative. My fear that our unconventional family life might harm them has begun to fade. I have nearly completed my part in raising them. I see a time of new freedom for me. A time to pick up threads of my creative life left behind at age twenty-six when marriage and family took over my focus.

By the time my birthday actually arrived, I felt happy and excited. Two days before, I had a dinner party upstairs at Chez Panisse surrounded by ten wonderful women friends. Alice Waters made a beautiful feast. I felt skinny and terrific in a black Donna

Karan bodysuit and wrap skirt. Everyone looked radiant. All the gifts had something to do with flowers, a glass basket of miniature wild roses, a vintage flowered dressing gown, a silk scarf with a floral design, a small flowering tree, a photograph of flowers. I felt as if it was a message to me about blossoming. I told the story of visiting a Chinese fortune teller years ago who said, "Your life is like driving a Rolls-Royce over a bumpy road until you are fifty, and reach the pavement." The road ahead looks smooth.

The next day Sofia and I left home in Napa and flew to Washington, D.C., to celebrate with Francis and Gio on location for Francis's thirteenth feature film. Roman arrived from New York City where he is attending New York University. I told Francis what I wanted was to do something I had never done before. On the Sunday morning of my birthday he said, "Get dressed, we're going out to brunch." We drove to the river. I guessed he had made reservations at a restaurant overlooking the water. Instead he led us down a gangway onto a boat. A dozen friends in Washington for the film production were already aboard, along with food, champagne and a band of gypsy violinists. We sailed slowly down the Potomac, stopping for a private tour of Washington's beautiful home, and returned as the river reflected shades of purple and deep orange with the setting sun. I opened the gift from the cast and crew. It was a beautifully faceted Baccarat crystal flower vase. Alex [Tavoularis], from the film's art department, took pictures of our family: Francis in the middle with Sofia and me each tucked under a large arm and Gio and Roman on either side as we sat on the back of the boat, our hair blowing wildly in the wind, smiling happily.

May 13, 1986

Yesterday was Mother's Day. Gio and his girlfriend, Jacqui, invited me for lunch. They finally arrived nearly two hours late, their arms loaded with bouquets. They had driven around Washington looking for flower stores not already depleted by holiday shoppers. They brought nine bouquets. We put them everywhere in the small apartment, arranged in my new crystal vase, in pots, pans and a wastebasket. I felt as if Gio was trying to make up for the hard times he has given me since his teenage years. This past six months he has changed, he is living with Jacqui, is happy and more self-confident and has grown closer to me.

After lunch they took me to the National Gallery and the Smithsonian. I was startled. I brought the children to museums frequently when they were young but when they became teenagers they refused to go. This was the first time a child of mine invited me to a museum. Gio had his camera; he took photos as we walked of Jacqui and me, of street people, of a crowded hot dog stand. I was interested to see what he chose to shoot, how he composed an image, sometimes on the diagonal. His photography skills are developing.

In the evening Jacqui made a salad and Gio barbecued steaks on the tiny terrace of our apartment, trying to keep the thick smoke outside. Francis got home just in time for dinner. We ate in a hurry. I had to catch the last shuttle flight to New York. Gio carried my heavy suitcase out to the waiting taxi. He gave me a lingering hard hug in his distinctive bone-crunching style.

A few hours later I arrived at our apartment in New York City in the Sherry-Netherland hotel, and entered through the side door into the little kitchen. Piles of dirty pans and dishes crowded the stove, the sink and tiny counter; the smell of leftover tomato sauce and garlic overwhelmed the small room. Roman, looking tousled and sweet, gave me a kiss and a hug. As I stepped further into the apartment I could see his clothes in mounds on the floor of the bedroom. He said, "Yeah, I worked out a system, I only have to go to the laundromat once a month." There were guitars, drum pads, tapes, books and art projects strewn over the sitting room. His friend Greg was there. It looked as if they were having perfect college student fun.

I was happy to have seen two of my children on Mother's Day. I opened the doors to the part of the apartment that is usually kept locked and rented by the hotel when we are not using it, where I would be staying. It was clean and spacious. I noticed a smear of tomato sauce on the dining table. The boys confessed they had sneaked in with their dinner.

Today I spent making calls for apartment maintenance; the air conditioner isn't working, the shower ceiling is peeling. I waited for the new bed and headboard to be delivered and installed. There wasn't time to go out. I only took a few minutes to run across the street and look in the windows of Bergdorf Goodman; they often appear as if they are sculptures, well composed with witty elements and good lighting. The mannequins were wearing black cocktail dresses and standing in hundreds of broken white plates. Roman was still at school when I left for the airport. I was sad to miss hugging him goodbye.

Ice crystals are sparkling on the plane's oval window in the late afternoon sunlight. I am flying to San Francisco to be home for Sofia's fifteenth birthday tomorrow. I left some things unfinished in New York but am determined to be at home for her. Last night we talked on the phone. I was trying to complete arrangements for her party. She had changed her mind and wanted to go to a different restaurant after I had asked a friend as a special favor to get reservations at one she'd chosen. I could hardly hear her so I said, "Please speak into the phone, I can't understand what you're saying." She said, "My friends can all understand me. Why are you being so negative?" We began bickering. Finally, exasperated, I said, "I get along with my other kids, their girlfriends, my nephews, other people, the only difficult relationship I have is with you." She began crying. I felt awful. I told her I loved her and looked forward to seeing her.

When we hung up I could feel the emotion in my chest radiating out through my arms. I was furious with myself for being unable to transcend a typical teenage daughter and mother encounter.

I am feeling isolated, here on this airplane in a seat next to the window, no one beside me; the members of the family are in different cities and I'm somewhere in between. I feel the contradictions in myself, an ongoing theme in my life, as I both appreciate the solitude of these few hours and also feel lonely and left out. Francis and Gio are excited about the new film on location in Washington, D.C., Roman is enjoying school in New York City. I am going home alone to take care of Sofia, who at the moment doesn't want to be with me.

May 16, 1986 Napa

In the late afternoon I went for a walk. As the back door slammed a large blue heron rose up from the pond. The baby swans had grown from the size of fuzzy tennis balls to large footballs of feathers. Two beautiful pomegranate trees were in bloom, their leaves an intense chartreuse and the small blossoms vibrant vermilion, colors so garish they seemed unnatural. I walked down the lane with vineyards on either side of me and inhaled the perfume of dry earth and thick leafy vines stretched out in the sun. I picked up trash: an empty Marlboro package lying as if it were an ornament on the freshly plowed dirt, a flattened beer can at the side of the road, several small yellow plastic flags left by the telephone linemen. Along the north side of the vineyard where the furrows were smooth I saw lines of jackrabbit tracks in the dirt with dog prints alongside.

Sofia and I had dinner on the porch, then I took her to a friend's house to stay overnight. With just the two of us here now, she tries to spend as much time as possible at her friends' homes. She said, "It's no fun here anymore."

Francis called: "Thursday is the first day of shooting." He said he'd had good rehearsals with the actors and was expecting everything to go well. I asked him how the Nigerian student I'd hired to clean the apartment was doing. "She's doing OK except when she changed the sheets she put the top sheet on top of the blanket instead of under it. Otherwise the apartment is comfortable and I'm looking forward to you and Sofia coming as soon as school is out."

Since Francis completed *Apocalypse Now*, in 1979, he has made four films on location. *One from the Heart*, *The Outsiders*, *Rumble Fish*, and *Cotton Club*. Over the years I thought by the age of fifty I would surely have resolved basic issues that plagued me as a young woman. Instead I am still groping along looking for solutions. When I go on location I still find myself disoriented away from home and feel the contrast of being simultaneously in Francis's very stimulating creative environment and my own personal dullness as I shop for the mop, frying pan, kitchen towels, firmer pillows, fresh flowers, groceries, wastebaskets, trash bags, laundry detergent, doormats, shampoo, duplicate door keys. I feel cut off from my friends and my creative life. I imagined that at this age I would be wise and able to balance the elements of my life; instead I feel as if my brain is a rusting file cabinet full of useless information: markets, dry cleaners, hardware stores, clothing shops in Los Angeles, Manila, New York, Tulsa, Washington, D.C., and more. In my mind's eye I can see the dry goods store in Ogallala, Nebraska, where we lived during the making of *Rain People;* there I bought our two little boys shorts and tennis shoes. The grocery store had penny candy machines and an old freezer containing Eskimo Pies covered with frost. I often took the boys to a coffee shop where there was a kind waitress who didn't get upset when they made magic potions of catsup, mashed potatoes and peas in their milk glasses.

Roman was three and Gio was four and a half. Some days I drove them to visit Francis while he was shooting. Other days we went to the dime store and got water guns, balloons, or plastic trucks and went to the small park in town. While the children took naps in the hot afternoons I sewed sitting next to the air conditioner in our motel room. Or I read. I was reading *Siddhartha* when the news of Robert Kennedy's assassination came on TV. Tears ran down my cheeks, the book was so beautiful and real life so tragic.

MAY 23, 1986

Roman called from New York. His voice was happy: "School is almost over. I got on the dean's list and am invited to go to London on a summer study program." I think I was more excited than he was. "The air conditioner in the apartment still isn't working. The repair guy says it's not worth fixing." He said he found a notice left by the company that made the headboard for the new bed wanting an additional payment before they would attach the casters. My days are full of the necessary tasks. Today I checked on the progress of the painters in the guest cottage and met with the woman doing the drapery. A workman brought samples of materials to use on a wall that needs repair in Roman's bathroom. The gardener told me that Sofia's small dog has been running into the vineyard with the ranch dogs where she may get hurt and asked me to keep her near the house. He asked where to plant the potted hydrangeas that were left on the porch after Easter.

In the afternoon I drove Sofia's car pool. There were three extra girls who wanted a ride so all seven of us squeezed into our small sedan. The girls gossiped brutally about what different students wore that day. "Did you see her shoes?" "That skirt is her mom's, I know it is." They got out at the market in St. Helena. Sofia stayed in town to visit friends.

I ate an early dinner by myself sitting in a patch of sunlight on the front lawn with my tray in my lap. Sofia came home with Stephanie. I heard them upstairs giggling as Sofia applied a new product tinting Stephanie's long blond hair pinkish-red. I could hear her screech when they used my travel dryer and got her hair caught in the fan. When they came down to the kitchen they decided to make French fries and needed more potatoes. They wanted to go to the little Mexican market across the highway on the motor scooter. It is not legal to drive the scooter on a public street so I made them promise to park it on our side of the highway at the end of the private road and walk from there. I was relieved when they returned. They cooked hot dogs and deep-fried neat little slices of potato.

Francis called. "Tomorrow is the first day Jimmy Caan shoots. He hasn't worked for four years and he's nervous." He said, "Gio is working really hard. There are problems with the equipment in the video van and he is having to be very ingenious to keep it working."

Gio is very conscientious and really wants to do a good job for his father, and at the same time he has been developing a reel of his own work including a montage he shot for *Cotton Club* that was singled out in *Time* magazine's review of the film. Gio was the second unit director for Francis on that film and now he is growing anxious to go out into the world on his own.

Sofia wanted to drive my car the few hundred yards to Francis's bungalow and go in his hot tub. I was apprehensive because she hasn't driven at night alone yet. Francis advised, "Let her do it and call you when she gets there so you know she's not in a ditch somewhere."

She couldn't get the tub to heat so she and Stephanie came back to the house and got sleeping bags and went outside to sleep on the trampoline. Every inch of her wants to break out of an ordinary routine. I love her exuberant imagination and hate being the one who has to contain it.

May 25, 1986

I stayed up late watching videos. When I woke up the sun was streaming in and the phone was ringing. Francis said he has two days off for the Memorial Day holiday and he is going to drive out of Washington, D.C., into the country to try and take his mind off the production. "The first days of shooting went well, we're on time and on budget." But he had gotten a call from the head of the producing company. "They have 'reservations' about my new draft [of the script] and I have to work on it."

While I was reading the Sunday paper on the front porch, Gio called. He asked me for the telephone number of a video technician. He said he was having ongoing difficulties with the equipment and needed to get someone to come to Washington and help him solve the problems. He stayed on the phone visiting with me a long time and then put Jacqui on. It was the first time in many years he didn't just call, ask me for something, and hang up.

The last seven or so years Gio turned away from me, there were periods he hardly spoke to me. During the time it seemed like my marriage was about to end he sided with Francis. I was heartbroken although I realized he was taking the male position on his way to becoming a man. There was nothing I could do except wait for him to grow up and, I hoped, be more understanding. Also, there are aspects of his personality that are more similar to mine, quiet, introspective and nurturing, which are hard for a young man to reconcile with society's macho ideal. When he's home he often gets up late and sits at the kitchen table drinking a beer with his breakfast. He knows I disapprove. I go behind him and rub his shoulders through his blue bathrobe. It feels as if it's the only way I can let him know I love him no matter what. Now, the last six months since he has been with Jacqui, he seems to be letting me back into his life. I've been waiting an excruciatingly long time. When I hung up the phone after our conversation today I could feel my heart beating rhythmically, as if finally relieved of a gnawing pain. It made me feel better about Sofia, reassuring me that when she is older we will enjoy each other's company again.

I spent time in my work room doing research and selecting fabric samples for costumes I've been asked to design for ODC Dance Company in San Francisco, a frisky, innovative dance company that moved west from Oberlin College. I have known the lead dancer, KT Nelson, since she was a teenage babysitter for my young children. Through her I met the artistic director, Brenda Way, who saw some of my work and hired me. It felt good to begin focusing on a project of my own. In the afternoon I went to St. Helena to pick up Sofia at a friend's house. When we got home she spent several hours on the phone with Stephanie. They decided they wanted to go camping. I told Sofia she had to stay home and tend to her homework. She had a school report she hadn't started and a project that was due. She begged and promised she would work tomorrow. I told her she couldn't go, she had just spent two days and two nights with her friends.

I drove to a birthday dinner for a former employee but felt uncomfortable leaving Sofia alone in an unhappy mood so I left the party early. When I got home she was sitting irritably at her typewriter. She asked me again to let her go out. I said, "No." I felt bad about the way the evening ended.

May 26, 1986 [Memorial Day]

Sofia and I ate lunch on the front porch. We could hear rifle shots in the hills. The sounds cracked through the hot afternoon punctuating our sentences. Perhaps the vineyard workers were shooting at targets or hunting coyotes. As the shots increased, I wondered if a revolution had started and in our isolation here against the hills, with no television reception, we were the only ones who didn't know about it. The dogs, their fur full of burrs, were stretched out asleep on the cool boards of the porch. The moment didn't seem dangerous. After lunch Sofia returned to her typewriter. She had written four pages since last night. I read them and was amazed at how articulate and well written they were. "Hey, this writing is good, really good," I said. She seemed pleased with what she had accomplished and her irritation with me had subsided. She wanted to go to San Francisco and shop at the Memorial Day sales. I wanted to take her to do something we could enjoy together, but I didn't feel well. I finally said I was sorry but I couldn't go.

I can't understand why I don't feel well. I've been exercising and eating healthfully.

I have a small octagon-shaped room on the third floor in the turret of our old Victorian house which I have made into a space for solitude away from the busy household below. Our house is a large handsome Queen Anne–style Victorian, built in 1885. In the early seventies we lived in San Francisco and came to the Napa Valley looking for a little country house where our three children could play outside during cold, foggy San Francisco summers. Francis wanted a few acres of grapevines so he could make home wine.

As we looked at properties one day the real estate agent said, "There is a place you should see. It's not for you, not what you're looking for, it's the Niebaum estate and may only be for sale once in our lifetime. It's beautiful! You should see it while it's open." We drove up the driveway and saw the lawns, the elegant house under the branches of a grand old valley oak tree, the swimming pool and gardens set in over one hundred acres of vineyards and surrounded by untouched natural landscape climbing up to a distant ridge line. It looked like a movie set! We were enthralled.

Francis had just gotten a payment for *Godfather* so he made a bid of a sum beyond our wildest dreams, but lost to a consortium of twelve land developers who planned to sell off the house and vineyard and build sixty homes in the hills. Nothing the realtor showed us after that looked appealing. Then a few years later, much of the Napa Valley was zoned agricultural preserve. The land developers were not permitted to build and they wanted to sell. Francis responded aggressively and we bought the property in 1975. Suddenly we were owners of premium vineyards; Francis began to think about making not home wine but very fine wine in the tradition of the world-class premium wines that had historically come from the property. He said, "If you own a great race horse, you have to race it." He hired a winemaker and began developing a winery in an old coach house on the property.

My octagonal room faces into the upper limbs of the old oak tree. There is a built-in wooden window seat forming a wide shelf under the rolled glass windows; on it I keep a selection of things I collect from nature. In the center I lay a textile and make a kind of altar where I create changing arrangements of flowers, candles, photos and objects that have meaning to me.

A few years ago, actually it was very early in the morning of Memorial Day, we were awakened by a loud, horrific sound; the bedroom creaked and shuddered. It sounded as if a bomb had dropped. Gio slept in the room next to Francis's and mine. He cried out in the high voice of a frightened child, "Mommy!" It was disturbing; he had called me "Mom" for years and now his voice, at age eighteen, was deep and resonant.

We went out in the night to investigate. An enormous limb of the giant oak tree in front of our house had fallen, grazing Gio's room, shearing off the corner of the porch, knocking down a fig tree and landing on the driveway, flattening my car which Gio had driven that evening and hadn't put back in the garage.

That afternoon I went up to my third-floor room to meditate, looking for meaning, some kind of sign in the falling of a major branch from our family's giant oak tree when there was no storm, no wind. I felt a wave of fear but couldn't attach any significance to the event. All the members of the family were well. Roman and Sofia were out with friends. Francis was writing in his bungalow. Gio was downstairs watching the Indianapolis 500 car race, I could hear the distinctive high whine of racing engines rising up the staircase. How ridiculous of me to look for an omen in a random occurrence in nature.

May 29, 1986 Washington, D.C.

My mind keeps jumping back to Memorial Day afternoon; I was at home in my little room on the third floor looking out into the branches of the giant old oak tree trying to understand why I felt ill for no reason. The telephone rang. Sofia answered it downstairs and I picked up the extension. We both heard the strange, strangled sound of Francis's voice, as if he were speaking without breathing: "Ellie, we've lost our beloved son. Gio is dead."

My cries lifted me out of my chair. Sofia went to the other line and called Roman, then she came to my room in agony. I pulled her into my arms. She sobbed, "I never heard Roman cry before."

We learned that Gio and a friend were in a speedboat crossing the South River late on Memorial Day afternoon with the sun in their eyes. The friend drove between two boats without seeing that they were joined by a long tow rope submerged in the water. The rope snapped out of the water, broke through a railing and knocked Gio with such force against the back of the boat that he died instantly. The other young man was unscathed.

That night Sofia and I flew to Washington, D.C. The next days are memory fragments. I can see Sofia and Roman crying on the rented sofa in the apartment . . . Francis doubled over on the floor . . . the pain of seeing the family devastated layered on my own grief . . . the meeting I had with the priest to arrange a memorial service. For him it was just another appointment to schedule: "Yes, it can be in the late afternoon but not later than five. I have a dinner engagement at seven" . . . the first evening in the apartment, friends trying to comfort us, the phone ringing . . . looking in the mirror, seeing my face so changed, no longer looking vibrant and excited, younger than fifty, now seeing an unrecognizable old woman, drawn, red-eyed and frail . . . suddenly sinking to the sidewalk in front of the Hyatt hotel, sobbing hysterically, having to be supported by two of Francis's cousins . . . standing in the small side room at Arlington Chapel reserved for family . . . seeing Francis standing in his gray suit next to a bouquet of miniature white roses with a card from Bobby De Niro . . . sitting in the first pew of the chapel filled with family, friends, cast and crew, banks of flowers and afternoon sunlight beautiful enough for a wedding . . . friends speaking about Gio . . . Francis's father's music playing on the organ . . . the priest reading from Kahlil Gibran . . . a personal celebration of Gio's life rather than the packaged service I had feared.

May 30, 1986

Roman, Sofia and I went to the hotel room where Gio was living with Jacqui. She was there. We packed up his things. Sofia put on Gio's white silk jacket, she said, "It smells like him." We found the script he was writing. We told Jacqui she could have anything of Gio's she wanted. She put things in her suitcase, including the black slippers I gave him on his last birthday. I felt conflicted. I wanted to keep those slippers but knew I had to share my twenty-two-year-old son's history with this tall, brown-eyed, twenty-year-old woman with a vibrant smile who was his girlfriend for six months. Jacqui had been waiting on shore where the boys had let her out of the boat only minutes before their accident. When she learned what had happened she wept uncontrollably and confessed she was two months pregnant with Gio's child. A part of Gio continues to live, as if he knew that leaving us would be too unbearable so he left a gift.

JUNE 2, 1986

Yesterday I threw out seven flower arrangements. The apartment still has the faintly dank odor of dead flowers, all that remains from the dozens of arrangements sent to the memorial service for Gio. There were flowers in the crystal vase I got for my birthday and filled on Mother's Day. I am in an unspeakable rage. How could life so utterly and excruciatingly sabotage me, how could Gio abandon me just as we were drawing closer, how could he leave us and shatter our family? How outrageous my every thought is.

In my late forties I did a lot of therapy and personal work attempting to rid myself of old angers, lingering resentments and to forgive those who had caused me pain and forgive myself for my mistakes and the pain I've caused. I felt I was beginning my new decade in a positive, healed way. Now I feel as if I am back to zero, full of anger, heartache and darkness; a point I thought I would never slip to again. I thought I would just get lighter, happier and by the time the losses of old age set in, I'd have the wisdom to meet them. I never expected a knockout blow now.

JUNE 6, 1986

Wednesday Francis started back to work. The producers offered to close down the film but he wanted to continue. The demands of the production would be familiar, the days would be filled with hard work that would prevent the torturous reality of Gio's loss from pervading every moment. Shooting was scheduled for 6:00 p.m. to 6:00 a.m. Sofia and I stayed until after the lunch break at midnight. Francis was out on the set but we spent most of the evening in the video van with Roman. Francis asked Roman to come and take Gio's job. He canceled his study trip to London and came to Washington, D.C. I could see his misery. He lost the person he was perhaps closest to in all the world and he couldn't escape; each day he will be surrounded by reminders of Gio and will witness his parents' and sister's pain.

On the monitors we could see the set as Roman talked over the radio to the crew unreeling cable and positioning the rolling rack of video recording equipment. Gio's pillow was still under the console where he curled up at night during long waits for lighting on the set. Taped to the wall was a printout of a line Francis found in the console computer that Gio had put in when he was sixteen and first learning how to use the equipment: "Art Never Sleeps."

Francis continued for the weeks that followed to direct the film about the honor guards of Arlington Cemetery who bury the young men killed in the war.

Jacqui came to live with us. Ten family members were together on New Year's morning in 1987, when our granddaughter Gia was born.

September 7, 1991 Napa

Francis turned an old barn into a rehearsal stage and is here working with the cast of *Bram Stoker's Dracula*. Fourteen actors and crew members have been staying with us in the house and two guest cottages. My attention has been on details such as dry towels, the constantly ringing phone and dinner preparations. I am surrounded by people coming and going and have begun to feel hungry to be alone, but at the same time I am relishing the creative energy and the entertaining company around me.

In the afternoon I took two baskets and walked into the garden.

I could hear several turtles slide off rocks into the pond as I passed. The scent of roses, damp earth and lavender drifted up from the shady flower beds along the path. I crossed the dirt road into the bright sun and entered the vegetable garden. The zucchini plants were sprawling with gray blotches on their broad leaves but still I found a dozen new squash rising up from their centers. I cut them off and collected the deep yellow blossoms. In the heat I could smell the tomato vines thick and bushy leaning on posts. I picked the reddest ones, half filling both baskets. I added green peppers on top, then went to the greenhouse and gathered red-leaf lettuces, a bouquet of basil, handfuls of arugula and Italian parsley. My baskets were heavy and overflowing; I had to stop several times on my way back to the house to rest or pick up lettuce that had fallen out.

In the kitchen I put the salad greens in the sink and the basil in a vase. I scalded the tomatoes, peeled and chopped them, watching stripes of afternoon light cross vegetables, bowls and knives on the long wooden table where I sat.

As I finished cutting the zucchini into round rings, Patty, our housekeeper, burst into the kitchen with bags of groceries. We set to work pounding veal, slicing mushrooms, chopping parsley, drying the lettuce, roasting peppers. Francis's assistant director called from the stage to say there would be twenty for dinner; too many to fit in the dining room so we set the long table on the side porch. I was filling small vases with bouquets of pink roses and flowering oregano when Francis arrived with the actors and crew. While they took drinks to the front porch or went swimming in the pool Francis began to cook. He thought we hadn't flattened the veal well enough and he pounded it more.

Someone started the jukebox in the dining room; *Tosca* was playing. Francis fried the zucchini blossoms. People came in and out of the kitchen getting drinks from the refrigerator and tasting the hot squash blossoms, roast peppers and olives set out on the table. I could hear Tom Waits talking to his daughter on the phone in the hall about a homework paper she was writing on the topic of friendship. The pasta water began boiling and as Francis put the spaghetti in, I went out on the porch to light candles and invite everyone to come to the table.

I passed pitchers of water from our spring and bottles of wine. As I served our guests—among them Winona Ryder, Keanu Reeves, and Cary Elwes—I was reminded of the first time I had a star for dinner. I was young. Francis was directing *Finian's Rainbow* and had invited his leading lady, Petula Clark. She was at the height of her fame. I was so nervous as I was serving, I knocked a flowerpot off a stand near the table. It scattered dirt and debris over the floor at the heels of my guests. I was frozen with terror not knowing whether to stop serving and clean up, letting the food get cold, or continue serving and step in the mess. I did the latter and still feel perspiration rise on my neck when I think about it. Now as I looked along the table, the movie stars appeared no older than my children and didn't seem terrifying at all.

When I returned to the kitchen Francis ladled pasta into bowls while Patty and I garnished them with leaves of basil. We carried the full trays out to the porch. Francis sat down last at the end of the table and sprinkled his pasta with red pepper flakes. As the last light faded from the garden, Francis and I went back into the kitchen where he cooked the veal and I sautéed zucchini. We brought out platters and passed them family-style.

We all remained at the table in the candlelight sipping grappa and espresso. Polite conversation had fallen away long before. Tony Hopkins and Gary Oldman gave imitations of Richard Burton, Marlon Brando and Jack Nicholson. Explosions of laughter burst across the porch and into the trees, seeming to rustle the leaves in the darkness.

September 17, 1991 Los Angeles

Francis is doing final rehearsals with the actors in Los Angeles. I arrived from Napa last night and rode to work with him early this morning. He showed me a little office he had prepared in a studio apartment across the street from the rehearsal space. It was in an old building with a plaque in the front hall that said, "Built by Rudolph Valentino, Errol Flynn lived here." The carpets in the halls were an unappealing brown shag. The doors to the apartments were new and ordinary with cheap hardware. When we stepped into the apartment I was surprised; it hadn't been remodeled and had original 1920s charm. There were small windowpanes rimmed with vines, nice old tile, a built-in dressing table and roomy cedar closet. Francis had a table set up in the small living room with his writing supplies so he could add ideas into the script and new lines he got from improvisations during the rehearsal. From a file tray he took a new script his assistant had prepared for him with yesterday's notes.

We walked across an alley and into a large courtyard at the side of a church. There was a school attached to the church and the gymnasium had been rented for the rehearsal space. On the lines defining the basketball court, folding tables and chairs, apple boxes and props were set out. Along the side lines were portable clothing racks full of costumes and a table with a hissing coffeemaker, pink cardboard pastry box full of doughnuts, a stack of paper cups and paper napkins laid out in a fan. The actors talked together in clusters under the home team basket. The murmur of conversation echoed in the large hollow room, punctuated by the clack of folding chairs snapping open and a propman's screwdriver falling against a metal table leg.

It was the first time I'd seen the actors since their stay in Napa. They seemed familiar and friendly. Keanu came over and hugged me warmly as if I were a favorite aunt, then he loped back to a place by the table. Maybe it was only a hug for the boss's wife, but I treasured it. The color of his skin and hair, his height, the width of his shoulders, the casual easy way he wears his wrinkled T-shirt and scruffy blue jeans reminds me so much of Gio. Today is Gio's birthday. Suddenly I could see the last moments we were together on Mother's Day 1986, standing on the sidewalk in front of the apartment in Washington, D.C. I could feel our last hug, my right hand touching the thick, dark wavy hair at the back of his neck, my left arm wrapped across his T-shirt against the taut muscles in his thin young man's back.

I realized that while I was thinking about Gio I had unconsciously moved to a chair alone by the costume racks. I thought I was being very calm just reviewing thoughts from the past in my mind when a wave of grief welled up and spread across my chest into my throat and a low animal cry escaped from my lips. My face contorted as I stifled a moan and quickly concealed myself behind a row of hanging overcoats. Finally I regained my composure. I wiped my face on the striped sleeve of a man's shirt and slipped between women's dresses to exit by a side door. Outside, Tom Fox, the video technician, was laying cable and waved a cheery "Hello!" I could feel tears choking my voice and hurried across the street and up into the little office apartment where I could be alone. As I stood weeping by the window, watching the school children in the play yard below, deep wracking sobs rose out of my chest. As my body began to unclench I happened to look at my watch. It was just after 11 a.m., the time of Gio's birth twenty-eight years ago.

The phone rang. It was Francis's sister, Tally. I wondered how she had found me at just that moment. We talked for a long time. Finally my tears subsided. She invited me to come spend the day with her. "I'm OK," I said. "I think I just need to be alone." "Well, let's all get together for dinner and commemorate Gio's birthday. Pick the place and let me know," she said. "I'll ask Roman to decide," I told her. "It'll be a steak house for sure."

In the afternoon I drove to Jacqui and Gia's apartment. I could tell I was feeling better because I began to notice things around me, such as a man strolling along the sidewalk on Hollywood Boulevard wearing only swimming trunks and combat boots.

When Jacqui opened the front door a dank smell curled around me. As Gia ran into my arms, a gray rabbit hopped out from under the dining room table leaving a trail of round black droppings. "We're cleaning its cage right now," Jacqui said. I helped Gia wash the water dish and fold newspaper to fit the bottom of the cage. I told her, "Your daddy loved animals, you know. He had two rabbits when he was a boy, a brown one and a white one."

We sat on the couch and I read *Curious George* to her. She is four and a half and likes the story about a mischievous monkey. When she was tired of reading I told her it was Gio's birthday and the whole family was going to have dinner together. I said, "We'll get a little cake and you can blow out the candle." She thought for a few moments and said, "My daddy would be happy to have his little girl blow out his candle."

October 19, 1991

Last evening Francis and I watched rushes from the first day's shooting of *Dracula* on sound stages in Los Angeles. They were projected on the wall-sized screen in the bedroom. I pushed buttons on the control unit at the end of the snakelike cord until the bed was adjusted into a sitting position. We watched a scene with Lucy and Mina play over and over; the wide angles, the medium shots and close-ups, all the selected takes for one scene. I couldn't keep in mind the subtle differences between takes, couldn't imagine how Francis knew he wanted the editor to use take nine instead of take thirteen. I watched the endless repetition as if it were a strangely fascinating avant-garde film.

I drove to the studio this morning to visit the set. Inside a huge stage at Columbia Studios a grand Victorian mansion had been built. I loved seeing the furnishings, all the rich silks and brocades in a perfect harmony of muted color. Francis took my hand and said, "Come see this." He led me to the bedroom to look at the large round headboard for Lucy's bed with its carved bat designs and thick tassels.

The room opened onto a terrace overlooking the garden. We walked down two flights of wide stone steps to a fountain and a pond with water lilies blooming. Beyond, I could see the entrance to the crypt and a hill with family gravestones. There was a rose arbor and a maze of high hedges. Francis said, "All this garden is built in the pit of the stage where Esther Williams's swimming pool once was." He was called to the first camera position in the great hall. I roamed around, interested in the way real and artificial plants were intermixed. The painted fake stone walls had drifts of real ivy and moss. A greens man was burying the last pots of flowering shrubs next to the pathway.

I went back up to the main house set and was happy to find my friend Eiko Ishioka, the costume designer. She pointed out an arrangement of flowers that she wanted the set dresser to change because the colors of the blossoms were too bright for the subtle scheme of the room. We walked to the bedroom set. She said, "I ask art department to get many collections exotic things. Lucy is rich girl. She would travel around world, bring back many things." The set dressers were arranging collections of small Oriental masks, cut-glass bottles with ornate silver tops, boxes of unusual butterflies, little silk purses, ivory carvings, and hatboxes on the chests, bedside and dressing table. There were boxes of things still wrapped in tissue paper stacked on the floor. I thought about Eiko being so involved with the visual look of the film, concerned about the many details outside her department, her strong opinions and fearlessness in expressing them. She and I have talked about how I am more Japanese in manner, more quiet and shy, and she more assertive and American in ways. She pointed out the fake blossoming wisteria vines hanging over the door to the terrace: "That shade of lavender too strong. Needs to be softened." I hadn't noticed it; she was right.

We walked together to the camera position. Winona Ryder had come onto the set for a rehearsal in her costume; she had a perfect Victorian figure, a tiny wasp waist and full bust. Eiko looked sharply at Winona's dress, then adjusted the fabric falling imperceptibly askew. The dress was made of pale absinthe-green silk taffeta with intricate embroidery on the bodice. The full skirt had hundreds of knife pleats at the waist and a draped bustle with yards of fabric cascading to the floor. It was a work of art.

November 9, 1991

I flew from Napa to Los Angeles and took a taxi to the studio. As I passed by the big open doors of Stage 30 I could see bulldozers pulling down the last of the beautiful mansion set. There was a dark gaping hole where the English garden had been. I found Francis in Stage 23 on the asylum set. We were happy to see each other. As he released me from a lingering hug, I could see the crew rushing between their supply areas and the set, working on last-minute details before the first shot. The cavernous dungeonlike rooms were wonderfully horrifying, with rock walls oozing slimy water. Francis pointed down a deep musty corridor and said, "See that?" Suddenly I realized that the set was quite shallow and the vastness was created by a huge wall of mirror artfully covered in rock at the edges.

Tom Waits stepped out from one of the chambers in his costume. His hair had been shaved up the back in odd little ridges. The front, left long, was sprayed gray and stuck out from his head. His teeth had been stained black and brown and he wore filthy long underwear and a torn, dirty Victorian coat. He had pointed period shoes, unbuttoned, flapping open on his dirty bare feet. Each of his hands was covered with a bizarre cagelike glove made of dark stained leather around his wrist and thin bent metal rods over his fingers with leather caps at the tips. He held a battered tin plate with his asylum food, a moldy crust of bread covered with a squirming mass of maggots, strange orange worms, dead flies, a large potato bug and a selection of beetles. Tom was gently pushing them around the plate saying, "Hey, you, move over."

The bug wrangler was standing nearby. He had several additional tins of maggots and beetles. He occasionally prodded the contents of Tom's plate to make sure they were all moving. He had an assistant with several boxes of candy beetles that were added to the plate so that when Tom picked up something to eat in a scene he could select the candy. Tom was having difficulty picking up anything with his caged fingers. Eiko and the propman were called in. They tried putting honey on Tom's leather fingertips so the candy insects would stick. It didn't work. They tried double-faced sticky tape and then spray adhesive. Tom was very patient as he tried hard to pick up worms from the wiggling mass. Finally the shot setup was complete and they had to shoot. They decided to frame over Tom's shoulder and let the second unit get shots of him actually eating from the plate.

November 11, 1991

Francis got a wake-up call at 5:45 this morning. As he was leaving for the set, he said, "What are you going to do today?" I found myself in the early gray light slipping into a familiar depression. Part of it is being on location in Francis's domain where he goes to work, intensely focused on his project, and I attend to little tasks. I thought of all the things I want to do at home and felt anxious to get back to Napa. Of course I am free to leave Los Angeles, but Francis and the children are here.

In the afternoon I went to the studio and found Francis in the Silverfish [video van] reviewing what he'd shot that morning on one monitor and, on another, watching the progress of the crew on stage setting up a new shot. As we sat in the dim light, his producer Fred came in with a folder of papers and began discussing our financial situation: "It looks as if next year some of these debts can be retired." We still have debts from the millions of dollars in losses incurred during the early '80s when Francis bought Hollywood General Studios and made *One from the Heart.* Both of which turned out to be financial failures. Deep inside I know I hide the fear that if something happened to Francis I would be responsible for those debts with no possible way to repay them.

November 12, 1991

I drove to meet Mary Patton, a friend since college, for breakfast at a new place on La Brea next to a bakery. I haven't lived in L.A. since Francis made *One from the Heart* in 1980. I lost my way.

When I arrived Mary was standing outside the restaurant. As I parked I could hear a scolding voice in my head shouting at me, "Why can't you be on time? Why didn't you start earlier? Your life is so easy compared to Mary's."

Mary looked pretty wearing a jade green silk blouse, her naturally curly blond hair framing her smiling face. Only the crease cutting deeply between her eyebrows hinted at the pain she is enduring. We sat in the atrium in the bright morning light. I ordered toasted walnut bread with goat cheese, curious to try new California cuisine. Mary had hot seven-grain cereal, the healthy kind my mother made me eat as a child when I wished I could have Wheaties.

Mary played the ingénue in Francis's first feature film, *Dementia 13*, where Francis and I met while I was the assistant to his art director. Mary's two boys, Geoffrey and Tyler, played with Gio and Roman on location in Nebraska during the making of *Rain People* in 1968 and in New York City during *The Godfather* in 1971. Now Mary is the script supervisor for Roman, who is shooting the second unit on *Dracula.* She talked about working for him. "Roman is so calm, so intelligent. He's really doing a great job! Everybody on his crew loves working for him." She said things I wanted to hear but as we got up to go, I felt I had failed. I had intended to be a compassionate friend for her, encourage her to speak from her heart while I listened. Her son Geoffrey is dying of AIDS, he has recently taken a downturn. She tries to honor his wish to be independent, she stops by his apartment daily but tries not to hover. Gio died instantly; I did not suffer in advance. I am awestruck by Mary's strength, how she can have breakfast with me, go to work and go on with her life.

In the parking lot Mary said, "I'm on my way to see Roman's rushes." I hadn't seen any of Roman's work so I followed her to the studio. We parked and walked to the main building and down into the underground screening room. The director of photography and the camera operator were already there. We sat down in the plush seats. Roman arrived with his briefcase, his hair mussed from riding his black studio bicycle hurriedly across the lot. He sat down in the row in front of me, leaned over the seat and gave me a quick kiss. The lights were dimmed. I was relieved that no one could see tears suddenly squeezing out of the corners of my eyes. My deepest fear is that something could happen to him.

The first shot came on the screen. It was a series of spiders and beetles crawling over Tom Waits's eyeglasses on the asylum floor. The last shots were of Tom putting the live bugs and worms in his mouth and chewing. One shot ran over and you could see him spitting out a beetle and laughing.

November 14, 1991

Last night Francis and I went to a birthday party for Carrie Fisher and Penny Marshall at Penny's house. Several times during the day I felt waves of dread. Some of my most uncomfortable moments were at Hollywood parties years ago. In the late sixties Francis was the hot new young director in town and invited everywhere. I remember going to parties at famous people's houses and not knowing anyone; finding myself sitting in a chair at three in the morning on Joan Collins's deck, everyone in the pool swimming nude but me. Living in Northern California has been a welcome shield.

The invitation was for 7:30. We arrived well after eight. We were perhaps the third couple to enter the huge front door. I was happy to see Penny just back from six months on location. I like her Italian warmth, she gave me a real hug. She said, "I'm still using the code number Gio put in the lock on my front gate." I had a memory of coming to her house when Gio was dating her daughter, Tracy. ⟦I slipped into the powder room to calm my emotions.⟧

The house began filling with people; I could see Carrie moving through the crowd greeting friends. I met her in the hallway outside the bathroom. I said, "I read *Postcards from the Edge*. You're a really terrific writer!" She fanned her arm in the air, dismissing my compliment. I asked her if this was a special birthday. She said, "It is for me. I'm thirty-five and don't have any children and no prospects." Her voice was pained. I said, "Listen, you have ten good years ahead to find the right man and start your family." I told her, "I was thirty-five when Sofia was born. When I was pregnant with her, people looked at me as if it were rather unseemly for such an old woman to still be having sex."

I was surprised to find a number of people at the party I knew and was glad to see. I talked to Mary Kay Place. We have met occasionally over the years and always liked each other. I asked what she was doing. She said, "I'm completely frustrated because the jobs I'm offered are material I don't care about. I want to do something that sheds light on how we can make the world better." Teri Garr joined us and said, "It's true. The scripts I've been getting are terrible."

A number of people told me they had seen the documentary I shot, *Hearts of Darkness*, about the making of *Apocalypse Now* and complimented me on it. It felt strange to be associated with a film of my own. It was the first time I thought anyone in the film community could see me as a person other than "Francis's wife." Several people spoke to me admiringly about my long marriage. I saw only two other couples who had been together 25 years or more. In the late sixties and early seventies when people I knew were exploring open marriage and getting divorced, I felt I was sometimes regarded with disdain, as if I were boringly old-fashioned and unadventurous. Now some of those second marriages have come and gone and my life's path seems appealing.

At one point I was standing by the pool talking to Francis's agent Rick Nicita. Rick said excitedly, "Ellie, this is an 'A' party. Definitely an 'A' party!" Over his left shoulder I could see Norman Lear, Bud Yorkin and their pretty young wives talking with Dan Aykroyd and Lorne Michaels. Over his right shoulder I could see Glenn Close, Barry Diller and Anjelica Huston in the crowd. I felt as if I had a ticket for a front-row seat at a Hollywood party.

November 17, 1991 Napa

There are three stacks of mail and the message pad is filled. I'm spending the day at my desk; looking up only occasionally through the rolled glass windows to see wavy images of new red leaves on the Japanese maple tree in the garden, watch a jackrabbit hop across the lawn, notice the dry curled fig leaves lying like brown gloves on the gravel driveway.

This evening I am sitting at the kitchen table chopping carrots. I had the urge to make a big pot of soup for the family coming home this weekend, as if that could somehow balance us all. I went outside in the dark with the flashlight and walked to the greenhouse for parsley and basil. In the moonless night I could hear my footsteps in the gravel and smell the fragrant air. The aromas of pine, eucalyptus, and damp earth at the edge of the garden evoked childhood memories of Girl Scout camp. I remembered my excitement at those exotic smells, so different from the salty sea air at the beach where I grew up. I remembered walking with my flashlight to the tent I shared with ten girls. In Bunk No. 9 Benita Ship wet the bed. The acrid smell from her thick sleeping bag and kapok mattress mixed with the smells of pine needles, dusty floor boards, and canvas.

I could see myself outside in the dark starry night standing in a circle focusing my flashlight toward the sky; hear our leader Mrs. Tornquist's quavering voice say, "Now Eleanor, point out Orion's Belt for us," as I try earnestly to qualify for a Star Finder merit badge.

Now as I look up into the deep indigo above me, I can see the Milky Way and the Big Dipper but I can't find Orion's Belt. I imagine Gio racing among the stars in a red Ferrari. And I am suddenly struck with worry that he'll be cold.

November 22, 1991

Yesterday was Thanksgiving. I led family and friends out to the vineyard to pick several basketfuls of tiny wild mustard leaves from the new growth on the ground between the rows of vines. I cooked them for dinner flavored with bacon and onion. I wanted my children to learn there was something edible underfoot they could pick and eat for pleasure and, if need be, for survival. It reminds me of my grandfather who lived to be one hundred years old. As a young man he harvested wild mustard professionally in open fields all over what is now the sprawl of Los Angeles. He taught me to appreciate its slightly bitter taste.

December 9, 1991

It is evening and I am in the kitchen seated at the long butcher block table drinking tea. The tall windows are black and shiny, reflecting the room. In the glass I can see the stove, it appears to be black but it's really dark green. I recently had it lacquered at an auto body shop after a housekeeper scrubbed the outside with oven cleaner and large patches of black enamel peeled off. I actually prefer it dark green. In the window my reflection is overlaid on the stove. Today I got up for the first time after five days in bed with the flu. My hair looks exactly the way I've seen homeless women wear theirs as they sit beside shopping carts filled with plastic bags of belongings. My skin is blotchy without makeup, my shoulders slump in my terry cloth robe.

From my sickbed I watched the light change on the fall foliage outside the window; yellow leaves still hang in thick clusters on the gingko tree, the vineyards are ruffles of rust-red. I thought about how it would feel to be sick in the last century, be a pioneer woman and have to get up and build a fire to keep from freezing to death, to get wood, cook something as simple as hot cereal, boil water, and stir the pot for thirty minutes instead of popping a bowl in the microwave. I imagined what it would be like to be sick on the frontier with a husband away; left alone in a cabin with four children under the age of six. Our housekeeper brought me lunch on a tray.

December 13, 1991

A thick fog had descended on the valley. I couldn't see across the garden; the vineyards disappeared. The air was damp and icy. All day I stayed in the kitchen with the oven door open, warming the room; making the table my office. Francis called in the late morning. He told me about shooting the big scene where Harker meets Dracula. Then he said, "We worked till two this morning. The shooting schedule is going from days into nights. It's already time to go back to work."

In the late afternoon the fog lifted. I drove to the town of St. Helena. I'd been so engaged in the world of my kitchen, driving down the highway suddenly seemed exotic. I found myself interested in the colors of cars, the shapes of trucks and the rhythm of distances between them.

I went to the market. Light pouring from the doors looked so alluring and I was drawn into the aisles of beautifully lit items, freshly sprinkled lettuces, pyramids of oranges, bins of nuts, cases of meats and cheeses laid out as if each package contained jewels, shelves of shiny new magazines. I thought about my trip to Russia, and how it would feel for the women I saw in the suburbs of Moscow to walk into this Safeway.

At the Russian market I visited during my trip two years ago there was a long line outside the door, each person waited for a turn to enter and buy what was available that day. Under four dangling light bulbs attendants served customers from a large wooden bin filled with round loaves of bread. There were several big cheeses on a table and one shelf with cans of Bulgarian green beans. The rest of the shelves and cases were empty.

December 23, 1991

The family is home for the holidays and Francis and I took a walk in the afternoon. It was clear and cold. We walked to the back vineyard. It was the first time we'd been there in several months. Fourteen acres of old vines were pulled out after harvest and the ground was plowed. It changed the landscape dramatically. I missed the rows of dark twisted trunks. Some of the vines were more than sixty years old and no longer produced enough fruit to pay the farming costs. I thought I felt a kind of after-impression of the vineyard being pulled out by the roots as if they were many rows of old teeth. I wondered if the earth could feel it. I thought about becoming an older woman and not producing like a new, young one.

At the north end of the vineyard we walked into the trees. In a clearing we found great clusters of mushrooms growing on the ground near decaying logs. They looked as if they were chanterelles but I was afraid to take a chance. We found ruts of an old dirt road that went up over a hill we had never walked in all the years we've had this property. At the top we sat down panting. Below us were old silvery-gray olive trees with a blanket of brilliant green new grass on the ground beneath them. In the distance rust-colored fall leaves mixed with evergreens on the hills. There hasn't been a winter storm yet and fall colors are lingering longer than I've ever seen them.

We walked downhill into the old olive orchard; the canopy of branches closed over our heads. Francis said, "We need to get these trees pruned. We should be harvesting olives and making our own oil." When we came out of the grove we followed a dry stream bed northwest, then slowly angled up the side of the ravine to walk along the crest of the hill. Francis was some distance ahead of me. For the last six months he had been exercising and now walked too fast for me. I caught up at a fence which appeared to be our property line. We could see a TV satellite dish on the next hill and a stretch of new fence. We hadn't been to that corner of the property since 1975 when we bought the ranch and were driven along the boundaries in a jeep.

Francis wanted to return a different way. I would have been content to retrace our steps. We took his way and climbed down a steep ravine, crossed over a dry stream bed and struggled up the opposite side where we found a narrow deer trail and followed it south. Eventually we arrived at the meadow where the old PBR [river patrol boat] used in *Apocalypse Now* sits deteriorating. It was brought here at the end of shooting in the Philippines. Francis hadn't resolved the story and during his struggle in the editing room he wrote new scenes for Martin Sheen set on the boat as he read the dossier about Colonel Kurtz. The PBR was put in the Napa River and the scenes were shot close on Martin so the local background was out of focus.

We passed the barn where Francis rehearsed *Dracula* and got on the dirt road leading back to the house. When we got home Francis looked at his pedometer and said with satisfaction, "We walked four and a half miles!"

December 28, 1991

After dinner on Christmas Eve we tried to guess what our gifts were. We were making wild guesses but Francis guessed exactly what I was giving him. I had to lie and not show my surprise. I felt sneaky even though it was in fun. It reminded me of times in my life when I have lied to protect something personal. This led my mind to dark thoughts of painful experiences and quickly to my most painful, Gio's accident. Suddenly I felt nauseous, aching with despair, desperate to have him home with Roman and Sofia, Jacqui, Gia, Francis and me, in our warm house together with the little forest of five pine trees cut from our hill sparkling with glass ornaments and, hanging near the bottom, an awkward red felt Santa Gio made as a child. I tried to let the pain wash over me, not deny it, but not drag the rest of the family down with me.

I went upstairs to my octagonal room on the third floor. I took out a colorfully embroidered cloth I got in the Philippines and laid it on the wide window ledge. On the cloth I put photos of the family, four candles, and a little pack of Japanese cards with flower designs that Gio had given me. I sat in the flickering light and let my sobs rise up out of my heart.

December 30, 1991

It has rained hard most of the day and evening; the first real storm. The wind has blown the last of the fall leaves from the trees. Tonight the electricity is off. It feels as if the storm is cleaning the last of the old season away, scouring the garden, the hills and vineyards, making way for the new year.

JANUARY 3, 1992

Last evening we had dinner together in San Francisco, then Francis stayed to work with the *Dracula* editors and I drove to Napa with Roman. As I left Francis said, "Women choose their children before their husbands." It was more of an observation than an indictment but its truth made me wince.

I liked driving enveloped in the dense blackness of country roads at night. Roman and I talked about the exhibit of early Russian stage set and costume designs we had seen in the afternoon. He told me about a tradition of Russian circus performers who wore costumes that were rigged to change dramatically. "For instance, a man would pass behind a tree trunk on stage and emerge in women's clothes," he said. I realized I was treasuring each moment with Roman with an intensity brought by Gio's loss.

This afternoon we went for a walk. I wanted Roman to get out of the house, see the changes in the property and grow to know what would one day be his. As we walked along the dirt road he stepped into the vineyard and picked baby wild mustard leaves to nibble. I led him to the back vineyard where the old vines had been pulled. The earth had been freshly plowed. It was the color of ground coffee and fragrant. At the end of the vineyard I showed him the old overgrown road Francis and I had discovered. He went up the steep incline effortlessly. I fell behind, my heart pounding. We walked down rapidly into the olive grove. Roman said, "Mom, we should get these trees pruned and harvest next year's crop." Francis and Roman both saw the old orchard as a new project. I was content just to walk under its tall leafy canopy.

We went over the next hill and followed the tractor road down past the storage building. Roman's old VW van was parked alongside it. He looked in the dusty windows. During the year after Gio's death he drove the van across the country alone. I felt it was an attempt to exorcise his pain. The following year he formed a band with three friends and crossed the U.S. and back again in that van. They played a rigorous schedule of dates at little clubs along the way. I remember getting a call from a pay phone with loud highway noise in the background. "Mom, the van broke down and we're waiting for a part to fix it. We're someplace outside of New Orleans. The four of us are staying in a motel room for $30 a night. Don't worry."

JANUARY 5, 1992

Francis and Roman flew south today; they return to the *Dracula* set tomorrow and begin the last four weeks of shooting. Sofia registers for classes in Los Angeles and begins the new semester this week. She is excited and happy about art school. I am here on this beautiful estate, but my work is not inspiring to me. I began the day with a meeting about the gardens and roads, followed by a meeting to deal with some petty theft that has occurred on the property. In the afternoon I attended a meeting at the winery, followed by a meeting with a builder to review plans for remodeling our wine cellar.

JANUARY 6, 1992

Francis called in the afternoon and again this evening. He talked about how photography is the grammar of filmmaking: "The photographer is always trying to stick to the rules. I want to break the rules." He said, "The photographer and the director are where reality and fantasy meet." He talked about making a small film next where he could be his own photographer. He said when he is making a big film he can't go through his creative process, take time to confront the unknown until he comes up with a creative solution. "A big budget, big picture doesn't allow for a moment of indecisiveness."

JANUARY 10, 1992 LOS ANGELES

In San Francisco this morning I did two interviews for *Hearts of Darkness*. It has shown numerous times on television and is soon going to be released in theaters.

Afterwards I flew to Los Angeles and drove straight to the studio. I found Francis coming out of the production office and walked with him to the sound stage. The stage was gigantic and contained a huge set of a winter scene in the Carpathian Mountains. There was a curving country road winding into the mountains complete with full-size trees and gray sky. Freshly fallen fake snow covered the set. Two real blackbirds flew in the huge stage doors and scurried across the road. The extensive lighting made the winter scene incongruously warm. The cavernous sound stage was silent; the crew was on a lunch break. As I looked up I could see where the set ended suddenly near the ceiling as if it were a high-water line; beyond there was plywood, scaffolding with catwalks, rigging and theatrical lights. I loved seeing where the illusion of the set met reality. In life the line is so blurred. Outside the stage four horses pawed the asphalt street and Count Dracula's coach waited nearby. Francis said, "I've got the backbone of the film done. Now I want to go for the creative stuff."

We walked over to the stage where Roman was. It was dark and we stepped over cables and maneuvered awkwardly to where he was working on an effect. He was shooting a scrim, focusing on the words of a letter written on the scrim and then fading the light up on a person behind so the words appeared to disappear. As we hugged, I could feel a patch of scratchy new beard on his chin and tension in his body. The art department, which had put the words on the scrim, had made an error. In the script the last word in the sentence was "dreams" and on the scrim it said "memories." He had to decide if he should go to the expense of stopping the shot and correcting it, or keep shooting. I felt a powerful force in my body as if my cells had been programmed: "Help your son solve his problem." I left the stage as quickly as I could.

I walked back across the lot and into the wardrobe department to give a New Year's hug to Eiko. She looked pale and exhausted. She has worked obsessively to realize her unique vision of the costumes; working in a foreign country on her first big film. One of the young actresses doesn't understand Eiko's work and resists wearing the costumes; insists on changes that torture Eiko. She said, "When I finish best dress, perfect for her, she say, 'No, Eiko, I don't think I look good in that color.' "

I found Francis again to say goodbye. I was already late leaving for the house to change into evening clothes for the ACE Awards (for excellence in television programming; *Hearts of Darkness* was nominated). I wasn't quite ready when the limousine arrived to pick me up. When I reached the Universal Hilton ballroom I was among the last people to be seated. There were fifty-six awards to be given out before dinner. I felt detached, having attended so many events with Francis when he was up for an award. I had learned to maintain a kind of emotional neutrality, so win or lose he knew it wasn't the award that was important to me but his creative vision. As a child I was told stories of famous artists who received no acknowledgment during their lifetime and who only became well known after their death. Also it was hard for me to feel excited about this award because although I did shoot the sixty hours of film that was the source of the documentary, it was sixteen years before and my life had moved on. It felt a bit as if something I'd done in college was suddenly noteworthy.

The ceremony began and *Hearts of Darkness* won one of the first awards. I went to the podium with the producers and writer/editors, five men. The award was given to me to hold. It was the shape of a silver ace of spades standing on a black base. It looked as if it were a prize for a Las Vegas blackjack tournament.

Doug [[Claybourne, the producer]] made a short speech expressing our gratitude and we were whisked off stage into a lobby area where the award was taken from me. I learned it was a dummy and recycled back into the auditorium for another winner. We were directed to a checkout booth to sign up for the real award to be engraved and sent later, one for each of us. We stayed out in the lobby drinking mineral water at the bar and talking until we felt obliged to go back into the ballroom. We sat through awards given for categories such as best "Game Show Special or Series," "Recreation and Leisure Special or Series," "Short-Form Programming Special," "Educational or Instructional Special." When the final award was given a huge cheer went up from the audience because dinner would be served. I went to the phone and called Francis. He was out on the set so someone was sent to tell him I won. After dinner our group piled into the limo. The driver was irritable when I asked him to take us to the movies. I caught myself as I started to apologize. We drove to the Universal theaters. It had been a long time since I'd been out with five men on a Friday night.

JANUARY 14, 1992

Yesterday morning I went to Gia's school. It was her day to celebrate her birthday and bring her family. She was seated in front of the children with me on one side and Jacqui and Roman on the other. She had a little bulletin board with family pictures which she talked about. Then it was the children's turn to ask her questions. They asked her favorite color, "pink and gold"; her favorite place, "McDonald's"; her favorite dinosaur, "brontosaurus." I wondered what the children said to Gia about not having a father.

In the evening there was a screening of *Hearts of Darkness* for the press at the Village Theater in Westwood. When I arrived, four TV news teams rushed forward and did brief interviews with me, Martin Sheen and the producers. There were press photographers and autograph hunters. I could see Janet Sheen standing to the side where I usually am. It felt strange to be thrust in front of the cameras for something I'd done. We didn't go in to the screening. The cast and crew had already seen the film so we stayed in the lobby and visited. I was glad to see Janet. I have always admired her. She seems to be a happily devoted wife and mother of four and although she is artistic herself and paints, she doesn't seem to be frustrated or diminished by devoting herself to her family, whereas I have an ongoing internal war, a conflict between wanting to be a good wife and mother and also to draw, paint, design, write and shoot videos. I focus on the family and imagine there will be time for my interests but there rarely is.

I was especially happy to see two of my favorite special effects men whom I hadn't seen since the Philippines. We talked of the nights we'd spent together huddled in huts in the rain waiting for the signal that the security guards had swept the surrounding jungle and everyone was safely in place so they could set off the big explosions. "There will never be anything like that again."

As people came out of the theater when the film ended, they were overwhelmingly complimentary. I was surprised at how awkward I felt. I knew so well how to be the silent, gracious bystander when Francis received attention but I didn't feel at ease responding myself. And what can one say? I wasn't able to think of anything that didn't sound like a cliché. I hadn't tried to make a major documentary. I simply tried to record, as best I could, Francis's creative process while he made his film. Fortunately I was able to hand-hold the camera steady and I have a good eye.

My experience of shooting brought back memories of the time I fell in love with Francis when he was making his first feature film. I was a free-lance designer and had gotten a job on the production as the assistant to his art director on *Dementia 13*. In my naïve and romantic young mind I imagined Francis would continue to make small independent films and I would work with him. Instead we soon had a family and Francis's productions grew large and he worked with experienced professionals beyond my skill level. My ambitions to be a working artist fell by the wayside. On *Apocalypse Now*, even with typhoons and monumental difficulties, it was oddly one of the best location experiences of my life, because I too was working on set.

When I got back to the bungalow around midnight, Francis wasn't home yet. I called the Silverfish. Tom answered and said, "He's out on the set in a big complicated shot with a lot of horses and snow. He probably won't be home for a couple of hours." I sank down on the sofa feeling sad that he hadn't been able to be with me for the evening to see work I had done being so well received.

JANUARY 15, 1992

I dashed to the airport from the set to catch the last flight of the evening from Los Angeles to San Francisco. I had flakes of fake snow still stuck in my hair and in the cuffs of my sleeves; bits were clinging to my black jacket as if it were oversized dandruff. I could feel scratchy pieces down the back of my neck. I shook out my jacket at the airport curb and brushed myself off as well as I could, but when I boarded the plane the stewardess said, "Looks like you've been to quite a wedding party."

An hour ago I was in a snowstorm on the huge stage where Francis was working. I was riding a camera truck with him which went fast forward and then backward fast in the center of the stage while a team of six horses pulling Dracula's carriage, gypsy horsemen and the principal actors on horseback gave thunderous chase along an oval track around the cameras. Through the cameras they appeared to be traveling over a long snowy road in a wintry forest at sunset with the Carpathian Mountains in the distance. The air was thick with dust from the dirt road, fake snow particles and machine-made smoke. A production assistant gave me a painter's mask. The crew were all wearing them over their noses and mouths and lifting them up to talk. The first AD, the director of photography and Francis, who had to give frequent directions, wore their masks dangling limply around their necks or not at all. It took about thirty minutes between each take to set up the shot.

When everything was ready the smoke machines began laying in the fog effect; when that was thick enough the snow would start to fall. Two big fans on top of scaffolding towers blew thin chips of plastic snow over the camera truck and into the scene. The cameras rolled, "Action!" was called and the horse-drawn carriage and horsemen would race around the track shooting at each other. On the second turn, one of the stunt men would be shot and fall from his horse over an embankment and land on pads. When Francis called, "Cut!" the camera truck rolled back to the starting position with all of us brushing fake snow off ourselves. Francis, the photographer, the AD and the stunt coordinator crowded around the video monitors on the truck and watched the footage from each of the three cameras to evaluate what they'd gotten.

Roman was called from his shoot on another stage to come set up a camera in position close to the pads and shoot a close-up of the stunt rider falling. Huge panels of lights made the stage very warm. Between shots the actors were helped out of their heavy winter coats and gloves, and the sweaty horses were taken outside into the night air. I stayed for three takes then raced to the airport.

Now as I lean back in my seat on the plane, I have the familiar heavy feeling like a sandbag is sitting on my chest. I am leaving Francis and the children in L.A. and already miss them. At the same time my toes are twitching in my shoes, anxious to be walking in the garden at home; my fingers tingle in anticipation of holding pencils again and working on some unfinished drawings in my room.

NOVEMBER 17, 1992

Bram Stoker's Dracula was released in the U.S. on November 13th. Francis didn't want to be at home caught up in tension, waiting for news about what the film grossed on its opening weekend. To get far away we traveled to Antigua in Guatemala and stayed with John Heaton, an expat friend who has an extraordinary house decorated with fine antiques and textiles from the region. Francis thought we would have relaxed days out of touch with U.S. news but he discovered John had CNN and of course a telephone. So we drove further to the town of Panajachel and stayed in a little cottage overlooking Lake Atitlán with no phone and no television. On the Monday after *Dracula*'s opening weekend Francis couldn't contain his excitement and curiosity any longer and sent me down to the little town to call his producer Fred Fuchs. The only place to make an international call was at the office of the telephone company. I entered and was directed into a booth. An operator connected me and when Fred came on the line his voice was very excited. He told me the number of millions the film took in at the box office during the three opening days. I was thrilled! On my way back I decided to tease Francis. I wrote down a series of numbers on little scraps of paper. When I got to the cottage Francis was anxious; he was excited and scared and said, "OK, tell me." I gave him a little folded piece of paper with the number 17 written on it. He opened it, "It made 17?" I could see him reconciling himself to the news. It was OK but not really great. I gave him another paper. He opened it. "Four. What does that mean?" I said, "Add it up." "You mean it made 21?" He looked brighter. I gave him another scrap of paper and another until the last one and he said in total excitement, "It made 34 million?" "It did!" We both knew this meant the film would pay off all our debts and earn even more.

In 1992 the opening weekend was huge. *Bram Stoker's Dracula* became the ninth-biggest box office grossing film in history at that time. When the profits were distributed we paid all our debts which had been hanging over our heads since 1981; then Francis said, "Ellie, I'm putting any additional money in T-bills and very conservative investments so we won't ever have to worry about our finances again." In 1995 the property adjacent to ours, which had originally been joined with our estate, came on the market. It had a beautiful historic château built in 1880 that was the home of award-winning Inglenook wines plus 90 acres of fine vineyards. Francis said, "I know what I told you, Ellie, but we can't pass this up." The property was purchased with our savings and our winery began its growth from a small endeavor in an old coach house next to our home to a major Napa Valley wine estate.

Part Two

April 4, 2002 Napa

In late February of 2000 I was alone in the house. Early one morning I was awakened by a thunderous cracking sound and felt the house shaking violently. I thought it was an earthquake. The big one. I leapt out of bed intending to hurry and stand in a doorway. When I was fully upright, the noise and shaking suddenly stopped. It was strangely silent. I noticed the room was darker than usual, then I saw the windows covered with leaves and realized a branch of the giant valley oak tree in front of our house must have fallen. I grabbed my robe and put it on as I ran downstairs. The entry hall was dim; more foliage screened out the light. I hurried to the back door and out onto the porch. A worker was running in from the vineyard, his brown face ashen gray with fear. He had come to carry out the dead lady—then he saw me and his body slumped like rubber in relief. I walked around to the front lawn. It wasn't a branch; the whole giant oak tree had fallen on the house. Huge limbs had gone through the roof of the third floor into the room above my bedroom and through the walls of the bedroom next to mine. Branches surrounded my room so closely they had broken the screens but miraculously not the antique rolled glass windows. Upended roots appeared to claw the air and enormous branches looked as if they were grasping the house. It seemed unreal, as if it were a set for a horror film. I expected to see Roger Corman dash across the lawn pleased with the look of it, complimenting his art department, anxious to get the first shot.

I felt giddy, I was alive! My legs were trembling; I sank down onto the wet lawn. Just days before the house had been full of family and friends, every room occupied. I called Francis in Reno where he was on a retreat working on a script. (He likes to go there where he can stay up all night, be able to order 24-hour room service, go down to the casino and see people, activity, any time of the day or night.) The phone rang a long time, he answered it groggily. He was heartsick at the news and hugely relieved that no one was hurt. I called the children. It was as if we had lost a treasured member of the family. All of us had swung on the old swing that hung from a huge low branch, had Easter, harvest and birthday parties in its shade. Each year we watched the seasons change on the tree. We saw the leaves fall and the gardeners rake them up for days, we enjoyed winter sun through bare branches, admired the thick green moss that grew on its north side, saw buds form and tender pale leaves appear that grew into dark leathery summer shade.

In February 2000, it had rained an unusual 22 days. The tree was very heavy and apparently older and weaker than we knew. The rain-soaked earth suddenly sank on the side next to the house and the tree fell over. We had the rings counted. It was 308 years in age. Our house was built in its shade in 1885. We have lived in it since 1977, when we returned from the Philippines after Francis made *Apocalypse Now*.

While the restoration of the exterior was being completed Francis and I stayed in the house, sometimes doubting our wisdom as the pounding and sawing began each morning promptly at seven and the workmen talked about what they'd done the night before as they repaired the roof outside our bedroom window. Now we are moving out so they can do an extensive renovation of the interior; creating new bathrooms and closets from several small bedrooms, updating the plumbing, electric and heating systems. We are going to install a handsome elevator to access a redesigned wine cellar in the basement and two new guest rooms on the third floor. I have begun sorting, discarding and packing all the things that the family accumulated over twenty-five years. Everything must be taken out of the house. During construction Francis and I will stay temporarily in a small caretaker's apartment a few hundred yards away.

APRIL 8, 2002

Today I am in the dining room with cardboard boxes open on the floor, tissue paper and a tape dispenser on the table, to pack up the drawers of the handsome built-in buffet adorned with clusters of grapes carved into its decorative surround. The drawers have burled oak fronts and are filled with table linens.

The first drawer contains stacks of cotton napkins and place mats, each with embroidery or appliqué. I bought them in Hong Kong on trips from the Philippines during the making of *Apocalypse Now*. In the next drawer is a 144" long tablecloth of exquisite snow-white linen with a pattern of finely embroidered dots, a gift from the French actress Carole Bouquet, given to us after she and her family stayed in our guest cottage. It is breathtakingly beautiful; I would never have had the courage to buy it myself. We use it for Thanksgiving dinner. There are sixteen matching napkins. The drawer below has two stacks of cotton print cloths from the '40s collected at swap meets by myself and friends. I'm drawn to the designs of the period featuring images such as cactus, cherries, fruit baskets and morning glories. We use them on the table in the kitchen or for casual lunches on the porch.

In the bottom drawer there is a large hand-crocheted lace tablecloth. Each tiny, even ivory looping stitch is perfect. It was made by my high school girlfriend Donna's mother as the booby prize for the last one of our group to get married. When I was twenty-three, all my friends were married; I was the "old maid" and the tablecloth was given to me.

In college my mother had urged me to major in elementary education and get a teaching credential, "Just in case you don't marry and have to support yourself." I worried her by graduating with a degree in art, then surprised her by becoming a free-lance designer, supporting myself and traveling the world with no husband in sight. It was on one of my adventures that I traveled to Ireland to work as assistant to the art director on a low-budget film, where I met Francis. Our romance began. The next year we married. I was twenty-six years old; there were major sighs of relief from my family and friends.

I grew up in a small town and was a teenager during the 1950s. My generation was taught that getting married and having a family was a woman's goal in life. The only working women I met were unmarried schoolteachers or nurses, and both were considered slightly unfortunate. When I married and had children I expected to automatically be happy. When I wasn't, I couldn't understand why. Over the years I went to highly regarded psychiatrists and psychologists (three men and one woman) and asked what was wrong with me. I had it all, a loving and successful husband, a big house, healthy children. I was mystified by my depression. Not one of them said, "You're a creative person, you need to pursue your creative life or you'll feel depressed."

Sofia's generation is so different. She and her women friends understand that marriage and family can be parts of a fulfilling life but they also have career aspirations. It mystifies me how I could have been so culturally brainwashed, so unaware. I am horrified. I suffered and vented my frustration on Francis and our children. Francis couldn't help me. He worked hard to excel in his field and provide well for his family. He couldn't understand why I wasn't totally happy caring for our beautiful home and being a good wife and mother. Recently I wrote down my regrets in extensive detail. I rewrote them over several days and then carefully burned the pages, hoping to release their grip, hoping to forgive myself and forgive those who lacked understanding around me. I think it helped.

APRIL 16, 2002

The maintenance men are moving out the dark polished wood secretary standing in the little living room. In 1977 it was shipped to us from the Philippines after *Apocalypse Now* in a container of furniture from the French plantation set. The upper section has shelves behind glass doors, where videocassettes were lined up until they were slowly replaced by DVDs. There were small partitioned spaces for stationery which we filled with decks of cards, score pads and dice in a leather shaker. The drawers below once contained children's toys but in recent years were filled with poker chips, Monopoly, Risk, and a green felt cover I had sewn for the game table. When the moving men removed the bottom drawer there was a small yellow plastic taxicab lying on its side on the floor.

NOVEMBER 9, 2000

The morning after the presidential election, the taxi taking me to the airport arrived at 6:15 a.m. It was a small van, the type that accommodates a wheelchair. The driver placed my bags in the front and the wide middle seats. (I had a lot of luggage, including a case of sound equipment and a camera case, as I was on my way to Luxembourg to shoot a documentary of Roman making his first feature film.) The smell of cigarettes rose from the driver's jacket. His dark hair was rumpled and he needed a shave. He told me to sit in the far back. "It's more comfortable back there, trust me." As he buckled his seat belt he shouted, "It's not over! They're going to do a recount in Florida." I was startled; the last thing I'd heard on TV as I went to sleep the night before was that Bush had won the presidency. "All those heads of state from around the world sent Bush congratulations," he said loudly. "But it's not over! And the recount can be a chance to stuff the ballot box."

Listening to the way he rolled r's on his tongue, I asked him where he was from. "El Salvador. You know what they do down there? When the ruling party doesn't win, they demand a recount. They do it over and over, maybe ten times. In each recount the government in power gets more votes until they win. Until recently, there was a lot of ballot box stuffing down there. Believe me, it could happen here.

"Do you watch a TV program called *That '70s Show*?" I say no. "I watch it to see a really pretty girl that's on the show. So one day I get a call for a pickup at a bed-and-breakfast in the Haight. It's two girls and one's the one on the show. They get in and right away start making out, and I mean really passionately. Then she says to me, 'Do you know who I am?' I say, 'Yeah, I see you on TV. I always watch you. I have the hots for you.' She just giggled. I don't know if she really is a lesbian. You know, Hollywood people try things."

"The other day, I stopped for a guy in the Castro. He gets in and says, 'Just drive around, anywhere.' Then he takes out a fifty-dollar bill and says he'll give it to me if I'll drive him around for two hours in the trunk. I take the fifty and say, 'OK, but only for thirty minutes.' So I stop the cab, open the trunk and he climbs in. I drive around and in exactly thirty minutes I come back to the place where I picked him up. I stop at the curb, open the trunk and he gets out, looking very happy."

I worried that his next story might be too much for me, and was relieved to arrive at the airport curb and jump out. He lifted my luggage onto a cart and I pushed it hurriedly inside the terminal.

I waited a long time at the counter while a frustrated, apparently new employee consulted numerous times with the next agent over how to go through the maze of procedures on his computer to issue me a frequent-flier-award round-trip ticket to Luxembourg with stops in Chicago and Zurich. His voice burned with irritation. I was sorry to cause him grief so early in the morning. I glanced down the counter to another station that had already checked in five passengers while I waited. The agent there smiled at me and when he was free he came over. "I've seen you before. Aren't you with Niebaum-Coppola winery?" I nodded. He said, "I thought so. Beautiful winery, by the way. I saw you there one day with Penny Marshall. You must be with Special Guest Services. I saw you here too at the counter once when Mr. Coppola checked in." He grinned and hurried back to his station. My agent smiled, finalized my ticket with a flourish and, taking my extra baggage without charging me, he said, "It's been a great pleasure serving you."

Now on the flight to Zurich out the window I see a thin line of horizon equally dividing the deep blue of the night sky and the black earth below. Pinpricks of light form a complex spider web pattern on the velvet black ground. The pilot is speaking. "Good morning, everyone. I hope you've had a comfortable flight so far. On your lefthand side you can see the lights of Paris . . ."

Yesterday when I boarded the flight there was already a man in the seat next to mine; he had on earphones plugged into a CD player. He was in his forties, wearing blue jeans and a black and gray plaid sweater. When dinner was served he unplugged. It feels awkward to me to dine so intimately, occasionally touching elbows, but not speaking. Finally I said, "Are you traveling for business or pleasure?" He smiled and said, "Pleasure, I wish . . . no, it's for business, but I will have a free weekend. Maybe I'll go to Berlin or Milan." Silence. "May I ask what business you are in?" "Yeah, tires. The company I work for supplies the material to retread tires." "How interesting," I say, thinking of groves of exotic rubber trees. "I imagine you travel to rubber plantations in Africa." He laughs. "Only about 5 percent of a tire these days is natural rubber; the rest is synthetic, it wears much better. Our business is retreading truck tires." He continues, "The tire lasts much longer than the tread. There's no profit margin in retreads for cars in the U.S. where you can buy a new tire for $80. But trucks are another story. Our company provides materials in the U.S. and Europe. Of course in Asia and Africa they can still turn a profit retreading car tires."

I became curious about how long it would take him to say something or make an inquiry that would lead to a dialogue. Men who don't view you as a potential sexual partner frequently don't check to see who else you are.

He continued, "I live about sixty miles south of Chicago. I have two daughters, seven and thirteen, who go to Catholic school. It's convenient because my wife works at the school in the area of fundraising." The flight attendant removed our dinner trays. He leaned back and put on his earphones.

APRIL 24, 2002

Into the give-away box I place a dusty pair of too narrow black patent leather loafer-style shoes that look good but are not comfortable. They were expensive; the salesman at Bergdorf Goodman told me they would "stretch to perfection." They didn't. It is very hard for me to discard something that is not worn out. I am deeply conditioned by the thrifty values of my childhood. I was taught to save rubber bands, iron used Christmas papers and ribbons for wrappings the next year, open used envelopes and write grocery lists on the clean paper inside. My life turned out so startlingly dissimilar, with completely different rules for survival. I remember the last time I wore these shoes.

MAY 15, 1998 LOS ANGELES

I am outside having brunch in the courtyard of the Polo Lounge at the Beverly Hills Hotel. My feet hurt in my too tight patent leather loafers. I'm sorry I wore them. Francis and Sofia are seated across from me talking intently. I am looking at the light falling on the centerpiece bouquet of miniature orchids and their pattern of shadow on the white tablecloth. I can smell star jasmine climbing the columns supporting the mushroom-shaped roof over our heads. I hear the clinking of silverware on china plates punctuating the murmur of conversations woven together around me.

Yesterday was Sofia's birthday. She turned twenty-seven. She is beautiful in an imperfect way. The bump on her nose is prominent in the light falling on her face. Her brows are pinched together as she concentrates on what Francis is telling her and writes notes in the red leather agenda he gave her for Christmas. She is going to direct her first feature film starting next month. It is a low-budget production with a script Sofia wrote from a book called *The Virgin Suicides*. I can hear Francis say, "Sit right next to the camera so the actors see you; see you're in control. Remember the actors' hands are almost as important as their faces. Hands are very expressive. If you cut hands out of the frame you're losing 30 percent of the performance." I am very happy for Sofia, happy that Francis is being such a good father and mentoring her, but I also feel a hot, aching jealousy in my chest. I'm trying to just notice my emotions, the way I was instructed in Zen meditation, to neither wallow in them nor push them aside. My father died when I was ten. I felt handicapped as I made my way into the adult world without his support and guidance. My mother gave me good values but she couldn't help me in the outside world. She didn't go beyond her home. Her sisters-in-law were all excellent homemakers, good cooks and seamstresses, made jams, casseroles and curtains. My mother wasn't interested. She was considered eccentric and fought depression. She wanted to be a librarian and spend her days with books but work wasn't an option in her marriage, in her day. She read a lot and neglected her housework. My teenage rebellion consisted of baking perfect lemon meringue pies, sewing all night and working two summer jobs; things my mother didn't do. As a young adult I longed for my father. He had gone to art school in France, worked in Mexico and been a political cartoonist for the *Los Angeles Examiner*. I felt terrified as I dropped out of college for a year, traveled in Europe and changed my major to art. I imagined my father would have encouraged and mentored me.

Francis and I married quickly in Las Vegas. I hadn't met Francis's parents. When I did I learned he was from generations of Italian men who believed a woman's life work was caring for home and children and supporting her husband's career. Francis knew I had artistic aspirations but expected they could be pursued at home in my spare time. By the early seventies we lived in a big house with our three young children. I was no longer interested in making lemon pies; my thoughts were about conceptual art and pushing the boundaries of what sculpture could be. In Roman's nursery school car pool, I discovered another mother was artist Lynn Hershman. She thought my ideas were interesting. We had intoxicating conversations and created several conceptual art events together. One of our more infamous was held in 1975 in our twenty-two-room Victorian house in San Francisco. Fifty board members from the Los Angeles County and the San Francisco Museums of Modern Art came.

When they arrived, Lynn and I were out of sight, downstairs in the screening room with a closed-circuit television connection to the living room. We spoke to our visitors over a large monitor. They could converse with us but only interact with our electronic images. We invited them to take a self-guided tour of rooms in the house where we had placed exhibits. I knew the audience wasn't as interested in our art as they were in coming to Francis Ford Coppola's house where it was known he kept his five Oscars. In those days when a man won an Oscar, a miniature Oscar was given to his wife to wear on a chain around her neck. I had a jeweler file off the little loop for the chain at the top of the head of my five tiny Oscars, then removed Francis's from the lighted glass case where they were always kept and displayed my miniature gold statues in their place.

In an upstairs bedroom Lynn exhibited Margo St. James, the

president of an organization attempting to unionize prostitutes, COYOTE (call off your old tired ethics). I paid Roman and Sofia to stay in Sofia's bedroom with a TV monitor playing a video of her birth. There was a cord across the open door and a sign that said, "The artist's most important work, expected to take 21 years to complete." On the long wall of the second-floor hall I hung a series of fifty photos I'd taken of my friend Joyce Goldstein standing in front of her closet wearing different clothes, from underwear to evening wear. She was on hand that night, continually appearing in different outfits. In the kitchen the guests were directed to peel a potato and then read a quote from the artist Joseph Beuys which said, "Peeling a potato can be a work of art if it is a conscious act." There were two large cooking pots labeled "Art" and "Not Art." Each guest had to decide whether his or her peeled potato was art or not and drop it in the appropriate pot.

Francis was out of town when Lynn and I staged this event. From what he heard about it, he saw neither the art in it nor the humor. His feelings were hurt. He thought I was making fun of him, his Oscars, our house. He worked long and hard on his films, and thought conceptual art was too easy. "So some guy shoots himself in the arm [Chris Burden] or pisses off a ladder in a gallery [Tom Marioni] and that's a big deal?" The only thing Francis finds OK about that period is a Joseph Beuys sculpture I bought him that he didn't like at the time but is now worth thirty times what I paid. I was not a good wife by his definition or mine.

My thoughts came back to the brunch table at the sound of my fork dropping as the waiter cleared my salad plate; it glinted silver in the sunlight as it hit the brick floor. At a table across the patio I see Donald Trump, he is seated with a girl seven or eight years old. The girl's dress is pale pink starched cotton with lovely hand smocking and lots of ruffles ironed to perfection, something you never see a child in L.A. wear. I'm always slightly surprised to see a celebrity, not quite believing they are real. People imagine I hang out with famous people all the time. I don't. We live in the country. The famous people I meet through Francis are usually artists focused on their work which is often different from the celebrity personas they inhabit on late-night talk shows.

I think of the Polo Lounge as a relic. It was once a legendary hangout for old Hollywood stars and deal makers, but now the hotel has new owners, the food is unexceptional and it seems as if it's a Beverly Hills tourist attraction. We come here occasionally for breakfast because it is close to our bungalow in the hills and it's fun to sit in the big curved booths where movie history was made. Maybe it's still being made. I can hear Sofia saying, "I want the camera to be static, not move around." Francis replies, "So use a forty-millimeter lens. I shot the whole *Godfather* with that. Beware of high angles or low angles. Say the actress stands up, do you want the camera to pan up? No, you don't want to be looking up her nose. Just let her move out of the frame."

April 26, 2002 Napa

Boxes of art books and catalogues of shows are packed and ready to go to storage. They are on the back porch waiting for the maintenance men to come with the pickup truck and move them. I opened the lid of the top box and noticed the chartreuse cover of a large catalogue for a show of paintings by Chuck Close.

November 7, 1991 New York City

I'm in New York City for a few days overseeing painters working on our apartment in the Sherry-Netherland hotel. Today I ate lunch alone in a Japanese restaurant nearby. I've been there so often that the host, a very tall Asian man, smiled broadly when he saw me and escorted me to my favorite place near the middle of the wide polished wood counter. I ordered Lunch No. 3 as usual. At a table behind me I could hear three women speaking German. The sound became a counterpoint to the Japanese flute music playing.

After lunch I walked to the Metropolitan Museum to see the Seurat show. I wasn't expecting to be more than mildly interested. I remembered the well-known painting *La Grande Jatte* from an art history class long ago and later when it was reproduced as a backdrop for a Broadway musical. Looking at the original large painting and the many drawings and studies, I realized I'd never noticed how separate each figure was. No one is talking to anyone else, engaged with another. The scene in a park is crowded with people yet each person seems to be in a private reflective moment. I had always thought the work was about capturing natural light at a certain moment using dots of color in the pointillist technique. I hadn't seen the emotional distance, the intense isolation, the implied pain. Maybe I hadn't been old enough.

I left the museum and took the subway downtown to the Pace gallery to see a show of the work of Chuck Close; huge faces painted from color photographs. They were painted in thousands of small ellipses, dots and lines of less than an inch. Up close the images are completely abstract. I had to stand across the room to see the painting come into focus as a portrait. I went back and forth looking at the way color was used. A small dot of orange next to a tiny line of violet and one of emerald would create a speck of cheek in shadow. A dot of pink, a line of orange and a touch of light blue would equal a bit of skin on the nose. I began to breathe irregularly, gulping air, my body as well as my mind responding to powerful art.

I tried to compose myself before approaching the receptionist to ask for a catalogue. She pressed an intercom button and spoke to someone behind closed doors. A perfectly groomed blond woman in a sleek gray suit appeared. She gave me a scrutinizing look. I inquired boldly about the prices. She said, "Everything in the show is sold. The range is from $125,000 to $250,000." I tried not to flinch visibly. I must have appeared calm enough because she continued, "He is working on a new body of work. Would you care to be contacted when it becomes available?" I gave her my card. She smiled when she read my last name and offered to take me downstairs to a storage area to see other works. I declined.

I went to a nearby coffee bar; my heart was still pounding. I sat for a long time savoring afterimages of the colors in the paintings and the portraits they formed. I wondered how I had happened to choose to see the work of Close and Seurat the same day; such related opposites. Seurat's pointillist figures were remote and faceless, set outdoors at a particular time of day one hundred years ago, and Close's paintings were of enormous isolated faces in meticulous pointillist-type detail, in the artificial light of a photographed moment. Why this work resonated so strongly with me was a mystery I tried to answer but couldn't. I watched the ring the bitter coffee was making on the inside of my paper cup.

April 28, 2002 Napa

Yesterday I stood on a stepladder clearing a high shelf in my closet. Under two dented felt winter hats I found a flattened white tennis hat with "O Boticário" in yellow letters embroidered across the front. It was given to me in Brazil.

Our 1997 family Christmas trip to the Galápagos Islands ended in Ecuador. Francis was invited to go on to Brazil by a film company who wanted to work with him. The invitation included the family, all expenses paid. Six of us went along. A private plane flew us from Quito to Rio de Janeiro, where we spent the night at the Copacabana Hotel. The next morning two limousines took us to a heliport in the city. We flew south for thirty minutes with a spectacular view of the coast and landed on the tennis court of a vacation residence on a private island. Francis and I were given the best bedroom suite. Water skis and a speedboat were at the dock. A French chef presided over the kitchen.

January 3, 1998 Brazil

The blue door of the bedroom is open and I can see across the small deck past a flowering hibiscus to a mango tree thick with vermilion blossoms framing the path down to a small cove. The water is lapping rhythmically on the fine clean sand. The sea stretches to the horizon where three small islands float as if in a Chinese painting with pale blue-gray silhouettes of the mainland mountains behind.

Francis and I were the first at breakfast this morning at 10:30 a.m. Slowly the others arrived. After strong coffee and tropical fruit we all walked down to the beach and waded into the warm water. We stood in water up to our armpits, wearing sunglasses and talking. I thought we looked as if we were part of a cheap Italian movie.

Our hosts are four brothers and their families. Guilherme is the youngest, twenty-eight, an ex–soap opera star who seems to be the one paying for our holiday. He is tan and handsome with intense blue eyes, a charismatic smile, mustache and small shaped beard. Philippe is several years older. He is stocky and muscular with a hairy chest and expanding waistline, a former professional soccer player. Cryso is the oldest, in his late thirties. He is very clean-shaven, tan, androgynous; he is a principal in an advertising agency in São Paulo. Theodor is thirty-five, thin and tan with dark animated eyes. He lived in the U.S. for six years and speaks the best English. Theodor and Philippe work for Guilherme. The brothers have formed a film company and received backing from ten banks for a total of eight million dollars. They plan to produce "A brilliant film with Francis Ford Coppola directing and Al Pacino starring."

Francis has told them he is writing his own project and isn't available to direct, that he is here to wish them well, encourage them to develop Brazilian cinema. "Don't try to get Al Pacino.

Work with Brazilian actors; you have a lot of wonderful actors right here." Guilherme talks of making a film that will "revolutionize the Brazilian film industry." Francis tells them, "Don't make one expensive film, make a group of smaller films and give yourselves more chances to have a success." Their hearts are set on one big project. They hope to become a dazzling part of the international film scene. They have never made a film before. Where we stand in the water, red and yellow tropical leaves and bits of coconut husks undulate around us, slowly floating toward shore. I can tell the four brothers aren't really hearing what Francis is saying.

We step out of the water, run across the hot sand to take turns under an outdoor shower in the shade of a tree covered with large orange blossoms. I put on sandals and a wrap dress over my wet bathing suit and join the others walking along the weathered dock to board a wide wooden sailing boat that has just arrived. We sit and motor slowly out toward the distant islands.

There are perhaps twenty people on board. The four brothers, Guilherme's twenty-one-year-old girlfriend, Patricia, and two of her friends. Patricia is very tall and thin. She has long flowing hair and is pretty but not glamorous. She doesn't have fashion model haughtiness; she has leftover teenager qualities that cling to her like baby fat. One of her girlfriends is very short, tan and perky; the other is ordinary, not too tall, not too blond, not too thin. The girls speak only a few words of English so I can't talk with them.

Yolanda is the matriarch of the family, at fifty-eight she wears a two-piece bathing suit which she wraps with a sheer Gucci scarf when she is not in the water. I am told she is the mother of seven. Her husband deserted her when her oldest child was twelve. Her sons are very affectionate with her. Two grandsons are along; Theodor's son, a boy of three, and Philippe's eight-year-old son Pedro. Yolanda is very attentive to them. Pedro is the son of Philippe and his first wife. Philippe drinks heavily and is affectionate but his mother brushes him away; she favors her oldest son, Cryso.

There is a handsome, tan, silver-haired Italian banker, Carlo, and his tall, thin, beautiful, seventeen-year-old actress daughter on board. We learn she has been in a long-running play in Rio. Carlo is eager for her to talk to Francis. Philippe makes frosty drinks from fresh limes, *cachaça* and ice; he passes out cans of beer and bottles of mineral water from a huge ice chest.

There are five in our group: Francis and I, Roman, my nephew Chris and Francis's cousin Regina. Davia Nelson is here representing Francis's company. Davia is a casting director and also does original radio shows for NPR. We are old friends and when she is not part of the business conversation we go to sit in the bow of the boat and talk where we can't be heard.

Francis is sitting next to Lucia. A handsome woman, the wife of Theodor and mother of the beautiful, brown, three-year-old Juan-Philippe. Francis met Lucia on a trip to Rio with Bobby De Niro four years ago. She is a tan, graceful woman; once a ballet dancer, now she creates flower arrangements for celebrity parties. She has filled the cluster of houses where we are staying with exotic arrangements. An exquisite orchid in a Chinese pot sits next to my shower. On the sink a giant spiral shell holds lilies. There is a familiar admiring affection between Francis and Lucia. I try not to let my mind dwell on what their relationship might have been during Francis's previous trip. It seems they kept in touch by e-mail and arranged this trip. I can see the attraction for Francis; a beautiful, tan, poised woman of thirty-five who is intelligent and capable. She has "produced" this vacation. I couldn't stop my mind from creating a fantasy about being the Chinese-style first wife and she the second. How she would manage all our houses so much better than I. I would spend the day in my art studio and come home in the evening to a beautifully organized household. But then my imagination does not want to continue to how the evening ends.

Philippe comes to sit beside me interrupting my thoughts. He tells me in an accent thick with drink, "You are very interesting, you are the most interesting, I love you." Then he looks in Francis's direction, turns back to me and says, "You are the balance, I can see you are his balance." Soon he has his arm around Davia, I can hear him say, "I love you, Olivia"—too drunk to get her name right—"we are married. No?" Davia explained to me that in Brazil it is customary to call a girlfriend your wife, a boyfriend your husband. She says, "I already have a Brazilian husband." Philippe says, "It doesn't matter, now you have two."

Our boat arrives in the bay of a tropical island. There are a dozen boats at anchor and a dinghy is ferrying people back and forth to the small dock. Along the shore, paths lead up to thatched roofs over large open-air dining tables set individually in the lush landscape. It is the restaurant where we will have lunch. Everyone on our boat jumps into the warm clear water and swims in a leisurely way to shore. I notice that I am the only person in a one-piece bathing suit, the only person with a flushed face, pale skin and spider veins on my legs. At the dock I don't have the covering of my wrap dress.

Everyone in wet bathing suits gathers at the outdoor bar. We are served glasses of an icy drink made with fresh mango juice and *cachaça*. It has the taste of a strong liquor, such as grappa. Glass pitchers with a crisp white napkin tied around the neck are filled with ice and the tangerine-colored liquid. I can see nearby tables set with thick ceramic plates. I am told they are made by the owner. In the distance a kiln is visible under a palm-frond roof near the water's edge. The owner, a thin, tan woman in her late fifties, presented me with a plate as a gift. It had one large leaf impression in the rough surface and a handsome shard of yellow and blue tile that she said was several centuries old, from a local colonial church. Platters of baked clams were served, then the owner told us there would be a delay before our table was ready; everyone walked back to the dock and got in the water. Philippe carried a goblet of the strong drink which he asked me to hold for him while he jumped in.

Tan young women in string bikinis giggled and frolicked as if they were sea lions in the small cove. Francis stood in the shallower water wearing his sunglasses, Onassis-like. Sailboats and sleek powerboats bobbed at anchor. Tan handsome people came and went from the small dock to the restaurant and back to the boats. Finally a waiter told us our table was ready.

We got out of the water into the humid hot afternoon and walked the short path to our secluded table in the shade of a thatched roof with a view of the cove. Eighteen of us sat on benches around the long table. We were served platters of fried squid and more pitchers of the strong drink. The afternoon light coming through the palm fronds speckled tan bodies, glinted off dark sunglasses, made patterns on the lace tablecloth. An hour passed and we received apologies from the kitchen; the restaurant was so busy it would be a while longer before our lunch was ready. Everyone got up from the table and went back into the water.

At 5:00 p.m. we were seated again and a giant skillet of paella was placed on a wrought iron rack in the center of the table. Next a huge steaming pot of seafood cooked in spicy coconut milk arrived accompanied by a rustic metal cauldron of rice, a dish of a yellow grain with raisins and a jar of small red peppers in oil. Yolanda served her sons and Guilherme's girlfriend, the rest of us served ourselves. The desserts were small plates of tropical fruit preserves accompanied by pots of whipped cream and walnuts. A tray of tiny cups of espresso arrived. The owner came to our table with her Nikon camera to take pictures of everyone and have her picture taken with Francis and Guilherme as they signed her guest book.

We swam back to the boat, climbed up the slippery white ladder and settled ourselves under the awning. As we sailed from the cove the salmon-colored sun was setting among clumps of dark storm clouds. Orange light spilled across the gray-indigo water. Patricia and her girlfriends put CDs in a boom box and danced in their bikinis on the forward deck. The brothers popped open beers. Roman found a piece of string and made a necklace for Pedro from the pop tops he had collected all afternoon. The boat swayed. I pretended to be asleep. I mentally replayed the day as if it were a foreign film in this exotic location with its exotic cast of characters.

January 4, 1998

This morning Guilherme told us we would be sailing to another island for lunch and a press conference to announce his association with Francis. I realized this was Francis's payback for our generous treatment: the private plane, limos, helicopters, the sandy cove, the French chef.

We were picked up at our dock in a big motor sailor that was owned by a tanned older man in faded red shorts. He was a banker from São Paulo, apparently one of the sources of funding for Guilherme's production company. He turned to me and said, "We are very glad you are here, it is very important to us that Francis has come." A light rain was blowing under the awning and my silk blouse was shriveling as it became wet and transparent. I had been told to expect pictures would be taken.

We drew up to a dock with flags flying the word "Caras" in large red letters; the name of a popular magazine in Brazil, a cross between *People* magazine and the *National Enquirer*. As Francis and Guilherme stepped off the boat several still photographers and a video cameraman photographed them. The misty rain had stopped and we were invited to sit in an area of lounge chairs with *Caras* towels folded neatly on each one. Francis settled on a bench at the perimeter, I walked around to see the view. Regina sat down next to Francis. From a distance I could see the photographers taking photos of Francis and Regina, thinking she was his wife. Finally the mistake was realized and an assistant came running to get me to pose with Francis. He wanted to be photographed in a different setting and we walked onto the beach and stood next to a boat named

Romantica. Francis has told me I look better in real life than in photos. I struggled to look relaxed.

After many photos were taken Francis returned to the bench in the shade and a pudgy young woman journalist approached him with a small tape recorder in hand and asked for an interview. She was so nervous her voice quivered. Francis reached out in a grandfatherly way and sat her on his lap. She giggled and awkwardly began her questions. We were served Mexican Sol beer from trays carried by girls wearing red miniskirts and blouses emblazoned with the Sol logo. I began to realize the entire small island had been taken over by the magazine, the beer company and a cosmetics company, solely to entertain celebrity guests and get photos of them with their products.

It started to sprinkle. The setup for the press conference was quickly moved from the terrace into the living room of the main house. Francis and Guilherme were seated on a sofa facing four production video cameras, their crews and a dozen still photographers and reporters. A woman from Telecine led the questioning. She asked Francis why he had come to Brazil and why he was interested in a co-production. She asked about what actors he liked and were there any he had in mind for this film. He said, "Our casting director, Davia Nelson, is here and she's going to be doing a search, a *procura*, for our cast throughout South America." He gestured toward Davia.

As the questioning continued, a woman who seemed to be a producer came over to me and said, "While your husband is doing this, wouldn't you care to have a massage at our spa?" It seemed thoughtful of her and sounded as if it would be nice so I said, "Yes" and followed her outside, down a flagstone path, to a series of small white tents set on the lawn. The tents had yellow sunburst logos on the sides with the name of the sponsoring cosmetics company, O Boticário, in large yellow letters.

As we passed the first tent I looked through the open door flap to see Cryso having a facial. I was ushered into a small canvas enclosure with a clear plastic roof and introduced to the masseuse, an attractive young woman in a white miniskirt. The producer said, "Take off all your clothes," then she disappeared. I undressed down to my cotton underpants which had a small hole on one side. She could speak no English and I no Portuguese; she motioned for me to lie down on my back. She massaged my feet and legs; I began to relax. It started to rain and I listened to the sound of the drops tapping on the plastic roof. She massaged my thighs and then my belly. I was startled as she massaged my breasts.

It began to rain harder and the plastic roof above me was beginning to sag as water collected in the middle. As I was directed to roll over, I felt some cold drops fall on my bare shoulders. In moments water was running from the seam in the roof onto my back and the table. I jumped up, wrapped a towel around myself and grabbed my clothes and camera bag. The attendant shrieked in alarm. Our nephew Chris happened to be outside and dashed in; when he saw the situation he got a broom and used the handle to push the ceiling up and let the water run off. I slipped through a tent flap into a facial compartment and hurriedly got dressed, then stepped outside and stayed under the O Boticário awning waiting for the downpour to pass.

Below, near the dock, a man ran by carrying an armload of umbrellas. I shouted but the noise of the rain and the palm fronds slapping the tents was so loud he didn't hear me. Finally, just as the rain tapered off and I was ready to make a run for the main house, a photographer rushed up under an umbrella. She said the producer told her she must have a picture of Mrs. Coppola at the O Boticário spa. In moments she had placed me next to a tropical flower arrangement with two beautiful attendants pretending to sign me in for my spa appointment. A tote bag of O Boticário cosmetics was put in my hand and a logo tennis hat was set jauntily on my head. As the wind whipped a potted palm against my leg, the photographer called out, "Now turn toward the camera and smile."

When I found Francis he was finished with his interview and was smoking a cigar. Several journalists were gathered around Roman. I stood at a distance and listened to some of the questions. "And what do you do?" Roman was answering so modestly I wanted to rush in and tell them, "He was nominated for a Grammy last year!" but I didn't. Then the young woman who had interviewed Francis sitting on his lap approached me with her pad in hand. She asked me, "How old are you?" I said, "I don't think there is a vital need to print that." She looked puzzled, then went on to ask, "What is your favorite thing about Francis? What is your secret to a long marriage? What do you do?" The host of a TV talk show joined us and said, "You know, she made that great documentary about *Apocalypse Now*." My young interviewer looked confused, said tentatively, "Oh yeah," and walked away.

The rain continued in sporadic showers. I saw a helicopter come in low across the water and land on a grassy knoll. I felt as though I had been in an elevator and it had suddenly dropped several floors. It was time for Roman and Regina to go back to Rio to catch the evening flight to Miami and home. We said goodbye and hugged hard. They got in a golf cart and were driven out of sight up the gravel road to the heliport. In a few minutes the helicopter passed over us and flew out over the water toward the dark storm clouds. Roman waved from the window.

When I could no longer see him I pretended to dry my face in a logo towel; I knew my fear was visible. I was thinking about the moment I heard our great friend, the rock band impresario Bill Graham, had crashed not far from our house in a helicopter during a rainstorm. I remembered huddling in an army tent with Bill while it rained in the Philippines during *Apocalypse Now*. He told stories about the bands he produced, how the Grateful Dead would never do an encore no matter how long the audience stomped and clapped. He always had to go to their dressing room and personally beg them to come back onstage.

It started to rain hard. We gathered up our complimentary tote bags of cosmetics, beach towels printed with Sol beer labels, logo sun hats and hurried down to the dock. The big boat that brought us was no longer there, the banker had departed, the journalists left in a different direction. Our group was put in a small speedboat. It had no top. As we picked up speed, the rain pelting us felt as if it were thousands of darts. We covered ourselves with the towels we'd received and put the hats over our faces.

When we arrived at our cove we were soaking. I wrung out my towel and wrapped it around me. I asked Theodor to try his cell phone from the dock and see if he could confirm that the helicopter had landed. It took him about half an hour to get a call through and come to tell me Roman and Regina were safely at the airport.

Part Three

June 31, 2002 Napa

I have always dreamed of living in a modern minimal home set in nature with soothing, spare spaces. Now that the children are grown we don't really need the big Victorian house and I find its old traditional design awkward for just the two of us. I've always felt I was living in the very beautiful nineteenth-century mansion of Captain Gustav Niebaum [the founder of Inglenook winery] that didn't relate to me or the time in which I live. Finally I asked Francis if we could build a small contemporary house for the two of us somewhere on our property to live the next chapter of our lives. He was surprised at first but warmed to the idea and decided our remodeled main house could accommodate special guests of the winery and fine wine dinners. The family could still use it for holidays. So we selected an architect known for his contemporary home designs and found a beautiful site, a knoll, on our hill among oak trees overlooking the valley. Now we are in the process of working on plans for the new house while we oversee renovations in the mansion.

For the time being we've moved into an old housekeeper's apartment next to the laundry. It consists of two rooms. There is a small living room with a kitchenette along one side, a dining table for two, a sofa and chair. The floor is covered with yellow and green squares of linoleum tile. A door connects to a small bedroom and bath. Francis says he likes it. "Now I can always see where you are."

My life used to feel as if I were living in an opera with 20 rooms filled with family and guests, huge dinners, large kitchen, dining room with patterned wallpaper, Oriental rugs and stained glass windows, and surrounded by wide porches. Now it's like a haiku. When Jay Shoemaker, the CEO of our companies, came to get my signature on some legal forms for the winery yesterday he looked around and said, "You're the only rich people I know who can live poor."

Unruly branches of a climbing rose press against the upper part of the window screen. Petunias and white begonias look in at me from a window box. In the distance I can hear electric saws, hammers, the screech of splitting wood, and the voices of the men on the demolition crew who are ripping the old sleeping porch off the back of the big house in preparation for renovation. Lying in bed in this small, plain, cream-colored bedroom with no art on the walls is soothing; images would feel too close, would press in on me. I'm thinking about people who have stayed in this apartment over the years. The longest was Ester, our beloved housekeeper from the Philippines who came home with us after *Apocalypse Now*. Recently Francis's young production assistant Lisa stayed here. She had lots of friends and overnight guests. She managed to create candlelit gourmet dinners for eight in the small kitchen–living room. Francis and I attended several, seated around a folding table between the sofa and refrigerator. When Gio and Roman were teenagers they used the apartment as their headquarters; they hung out a sign, "Wild Deuce Productions," and wrote a script together.

My thoughts are skipping back and forth as if my life is on a videotape in my mind that pauses randomly here and there. It has stopped on a scene in 1963 with the doctor who delivered Gio. I haven't thought of him for years.

When I discovered I was pregnant we were living in Los Angeles. I didn't have a gynecologist/obstetrician there so I got a recommendation from a friend whose affluent family I knew went to only the best doctors. She arranged an appointment for me with Dr. L., a noted physician in Beverly Hills. He was distinguished-looking with a kind of Jason Robards–style charm. After examinations he always called me into his private office. He'd quickly go over my medical chart and then begin chatting about people in the entertainment world. "I was talking to Jane Fonda yesterday and . . ." "I was playing tennis with a producer from Paramount when he . . ." He was pleased that my husband was a young screenwriter and frequently asked me who he was working with. Although Francis had begun working with several famous names, I always avoided telling the doctor. I felt his professional expertise in the delivery room was most important and there I'd have his full attention.

When I went into labor he phoned the hospital to check what stage I was in but didn't arrive until it was time to put me to sleep and have me wheeled into the delivery room as they did in those days. As my gurney rolled down the hall he appeared and, giving me a fatherly pat, said, "You'll do fine."

I was already so sedated I couldn't reply. Francis was out in the waiting room. "I'll go out and meet your husband," he said, and left. The next thing I remember was the doctor at my side. "You have a baby boy." In his next breath he said, "You didn't tell me Francis was working with Elizabeth Taylor!"

JULY 6, 2002

I'm sitting in a tiny patio the gardener created for us by using lattice and plants to screen out the clotheslines. There is a wicker table and four chairs that came with us from the Philippines. I've covered the table with a French picnic cloth and am eating a ripe peach from the farmers' market. All our good china is packed away, the peach is sitting on a plain glass plate I bought in Toronto to supplement what was in my hotel suite when I was there shooting a documentary for Sofia.

AUGUST 2, 1998

When I arrived from the airport last night and stepped out of the car I could smell the dark dry air with its perfume of grass, gravel, roses, oregano and, near the back door, cat food and porch paint that had baked in the afternoon sun. The house was warm with heat closed in from the hot August day. I went up to the bedroom, opened windows and took deep breaths of the cool fragrant air that had hovered over lawns, drifted through magnolia trees and along the arms of the giant valley oak in front of our house. I slipped into bed between smooth cotton sheets. Home at last after three weeks in Toronto. Francis is still in Europe. I miss him.

This morning I walked out the back door, across the driveway, to the pond. Water lilies were blooming, a bullfrog jumped as I approached, a bevy of quail took flight into the oleanders, blue jays squawked in the mulberry tree. In the vegetable garden dangling green beans begged to be picked, squash vines sprawled at the feet of tomato plants, dozens of zucchini protruded from under wide leaves, eggplants hung to the ground shining in the morning sunlight, cucumbers curled next to the fence.

I walked back to the house looking into the flower beds at the light filtering through thick canopies of old trees, casting patterns of shadow on roses, lavender and hydrangeas. I stood on the path and bowed my head in gratitude and wonder, wondering why my life's path is filled with such intense beauty, wondering if I am appreciative enough, doing enough in return. As I stood there I felt a heaviness on my shoulders woven of memories in the garden, the voices of children hunting Easter eggs, Gia and her friends running through on their way to the trampoline, to pick oranges or look for lizards, memories of walking into the garden to take solace after a quarrel, find a place to speak of divorce, of death.

I could feel the large handsome house ahead of me and my attachment to all the objects around it and in it, the wicker porch chairs that I bought in Manila after *Apocalypse Now* when I wondered if I would have a marriage and family to sit on the furniture by the time it reached home, the fabric on the pillows I got in London with Sofia. I can feel the things inside the house too, the Oriental rugs, paintings, carved woodwork, inlaid floors, densely patterned French fabric on the dining room walls. I feel all the beauty that surrounds me and also the weight of it. Although there is a side of me that adores rich pattern, it reminds me of chocolate mousse; too much of it makes me feel ill.

The documentary I was shooting was my fourth. This one is for Sofia to use to promote her first feature film, *The Virgin Suicides*. Sofia read the novel by Jeffrey Eugenides and wanted to make it into a film; however, she discovered a producing company owned the film rights to the book and had already engaged a screenwriter. Francis encouraged Sofia to not linger over her disappointment but begin looking for another property. On her own, she wrote a script. As it turned out, the hired screenwriter's work wasn't satisfactory and after some months Sofia was accepted as the writer and director for the project.

In Toronto I lived in a hotel downtown where most of the cast members stayed. My suite was business traveler's style, consisting of two small rooms with beige walls, colorless furniture and every convenience: coffeemaker, four dishes, refrigerator, microwave, fax machine, terry cloth robe. There was something very restful about having everything I needed but no attachment to anything around me.

I brought my video camera, hired a sound man and went each day to wherever Sofia was working and shot everything that seemed interesting. My feet ached from standing long hours, my right arm, shoulder and hand were sore from holding the camera. Shooting hours were often from 1:00 p.m. to 1:00 a.m. but usually went longer. When I got back to the hotel at 2:00 or 3:00 in the morning I was relieved to have only the book I was reading to take my attention.

Each day I felt unencumbered as I drove across the unfamiliar city to find the day's location at a school, a residential street, a cemetery, an industrial warehouse. I appreciated the familiar habits of the crew who said, "Good morning" at the beginning of the work day even when it started in the late afternoon or evening. My attention was on the drama happening inside my viewfinder. My miniature world was constantly fascinating to me. There I saw my daughter's triumphant smile when she'd given directions to an actor and he or she'd responded with an unexpectedly strong performance, moments of her frustration when the producer told her she was shooting over the budgeted allotment of film stock and had to cut back, moments when a difficult actor completed his days of work on the film and hugged her goodbye and I could see her affection and the hidden relief in her expression.

I recorded her wit with James Woods when his acting was broad and she'd playfully say, "Less *jambon* for the next take, please." On his last day she gave him a tin from a canned ham she'd had the propman mount on a trophy base to look as if it were an award. He laughed uproariously and said, "Hey, I love it! I really love it! You think I'm kidding but I'm going to put it on the shelf right next to my Golden Globe award and my Emmy."

I treasured the experience of being with Sofia in her world but I am now happy to be home. I walked up to my studio. The dirt road was hot as I came out from under the shade of the old trees near the stream next to the vineyard. Thick bunches of still-green grapes hung from the vines on one side of me and dense blackberry bushes with dark ripe fruit were on the other side.

Stepping into my studio I quickly shut the door to keep warm air from entering the cool interior. The building is constructed of straw bales. Its thick walls keep it cool in summer, warm in winter and invitingly quiet. It has tall barn doors and large windows. Our property is zoned agricultural preserve so the building was approved as goat habitat and has come to be known as Ellie's "barn."

I always had a spare room in the house for my work but building this separate studio space was a revelation. I hadn't realized what a toll it was taking to be in our home with a phone extension in my work room making me always available to interruptions and aware of the activities of the family. When I got a separate studio a quarter of a mile from the main house I felt as if I could hear myself clearly for the first time. I sat down at my drawing table. The white walls, the smooth wood floor and the silence soothed me. The large deep-set windows looked as if they were framed paintings of the natural world. I was reminded of the first page of May Sarton's *Journal of a Solitude*, when she is by herself in her house and she says, "It is here, alone, that my real life begins."

July 10, 2002

Our furniture and large items have been taken to a metal storage building on the property, but seasonal clothes and things we need access to are in the caretaker's cottage adjacent to our little apartment. I didn't have time to sort everything before it was moved from the main house. Today I went through a box that contained a mix of casual jewelry, spare buttons and several inexpensive watches I wear when I'm traveling in rugged terrain. Tucked into a small padded silk envelope I found two red strings.

Seven years ago Kwong Roshi invited me to have dim sum lunch at the Hong Kong Flower Lounge on Geary Street in San Francisco. He asked me to come at 11:00 so we could be seated before a line formed. He was already at a table by the window when I arrived. I hadn't seen him for a few years. There were a few more crow's-feet next to his twinkling eyes. His hair was an even half inch long and appeared to be growing out after having been shaved. He was wearing a plain flannel shirt; a navy cotton baseball jacket was thrown over the extra chair. Sometimes he wears monk's robes, sometimes his head is cleanly shaven, other times he has a regular haircut, some years he smokes, other years he doesn't. Only his smiling visage and his particular essence of inner peace laced with humor are always the same. After all his years of meditation, perhaps he has become released from the baggage of old angers, regrets and delusions that the rest of us carry around. I know he has had his share of pain and has overcome cancer yet he seems free, delighting in each moment.

He put on his reading glasses and perused the menu. He asked me if I was a vegetarian. "I'm not," he said. (Although the Zen Center meals are all vegetarian.) He ordered for the two of us. The waiter spoke to him in Chinese; he answered in English. When the waiter left he said, "The dialect I speak is from the south, near Canton, and considered the language of peasants so I don't like to use it." He ordered sweet rice wrapped in lotus leaves, steamed spinach dumplings filled with chopped mushrooms and water chestnuts, fried tofu skin stuffed with shrimp and vegetables, taro root, and Chinese broccoli with oyster sauce.

He told me about his trip to Warsaw for a conference with the Dalai Lama. The greeting committee had mistakenly gone to the wrong train station and he found himself alone welcoming the Dalai Lama to Poland. He gave me a photo; in it he is standing on the sidewalk next to the Dalai Lama. He said he had traveled to Warsaw a number of times in recent years. "When the government changed there and opened to the West, people were hungry for information about religion and sex." He spoke about his journey on the train back to the West. "Out the window I saw painful sights, people who had experienced devastating loss, and I also saw sights of magnificent beauty. I realized I mustn't turn away from the painful parts but, rather, breathe them in and then breathe them out, releasing them." I met with Roshi after Gio's death when the experience had invaded every cell of my being. I felt he was telling me now that the other part of the process was to exhale.

We talked about our children, his wife's sabbatical, Zen community members I knew and about the need for fund-raising. "I hope you would be willing to do an event for us in Rutherford." I said, "I can't do the event because I'll be away but you can use the grounds around our house." I told him an experienced event planner should be hired. He looked puzzled. I could see the ways of the material world were not his area of expertise. We consulted our pocket diaries and picked a date. He told me he was leaving in a few days for a vacation in Greece with his wife. I asked if he knew anyone there. He said, "No." He paused and giggled. "Isn't that good?" In conversation there is a traditional answer we expect. Roshi responds as if he is able to experience each moment for the first time.

As I got ready to leave he asked me if I would accept something he had made for me. He took out a red string with the two ends tied together. In the middle of the loop was a larger knot. Roshi said, "The knot is shaped symbolically like a diamond-cutting tool. It is worn around the neck. It symbolizes cutting through delusions so the truth can appear." He asked me to hold out my hands and he placed the string in one cupped palm, then he closed my other hand over it and he covered both my hands with his for a few moments before putting the string over my head. He said it was to be worn under my clothing and taken off for showers. He gave me three more for my family. That evening I told Francis about my lunch with Roshi and that he had given me a red knotted string for him. He didn't pay much attention.

I woke up in the night and was restless. In the morning I was tired and stayed in bed when Francis got up at 6:00. He is shooting a bittersweet film called *Jack*, with Robin Williams, Diane Lane, Jennifer Lopez and lots of children. Francis is particularly enjoying working with Robin and all the children. Most of the locations are nearby and he can be driven from home to the set. Before Francis left he came into the bedroom, woke me and asked for the string from Roshi. He said, "I didn't know which was worse, waking you up or not wearing the red string." I got out of bed and got it. I placed it in his big hands with my small ones around them, then put the string over his head. It got caught on his glasses but was in place under his Hawaiian shirt when he left for the set.

July 12, 2002

I cleaned my car thoroughly and found a missing CD from an audiobook under the passenger seat along with a rumpled theater program.

February 27, 2002 San Francisco

Last evening I went to see the opening night of the ODC Dance Company. It was their 31st season. It is so remarkable that a small dance company, a very underfunded sector of the arts community, can survive so many years and grow more vital. The artistic director Brenda Way's new piece was one of her best. It was called *Raking Light*. Today I am still seeing images in my mind of dancers' bodies in gravity-defying motion shimmering in strands of light inspired by paintings of Vermeer. At the celebration afterwards I hugged Brenda in congratulations. I could feel her body sag into me with relief, the doubts and fears of the weeks preceding the premiere of a new work finally gone; then she stiffened, and said, "My piece could be three minutes longer, don't you think?" Before I could answer, a board member approached with a potential new patron and she turned to them with her intelligent charm.

The dancers arrived at the reception. They were in their street clothes. Without their distinctive onstage personalities they were indistinguishable from other partygoers. After a few minutes I found myself alone picking from trays of canapés passed by bow-tied waiters. I was remembering going with Brenda and the dancers on tour to Russia and eating canned peas with slithery gray-pink wieners at a government hotel in Kirghisia, a hundred miles from the Chinese border.

July 16, 2002 Thailand

Chatri Yukol is a film director who has directed over thirty Thai films. At the Queen of Thailand's request and financed by the royal family, he directed *The Legend of Suriyothai*. It is an historical epic with a dramatic story including beautiful princesses, intrigue, royal poisonings and battle scenes fought by armor-clad warriors atop elephants. When it was released in Thailand in the fall of 2001, it was a huge success. Even though it was over three hours long it broke all box office records. The sound for the film had been mixed at Francis's facilities in San Francisco and Napa. I had met Chatri and Bee, his wife and the film's producer, while they worked in Northern California.

In the spring of 2002, Francis was hired by the royal family to re-edit the film, create a shorter version that would be of interest to an international audience. Francis worked in Bangkok for three weeks in April. During his stay he was invited to attend a state dinner at the Queen's palace in Chiang Mai. The Queen invited him to return to Thailand and bring me.

We made the ten-hour flight from Los Angeles to Osaka, Japan. After refueling, the flight continued for another five hours to Thailand. We had crossed over the international date line and moved ahead a day and thirteen hours. I was disoriented when we stepped off the plane in Bangkok. As we emerged from the passageway, a young man in a perfectly pressed custom-tailored uniform stepped toward us. He was accompanied by two assistants, a young woman in crisp blouse and skirt and man in dark slacks with white shirt and tie. They had been sent by the royal household; a security guard and two hosts. They took our carry-on bags and guided us to a special kiosk where, without standing in line, our passports were quickly stamped. At baggage claim our luggage was gathered and we were directed to customs, where smiling agents waved us through. A small van was waiting at the curb and we were driven through the night at high speed to the Sukhothai Hotel in downtown Bangkok.

This morning I awakened in this elegant tasteful room. The furniture with simple teakwood frames is upholstered in silver-gray Thai silk. The drapes are bronze-colored silk. The teak floor is laid in a handsome basket weave pattern. There is a wide black marble wainscoting. Burnt orange silk panels line glass-shelved niches holding antique plates with hand-painted slip designs. Stone temple carvings hang on several walls. Orchids bloom in lacquerware pots and a dark metal stand holds a thick, square glass plate filled with exotic tropical fruit. Every detail is simple, elegant, serene. Hotel decor in Asia is most often gaudy European style; rooms filled with fake French furnishings, faux Beverly Hills or Miami Beach tropical decor. This hotel's architect is French; as if it often takes foreign eyes to utilize local beauty well.

Over breakfast Francis talked about the original script he is writing. He talked about how he'd changed his main character to an older man and added an older woman, how he'd changed the younger woman's part. It felt as if he was seeing it come into focus, finally homing in on it after years of research and writing draft after draft. I thought about all the times I have listened to him talk about his work, never knowing if what I am witnessing is a memorable historical moment in his artistic work or just random brushstrokes that will be painted over in the months ahead.

Chatri was on the set of a new film he is directing, and shooting was taking place on a residential side road blocked off from a main boulevard. It had been dressed with street vendor stands selling food and drinks. Large glass jars of pineapple and watermelon juice stood on a counter next to a pyramid of fresh coconuts ready to be cut open, their milk drunk through a straw. Small grills sizzled with meats on bamboo skewers. Aromas of cinnamon and curry mixed with smells of sewage floated in the hot humid air. We were escorted by the young assistants of the royal household to the first camera position, where I saw Chatri and Bee.

When I met them both in Napa they always wore blue jeans and I never heard them called anything but Chatri and Bee. Now I realized everyone deferentially addressed Chatri as "Prince Chatri" or "Than Mui," which I learned translates as "Serene Highness," and Bee was called "Mom Chao," which means "Wife of Serene Prince."

An official photographer arrived and a flurry of pictures were taken of Prince Chatri and Francis talking together. Their lovely seventeen-year-old daughter Mangmoom was introduced to us. She spoke perfect English and was home from her Swiss boarding school for summer vacation. We were served a red iced drink from a silver tray. It was something I hadn't tasted for years, cherry Kool-Aid.

In the afternoon Francis and I were taken on a behind-the-scenes tour of the historic Grand Palace with its gold spires, intricate mosaic walls, marble floors, elaborate temples. We saw the tall altar that held the emerald Buddha, the great reception room with the king's throne and paintings of monarchs from the past. Paintings of their queens were in a separate room; there were no paintings of their consorts. The kings had many wives until recent times. Thailand is the longest continuous monarchy in the world, and I was amazed by the splendor of the rich ornamentation.

In the evening we were invited to Chatri's mother's house for dinner. The rooms were large and formal with nineteenth-century-style French furniture and Chinese sculpted carpets. There were lighted glass-front buffets containing the family's collection of dinnerware and crystal from the reign of King Rama V, Chatri's great-grandfather. There was a large painting of Chatri's mother and father in formal attire for their presentation at court. His father wore a high-collared red jacket with many medals; his beautiful mother, twenty years younger than his father, wore a Thai gown with a royal sash from her left shoulder diagonally across her chest to her right side waist. There were photos of his mother as a young woman curtsying before the beautiful young queen.

The house was hot and stuffy; the air-conditioning was shut off. Four maids chatted together in the kitchen, otherwise there was no one in the rooms. We were directed downstairs. When the door opened we found ourselves in a large room next to the garden. It was cold; two air conditioners were whirring. Perhaps twenty family members lounged on three groups of sofas or sat at round tables. The walls were covered with family photos. Chatri's mother commanded the main couch; an elegant woman in her late seventies wearing a lime-colored linen pants suit and heavy gold jewelry. We were introduced to the family: Chatri's brother, two sisters, their spouses, Chatri's children by other marriages, grandchildren of the family down to the youngest great-grandchild, a boy of four carrying a large toy dinosaur.

We were invited to sit at one of the round tables. I was seated next to Chatri's mother and instructed to call her "Mom" as everyone did. A dozen platters of different foods were brought to the table. I learned that in Thai cuisine there aren't separate courses except for dessert; everything is served at once. There were curries, dishes of seafood, salads, platters of vegetables and several kinds of rice. It felt familiar; as if I were at an Italian table with everyone talking at once, filling my plate, urging me to eat more. "You've hardly eaten a thing," said Chatri's sister, placing another packet of steamed fish wrapped in a banana leaf on my plate, more spicy green papaya salad, and a second serving of hot curried chicken. The wonderfully flavored food was the spiciest I'd ever eaten. My lips and tongue were ablaze; when I thought no one was looking I held gulps of cold beer in my mouth.

For dessert Chatri's sister served sticky rice topped with sliced fresh mango. Francis autographed *Godfather* DVDs for Mom. Affectionate goodbyes were said and we stepped into the thick, humid night air of the garden. Chatri and Bee showed us around the family compound. Each of Mom's six children has a large house and a smaller one for their grown children. No one moves away. Marriages bring new wives and husbands to the compound; only Chatri and Bee live five minutes away, next to their film facilities, and use their house in the compound for storing movie props.

July 20, 2002

We spent the day looking for large ceramic planters, carved wall decorations, and teak furniture for our new resort in Belize that Francis is building. In the Philippines Francis grew to like the climate, the exotic beauty of the jungle and tropical islands so he began looking for something like it closer to home. In 1981 he explored the new nation of Belize in Central America, which had just gained independence from Great Britain. There he found a run-down mountain lodge in the jungle near a river. Over the years we have transformed it into a desirable resort. Two years ago he bought a little inn with cabins on the beach near the fishing village of Placencia in Belize. Then last year every structure on the property was literally blown away by Hurricane Iris. Now we are building a much finer beach resort in its place.

The Bangkok streets were clogged with traffic. The driver didn't understand where we wanted to go and took us to many wrong destinations. The temperature was in the 90s and humid. We arrived back at our hotel tired and hungry. The café was already closed so we ate dinner in the elegant dining room. We began arguing loudly. I felt embarrassed but knew better than to ask Francis to lower his voice. He'd raise it further for sure.

The conversation evolved into what we were doing with our lives. Francis talked passionately about how his life was getting picked to pieces by all the obligations he has, the well-meaning but disruptive dates on his calendar: film awards, wine events, meetings for his homeless organization, his magazine, film productions, editing projects, dates for family trips, things he agrees to do then sees in frustration there is no stretch of time with uninterrupted days to write his own project, work on his own script, move forward toward making his film. "And you don't look out for me," he said. "You don't tell people I'm not available. You don't help me." He was so persuasive I began thinking of all the things I should have done until I caught myself and remembered he sets his calendar himself with his assistant.

I noticed how I have changed. There was a time in the not so distant past when I would have felt miserable and chastised myself, asked myself why I am not doing more for all the affluence I enjoy, all the travel and experiences Francis brings to my life. Now I recognize his frustration is his own. I picture him venting fumes as if they are clouds of gray exhaust blowing right by me. I hold my nose.

An hour later, he is at his computer making little jokes.

July 22, 2002

We flew north to Chiang Mai. Chatri and Bee joined us from a location in the mountains where they were shooting. We spent two days in a hotel that was built in a small valley surrounded by rice terraces. The crops were in rotation; some of the paddies recently harvested were golden-brown stubble, some were a thick lush green and some were newly planted with green shoots placed by hand in blue-black water. Workers in faded indigo pants and jackets, matching neck kerchiefs and pointed straw hats worked together at the edge of one of the low narrow dikes separating two paddies. Several times a day water buffalo were herded from one side of the valley to the other along paths meandering among hotel guest bungalows. We sat outside in our shaded octagonal pavilion leaning on decorative pillows, drinking papaya juice, overlooking the picturesque scene. I found it disturbing that people working in rice paddies under the hot afternoon sun were featured as the decor for our luxurious accommodations.

In the evening Chatri and Bee took us into town to visit the night market. I was enthralled by stalls with lacquerware from Burma and booths with textiles from Laos, Cambodia and China as well as the ethnic tribes of Thailand. Francis, bored, went outside and sat down on the curb, so Chatri took him to a café on the river while Bee and I continued exploring the market. Most of the vendors were women. I wondered how they managed their families. The stalls were open late into the evening; older children sat on the floor doing homework, younger ones chased each other through the narrow aisles, babies slept on mounds of textiles. I bought a beautiful small skirt with silk embroidery on indigo ikat woven in a mountain village in southwest China and a round Burmese three-part container made from lacquered horse hair and intricately painted. The next day we flew back to Bangkok. When we landed we were met by a car from the royal household. Bee had arranged that we be taken straight to a beauty salon. Francis, Chatri and I had haircuts, manicures and pedicures. Bee had her hair shampooed and styled. In the midst of my manicure a huge bouquet arrived. Bee told me that it would be my gift for the Queen. She wanted me to see it first before it was sent ahead to the palace. As I flapped my hands in the air to dry my nails, Bee instructed me in the protocol of meeting the Queen. "When you are introduced to her you will curtsy." I was startled. She showed me how. "Put your left foot behind and touch your right knee to the floor." I tried awkwardly.

By the time Francis and I were driven back to the hotel through the evening traffic, we had very little time to dress. Chatri told Francis to wear a black suit. Bee said I should wear a long dress. I had a long skirt and matching sheer jacket. I hurriedly practiced several curtsies in front of the large bathroom mirror. I couldn't get all the way down with my knee on the floor and be certain I would be able to get back up so finally decided to just dip, bow, and smile heartily.

At 7:30 a white Mercedes was waiting. A uniformed driver and a man in military dress with many colorful medals accompanied us. I realized that the man who looked as if he were a general was not a member of the military, because the Queen is not a member of the government; he was a high-ranking officer in the royal security force. After a twenty-minute drive we arrived at an undistinguished gate. The car took a sharp turn down a driveway paved with terra-cotta bricks that clacked under the wheels. Thick tropical foliage screened all that might have been visible out the windows. Suddenly we arrived at a circular drive in front of an exquisite nineteenth-century wooden Victorian building lit with gas lamps. The wide staircase was decorated with large arrangements of tropical flowers. A long tongue of red carpet descended down the center of the many steps. A woman who I learned was the highest-ranked lady-in-waiting greeted us, accompanied by the Lord Chamberlain of Crown Properties. He told us that the palace was the largest teak building in the world. As we ascended the stairs, I looked up and saw Chatri above us taking our picture.

We entered a large foyer which I found out was especially decorated for me. (Francis had told the Queen of my interest in textiles when he met her on his previous trip.) There were huge silver bowls with bolts of hand-woven silks swirling from them in artful displays. Many of the pieces were woven with gold and silver threads in complex patterns that looked as if they were nineteenth-century textiles made during the reign of King Rama V of *The King and I* fame. Guiding me around the room speaking of warp, weft and weaving techniques was a distinguished gentleman in charge of the Queen's art programs. "The Queen has a school and programs to preserve the ancient arts of Thailand. She teaches traditional crafts to the poor and unemployed, who learn to make a living with their beautiful work."

Chatri joined me and steered me toward walls with historical paintings and old photographs. He pointed to one faded photo of a group of women who he said were the wife and consorts of the King. They were all wearing the same Victorian blouses, Asian-style full wrapped trousers, knee socks and English shoes. Chatri said, "The woman in the center was the King's head wife. The one on the right is my grandfather's mother."

The lady-in-waiting came to tell me the Queen would be arriving shortly. "Would you care to wash your hands?" I guessed that was a signal for me to go to the powder room and check my hair and makeup before the Queen arrived and photos were taken. A few minutes after I emerged I was ushered into position at the side of the main door and the Queen entered. She was about my height, slightly plump, with jet black hair so perfectly coifed it looked as if it had been lacquered. She had clearly been a great beauty. Her round face was smooth and thickly powdered. She had a playful radiant smile and spoke with a soft breathy voice. Her movements were liquid and graceful, belying her seventy-two years.

We were introduced. I did my best to curtsy, but it was more of a dip. A member of the royal household staff handed me the bouquet Bee had selected for me to present. Pictures were taken as I ceremoniously placed my hands on the large arrangement of gardenias and red roses. It was so big and heavy the attendant got down on his knees in front of me and bore the weight of it out of the camera's view. A staff member placed Francis in the photo one step back but between the Queen and me. It was such a smooth maneuver I knew it had been performed countless times. I noticed that all the people bowed low as they came near the Queen. The first lady-in-waiting, a woman in her seventies, easily bowed down with one knee on the floor and stood up again gracefully. Suddenly Chatri bent down, lay flat on the floor and placed his forehead at the Queen's feet. It was the same formal bow I'd seen done in Chatri's film before fourteenth-century royalty.

We were ushered into a large octagonal room with a center table set for fourteen and numerous tables of eight on each side. We were seated at the main table with the Queen at the head, Francis on her right and Prince Chatri on her left. I was seated next to Chatri. The vice chamberlain of Crown Properties was on my left. Each place was elaborately set with six faceted crystal glasses and plates with gold designs. In the center of the table was an arrangement of orchids and two peacocks made of gold with every feather articulated. Chatri whispered to me, "See those birds? Each one is worth $250,000." He pointed out the Queen's evening purse resting on the table above her plate and said, "Its iridescent color is made from thousands of beetle wings." He saw that I looked amazed. "This work is done by people trained in the schools for traditional crafts sponsored by the Queen." Beyond Chatri I could see a table of eight ladies-in-waiting and a table of security guards in custom-tailored uniforms. Fourteen waiters in white jackets, flowing draped silk pants with blue socks, shining black shoes and white gloves stood one behind each chair at our table. They served the first course in unison, a bland consommé. It was followed by green salad. A silver tray was brought with four dressings. The Queen leaned toward me and urged me to try her favorite, a dark dressing with sesame seeds. It tasted as if it were oil and vinegar with soy sauce.

We were served filet mignon accompanied by miniature carrots and roast potatoes. I thought it odd to be having Western food at a royal dinner in Thailand. As we finished and I was expecting an elegant dessert, an array of platters with Thai foods were brought to the table, including three types of rice. The dishes looked much more delicious to me than what I'd already eaten. My spirits sank. I knew I would be thought unappreciative as I could barely eat anything more.

Throughout the dinner most of my conversation was with the vice chamberlain, on my left. I learned he traveled often to Europe to tend to properties owned by the royal family, including a group of hotels. His children were educated in England; his beautiful daughter, who was also at the table, played the title role of the historical Queen Suriyothai in Chatri's film although she was not a professional actress. The Queen had chosen her. Her mother was the Queen's favorite lady-in-waiting. He told me that five years ago his wife had died in a helicopter crash while in the Queen's service. He looked as though he might weep but quickly composed himself and continued: "The ladies-in-waiting accompany the Queen when she goes to her different palaces. There are numerous palaces all around Thailand. The King is in the southern palace this evening. He is less socially inclined than the Queen; he hasn't traveled abroad since the seventies, whereas she frequently goes to Paris and London. When she travels she goes on a Thai 747 with 60 people in attendance." The Queen apparently overheard part of the conversation and said in soft, precise English, "In New York I like to stay at the St. Regis Hotel."

I noticed that anytime during the long dinner when someone got up from the tables around us they faced the Queen and curtsied. At one point, a lady-in-waiting (about my age) came forward on her knees to deliver a message to the seated Queen.

The royal orchestra in formal attire played the Queen's favorite romantic pop tunes from the fifties. I looked around me at the soft thirties-style green of the room, with light from the grand candelabra and saw large portraits of royalty, enormous bouquets with five-foot stalks of orchids, white-gloved waiters, the Queen in a jacket woven with silk and gold threads and wearing a necklace of pearls bigger than cherries and a ring with a diamond the size of a walnut.

A few minutes after midnight everyone stood as the Queen said good night and departed with her ladies-in-waiting. Chatri whispered to me, "She's probably going to the movies now. She stays up very late. She prefers to go to the theater at 2:00 or 3:00 in the morning when it's empty and see films with her friends." I pictured the Queen finishing a long official dinner, changing out of her tight formal gown and heavy jewelry into loungewear, brushing out her hair and going off with her friends to see movies till dawn. As we were leaving the palace I was given a gift of three lengths of exquisite hand-woven silk, wrapped in mulberry paper, in a silk-covered box.

September 9, 2002 Napa

I went to the storage building looking for some art books moved from the main house. While I was there I noticed a box marked E.C., MISC. 3RD FL. I opened it and found things still covered with plaster dust that must have been picked hurriedly out of the rubble when the tree limbs came through the roof of my little turret room. Among the objects was a deco vase Sofia had given me and a blurry Polaroid snapshot I treasure.

April 12, 1980 Las Vegas

I am with Francis during a writing session and location scout for his next film, *One from the Heart.* Tom Waits, the composer and singer who will create the score for the film, is with Francis. Also Gio is here. He is sixteen and has recently taken the GED to complete high school and become his father's assistant.

Francis and Tom Waits are talking about the themes of *One from the Heart.* Tom is telling Francis in his raspy drawl, "Las Vegas is like a woman sprawled out in the desert getting a fix . . . mainlining broken homes . . . broken dreams."

I am taking photographs of Gio, Francis and Tom sitting around a table by the window. The room is dark; light rims Tom's forehead, illuminates his chin, a line of light outlines Gio's nose and Francis's gesturing hands. A new film is beginning.

Now I am eating in front of a window that looks out onto the floor of the casino with rows and rows of slot machines crowded with players. I can see a man in a wheelchair, in his lap is a paper cup filled with nickels and a spray can of shoe wax. On a small stage, a lady is singing into a microphone. A stuffed toy frog and toy monkey are attached to the railing in front of her.

Gio and I went to Woolworth's to buy supplies for Francis, colored pens, typing paper and note cards. Gio selected some shampoo for himself. A young black man in the aisle turned to me and said, "Are you a girl?" Then he saw Gio and asked, "Are you with her?" Gio said, "Hey, this is my mom." The man looked at Gio intently and said, "Say, how old are you? You got a mustache, and she looks so young." He eyed the Polaroid camera that hung from Gio's shoulder and said, "Let me take your picture." Gio handed him the camera. I stood there, with Gio, his arm around me, in front of the dandruff shampoo, in Woolworth's, in Las Vegas, smiling.

September 12, 2002 Napa

In that same box of dusty things I found a creased narrow paper wrapper from restaurant chopsticks that had been flattened out and saved because it had a child's drawing on it. Francis and I enjoy eating in Japanese restaurants and often took the children. When they got impatient I played games of hangman or encouraged them to draw on the white paper inside chopstick wrappers. At first I wasn't sure if this drawing was made by Sofia or Gia. Then I remembered.

September 10, 1993

Francis and I slept outside on the screen porch. I awoke early. The air was moist, the eucalyptus trees on the hill loomed mysteriously in the fog. I lay awake, warm under the down comforter, and let memories of the last few days cross my mind.

I took Gia to Los Angeles to put her in school. Jacqui is still working on location. She is the costume designer on a small film shooting in Montana. Jacqui's boyfriend took Gia to visit her over Labor Day weekend. When he brought her back I met them at the airport in San Francisco and flew with Gia to Los Angeles. I enrolled her in school and accompanied her to the orientation. I took her to the pediatrician, coaxed her out from under the examining table for a hepatitis B shot, assisted her with the mystery of collecting her first urine sample. I took her to the shoe store where she chose plaid sneakers instead of the plain white ones I favored. The clerk said, "They're the latest thing." I wondered if she has her mother's and her aunt's "style" gene.

Sofia met us at a Japanese restaurant for dinner. We three generations of women sat together discussing fashion, design and art. Sofia is excited about going to a new art school next week. On the back of the chopsticks' paper wrapper Gia drew pictures of girls with long hair, exceedingly long legs and wearing ice skates.

The next morning Gia was tired. I let her sleep until the last minute. We were a little late arriving at school and there was no place to park nearby. I didn't want her to be embarrassed by being tardy so we ran several blocks together. Gia thought it was fun. She was excited and laughing, "You are a really fast grandmother." We arrived in the school yard and were engulfed in a milling sea of children. She wasn't sure where to go, where her class was lining up. She could only see a few feet around her. A look of terror crossed her face, she clutched my arm. Across the tops of the children's heads I located her teacher holding a pink sign with her room number. As Gia reached her classmates and they drew into a line, her body relaxed. I gave her a hug and she was gone.

I went shopping and bought Gia a lunch box and a backpack. I returned to her school in the afternoon to meet the nanny who was driving Gia to family friends where she will stay until Jacqui returns from location next week. I was a few minutes early so went to peek into Gia's classroom. It was empty except for the teacher, who was in the room preparing the next day's lessons. I introduced myself and asked about Gia. She said, "Gia told me her daddy was dead and her mother was away on vacation."

In the early evening I flew back to San Francisco. Gia is the last child I will see off to the first day of first grade in my life.

SEPTEMBER 24, 2002

I received a postcard from Roman today. On it is a reproduction of a Wesselmann painting of red lips holding a cigarette with a curl of smoke rising up from its tip.

MAY 11, 1998 FLIGHT TO SAN FRANCISCO

I am on a plane at night. My tray table is like a little stage, the reading light a spotlight illuminating a clear plastic glass half filled with water center stage. The ordinary ribbed plastic glass is casting a magnificent pattern of dancing lines, ellipses and tiny dots. Does anyone else see it? I remember the first time I heard "We die alone; no one can accompany us or do it for us." Perhaps we also live alone a great deal of the time. I am the only person watching the fine diagonal weave of my jacket sleeve meet the soft ribbed knit of my T-shirt cuff, seeing the texture of my pale skin stretched over my fingers swirling the plastic cup creating the drama of shadow patterns on my tray table stage.

I am flying home from Chicago. Roman and I took a spur-of-the-moment Mother's Day trip to see the International Art Fair there. We both wanted to see the booths of art from galleries in Tokyo, London, Rome, Paris, Berlin, Mexico City, São Paulo, Seoul and major galleries in the U.S. exhibiting in one enormous pavilion on Navy Pier. We were exhilarated by the idea we could see a large survey of twentieth-century art all in one place.

I wore a tailored suit but had my most comfortable clunky walking shoes on. As I looked down I saw vineyard dirt still in their leather creases. Roman and I began systematically visiting every booth. Each one had as many as six walls or partitions hung with contemporary art and photographs. Sculpture occupied open floor spaces. There were a few video installations; one was playing the sound track from *Apocalypse Now* with images of a large sun rapidly setting and rising over and over.

In the midafternoon we came upon the booth of the John Berggruen Gallery. John is an art dealer I know in San Francisco. When he saw us he said, "Here, sit down in my chairs. The pavilion is a third of a mile long and there are six aisles. Think about it." As we rested, I admired a beautiful Matisse drawing on the wall; a classic ink drawing of a seated woman wearing a ruffled peasant blouse. Her face was simply rendered yet exquisitely expressive, and the way the brush strokes described the cloth of her blouse utterly thrilled me. Roman said, "You love it, Mom, you should have it. Get it!" I thought about why I would never buy a really expensive work of art. Why the burden of ownership outweighs the pleasure of seeing it. Seventeen hundred acres of land and everything on it feels as if it's all the valuable possessions I can bear. I marvel at how Francis can hold so much in his attention: the apartments in Paris and New York, the houses in New Orleans and Los Angeles, the lodge in Belize, the property he is bidding on in Costa Rica, the association with the film company in Brazil, all that is involved with the winery, his film company, the short-story magazine, invitations, requests, lawsuits and more. Some days I feel as if my mind is the size of a pebble and his is the size of Mount Rushmore. I am constantly trying to eliminate things from my scope of attention so I can hear my own voice more clearly. He seems to hear himself fine in a cacophony.

We finished looking at the last booth at 8:00 p.m. as the guards were shutting off the lights. I loved that Roman was as fanatical as I was about seeing everything. Outside a large crowd waited in a chill wind for scarce taxis so we walked more than a mile to our hotel. I was so happy to be with Roman, our arms linked, talking about what we'd seen. I haven't traveled alone with him as an adult and was apprehensive about whether we would be ill at ease without Sofia, Gia or Francis with us.

"So, if you had a lot of money to spend what would you have bought?" I asked Roman. "The Magritte." In my mind I could see a small rendering of a man's pipe with the words painted in careful script "This is not a pipe." "The Wesselmann"—a small painting of two identical images of red lips with lit cigarettes—"and the Ruscha"—a work on paper with the word "room" elegantly written in gun powder. We added up their combined prices; the total was $425,000. I gasped. He said, "I liked seeing art that is actually for sale; it's frustrating to know you can never own anything you see in a museum." We walked through a pedestrian tunnel passing under the highway fronting the lake. He asked me what art I wanted. I said, "Well, the Matisse of course and the Twombly painting for sure; and that little photograph by the unknown photographer, of his wife in a patterned sarong sitting on a flowered couch wearing a tiara in her fluffy hair. She looked so earnest as she posed to please her husband. I'm sorry I didn't get that."

Back in my room I lay on the bed with my aching feet up on pillows. I expected to be exhilarated by a full day just looking at art, but I felt I had seen too much. I was saturated and couldn't imagine ever being interested in art again. How can anyone care about work on paper or canvas anyway; surely all the images in the future will be electronic, be digital.

It was quite late when we went out for dinner. We were joined by a friend of Roman's and ate at a nondescript bistro near the hotel. At the end of the meal Roman ordered a double espresso. He explained, "I have to come up with a concept for a music video by tomorrow morning. I'll probably be up till 3:00 or 4:00." When we returned to the hotel and passed through the hotel lobby, I was startled to catch myself stopping to look at a small painting in a display case. I felt as if I was an addict. I'd overdosed on art only hours before and I was already looking for more. I could see Roman waiting by the elevator with a distant expression as if he were already at work scanning the video idea files in his mind. At the door of my room he said, "Wake me up in the morning when you are ready to go out and I'll get up even if I stay up late."

The next morning I waited to call him until 10:45 a.m., the last moment to order breakfast from room service before they stopped serving. He said in a groggy voice, "I didn't go to bed until 8:00 a.m. Order me something and call me back in 45 minutes. I don't care if my coffee is cold."

When he came to my room an hour later his shirt tails hung out and his hair was tousled. He slouched in the chair as he ate a half grapefruit and said, "I just couldn't get my concept to come together. I worked all night on an idea that never really panned out so at 7:00 this morning I gave up on it and did something completely different. I think it turned out OK. I faxed it to my agent in New York and the office in London. It's for a French band, we'll shoot in Europe."

It seemed so familiar. So many times Francis stayed up all night writing, sleeping only a few hours before going back to work. So often the creative process seems to include working very hard on something that never pans out and is finally abandoned only to discover something better.

Part Four

October 6, 2002 Napa

Looking for winter sweaters in storage this morning I came across a handsome scarf of gold lace backed with cashmere that was given to me by the costume designer Milena Canonero as she was packing up at the end of shooting *Godfather III*. "Ellie, you should have this, it was Kay's." I remember my discomfort when Diane Keaton once told me she modeled her character for Kay Corleone on me. I hated to think I was the inspiration for the quiet WASP bystander of Michael Corleone's deeds.

I am fond of Milena. She worked on three of Francis's films. When she did *Cotton Club* in New York, Sofia was twelve and liked me to take her after school to visit the costume department and see Milena's work, especially the exquisitely beaded showgirls' costumes and the bias-cut silk lingerie. Milena was nominated for an Academy Award for the costumes she designed for Francis's film *Tucker: The Man and His Dream*, and she designed *Godfather III*. As it turned out, Sofia was cast as Michael Corleone's daughter, Mary, in the film and Milena created everything she wore. All day today I've been thinking about experiences during the making of *Godfather III*.

May 7, 1989 Palermo, Sicily

I am standing on a terra-cotta tile terrace. In front of me are old gardens with orange, palm and pine trees. Bougainvillea and geraniums meander along the walkways leading to small curved balconies with stone benches in the high wall overlooking the small harbor. Sailboats pass and fishing boats are moored nearby. In the distance I can see the city of Palermo and the mountains behind rising sharply into a clear blue sky. We are here on a location scout for *Godfather III*. The last two days we have visited villas, churches and piazzas. This is my favorite phase of Francis's work; he is doing research and creatively envisioning settings for the film before the realities and difficulties of actually shooting set in. I appreciate the opportunity to see places unavailable to the public.

Yesterday the production team was looking for a house that would be Michael Corleone's home in Sicily. We were taken to the villa of a local baron who had an extraordinary collection of Greek amphorae found at sites in the local countryside. They were displayed in perfectly lit cases, in rooms with high painted ceilings and tall French doors that led to terraces and gardens. In the grand old library filled with leather-bound volumes, paintings of ancestors above the fireplace and real lion skins on the floor, we were introduced to the baron. He looked as if he had been sent from central casting, tall, slim and erect, with graying hair, handlebar mustache, and goatee. He wore a tweed jacket, silk shirt and ascot. His shoes were soft polished leather. He spoke English with a British boarding school accent and a world-weary attitude, as if he'd met every king and prince on the continent and a few filmmakers were a minor amusement in his day.

In the afternoon we went to meet the archbishop in Monreale (there are sequences in the script that involve an Italian archbishop). A young monk met us and guided us into a large room with centuries-old embroidered vestments hung on the walls behind glass. The archbishop joined us, a jolly man in his sixties who spoke animatedly in Italian. He wore a black robe trimmed with magenta piping and small covered buttons all the way up the front, a little round cap and wide magenta silk sash. Tucked into his sash was a heavy gold cross decorated with rubies, attached to a thick gold chain. He absently turned a large ring with a cameo of Christ between his thick fingers. An expensive gold watch was partially visible at his wrist and flashes of his magenta socks could be seen as he walked. He showed us through several rooms with beautifully painted high ceilings and old, patterned tile floors. Light filtered through tall windows with partially closed shutters. He opened

French doors and escorted us out onto a private terrace to see a magnificent view of the valley below, with terra-cotta-colored houses and groves of orange and lemon trees extending to the sea. Returning inside, we were shown into a large sitting room with heavy wooden furniture upholstered in burgundy silk brocade. Huge paintings in elaborately carved wood frames dominated the high walls. A young monk arrived carrying a tray of small cups of espresso and glasses of orange soda. We sat on the uncomfortable furniture and sipped our drinks while Francis interviewed the archbishop with the help of a translator.

We returned down a long hall to a heavy wooden door where the archbishop said goodbye and left us. The young monk opened the door and we found ourselves in a side chapel of a huge cathedral. The glow of candlelight reflected on gold mosaics covering the walls and ceilings in intricate patterns framing depictions of saints and biblical scenes. I could hear the murmur of hushed voices, the sound of clothes rustling and shoes on the stone floor. We stepped from the chapel and were in the midst of a throng of tourists. Looking up into the high main nave we saw the masterwork of Byzantine gold mosaic.

We were directed to exit by a side door and emerged into the bright light of a hot dusty street. Stalls selling tourist trinkets, noisy motor scooters, plastic signs advertising Kodak film, cars and parking lots surrounded us.

May 8, 1989

When I woke up this morning, the steep mountains behind the city of Palermo were pale formless shadows hidden in a dull gray haze. Francis had to leave at 8:30 to meet the mayor and the local cardinal. He was tired and irritable. I ordered coffee for him and tea for myself. Two pots of coffee arrived, which I didn't realize until after the waiter left. I called room service and had one of those traveler's conversations. I said, "Two coffees arrived and no tea," and he said,

"Yes, two coffees and no tea, is coming, Madame, right away," and hung up. Francis had an upset stomach, he drank water with baking soda and left. I took a long hot shower. As I stepped out, I discovered there were no bath towels, only a few thin linen towels next to the bidet. I fantasized about being at home sitting on the porch in Napa with a cup of mint tea, looking out across the lawn, past fragrant trees, to the bushy green vineyards.

May 10, 1989 Rome

The windows are open. I can see the tops of pine trees and terra-cotta-colored buildings. I am in a second-floor office at Cinecittà, the Italian film studio near the outskirts of Rome. Offices have been prepared for Francis's production here in the wing where Fellini used to work. A handsome new door says "Zoetrope/Italia." I can hear Francis's voice, loud and urgent as he conducts a script conference. The script for *GFIII* is due today. It will be submitted to Paramount in a few hours when it is morning in L.A. The last changes are being made before it is faxed to meet the delivery deadline.

This morning Francis was tired, on edge, after staying up most of the night writing. He wanted me to have a leisurely breakfast with him before he went to the studio. I got a call from the production office unexpectedly to go with Dean [Dean Tavoularis, the production designer] and his assistant Phillis [Phillis Lehmer, who traveled with me in Japan years later] to the Vatican to shoot research photos behind the scenes where the public isn't permitted. Francis was irritated, but I went. (The script has scenes in which Michael Corleone has dealings with the Vatican.)

Dean, Phillis and I were met by a special guide who drove us to the Vatican. At the entrance, our guide went into the security office and got a pass verifying our appointment with a monk he knew. He parked the car in a courtyard among the massive buildings and directed us to enter a side door attended by two tall, handsome Swiss guards. He showed our pass and we were permitted to take a wood-paneled elevator to the second floor. We learned that the elevator continued to the Pope's personal apartments. As we walked along the wide marble hallways with high vaulted ceilings I could see into enormous rooms with elaborate painting on the ceilings and walls. The floors were patterned with intricately inlaid marble designs. Each time we turned a corner out of sight of a Swiss guard, a new one appeared to check our pass. We arrived in the most spectacular room of all, outside the Pope's private chapel. We were the only people there and the sound of our voices disappeared in the vast expanses of silent marble. Our guide spoke to an attendant at a small side door and in a few minutes a monk appeared. He was a short gray-haired man wearing a black suit with a sprinkling of dandruff on his shoulders. He greeted us in a bored manner, took out a ring of large keys, found the right one and opened a door into a short passageway.

Suddenly, I felt the nearby sound of hundreds of people moving about on the marble floor in a vast room, their clothes rustling and their whispered voices. As we entered, I realized we were in the Sistine Chapel. I looked at the ceiling, enthralled, as I was hurried across the floor through the crowd to a roped-off area next to the altar. The monk spoke to a guard who unclipped a thick velvet rope and allowed us to pass into a small room behind the altar. Inside were a desk and a sofa. Worn-looking, richly patterned red silk covered the walls. We were told that it was the room where the Pope dresses before a service. We proceeded up a narrow staircase and waited at a doorway while the monk turned off an alarm system. We entered a room with heavy wooden closets lining the walls. The monk opened them to reveal glass cases containing shelves and shelves of high papal hats decorated with gold and real jewels. The top of one hat had an ornament containing an emerald the size of a lime. There were elaborately embroidered white linen undergarments and a case of ornate gold staffs. There were many shelves of elaborately decorated gold chalices, plates, bowls and crosses used on the altar. I noticed a gold hammer which our guide said is used in a ceremony when a Pope dies. "He is tapped on the forehead three times while his name is called." We were told a large assortment of silver altar pieces were used for mourning rites.

Slowly we returned back through the rooms. As we proceeded down the steps our guide instructed Phillis to slip the monk 100,000 lire [$80], which she discreetly did. We passed through the Sistine Chapel again and back to the point where we had first met the monk. We thanked him and he quickly disappeared.

Dean asked if we could see the Pope's meeting rooms and our guide informed him that power in the Vatican resembled an octopus with many tentacles and he would have to contact another monk some other day who had the ability to let us into that area. As we walked back through the great empty rooms in the direction of the elevator, I got a few last shots with the video camera in moments when the Swiss guards were turned away. The morning light coming through tall windows illuminated magnificently painted ceilings and patterned marble floors. We entered the elevator and soon arrived back in the courtyard where our car was parked. At the exit gate the guard took our pass. He peered into the car. We had put the cameras out of sight. Our guide drove us to Cinecittà, chatting about the ruins and things we should see while we are in Rome. I heard very little; I was still among the Pope's embroidered robes.

We spent months in California while Francis did script rewrites and continued pre-production.

October 8, 1989 Flight to New York

I am flying with Francis from L.A. to New York on the first leg of a journey to the location for *Godfather III*. Emotions move through my body along old paths. Yesterday I said goodbye to Roman on the sidewalk in front of the Sentinel Building as we left for the airport. I can still feel the imprint of his thick hair in my hand as my arms wrapped around his neck in a lingering hug. I won't see him until Christmas. A wave of pain mixed with fear settled in my chest. I remembered when Gio hugged me hard as I left for an airport. I never saw him again.

Last night in Los Angeles at the christening of Fred Roos's baby, we stood in the candlelight at the front of the church. Francis held the baby, I reached for his tiny hand as he waved it in delight over Francis's shoulder, perilously close to candle flames. We became godparents for the first time on the eve of starting *Godfather III*.

A limousine took us back to our bungalow in Benedict Canyon. The car had a furry camel-brown carpet. I thought about how much a child would enjoy crawling around on it. A deluge of memories of our children passed through my mind, my body. With Sofia in her first semester of college and Gia and Jacqui living in their own apartment, it is strange not to be constantly concerned about a child. Part of my mind is still checking on whether the carpet in the car is clean enough to play on.

When we arrived at our small house, Fred was waiting on the front porch with a box of videotapes. We settled into the living room and Francis set up the tapes to play through the TV. I watched as they went through the casting process, picking actors for the remaining parts, eliminating others. I thought how each person would feel when they got the news. I fell asleep on the couch, suddenly exhausted from the last weeks with cast rehearsals in Napa for those already chosen and preparations to leave home for five months.

October 20, 1989 Rome

When we arrived at Fiumicino Airport in Rome, a VIP car and escort met us on the tarmac and took us to the terminal ahead of all the other passengers. Our escort said, with excitement and a heavy accent, "Welcome to Rome. You are the director of the film *Stepfather*." When the young woman took our passports and read Francis's name, she called to the girl in the next booth and they giggled excitedly. At the baggage claim, one bag was missing. As I filled out claim forms, I reviewed the contents of the lost suitcase in my mind, and suddenly I felt I couldn't do without a single item, most of all the photos of the children. Entering the center of the old city was familiar and exciting. A car took us to Dean's apartment, where we had a simple home-cooked dinner together. Our rented apartment was not ready so we stayed the night.

October 23, 1989

The days are passing and I find myself once again in a familiar situation with Francis: he is excited in the throes of production preparations, and I am dealing with mundane domestic problems. When we arrived at the apartment rented for our location stay, it was filthy. The cleaning lady worked for half a day and left. Our friend Paula who lives nearby came to help me. We packed up seven cartons of the owner's personal junk: broken appliances, stained place mats, cracked vases, ugly bric-a-brac and chipped dishes. We threw out old food, stale seasonings and broken utensils. We defrosted the freezer and cleaned out bathroom cupboards, tossing out sticky half-used toiletries and packing up the old hair dryer, brushes, clogs, hot water bottle, shaving equipment, nail clippers and more. The faucet dripped and the toilet seat hinge was broken. It was chilly in the apartment and the heater didn't work. Now several days have passed and I have nearly gotten things in order—today only the kitchen sink is stopped up. My frustrations feel real enough to me, but are once again so completely insignificant in the life that surrounds me. Francis's problem is that although he has rewritten a part many times to please Robert Duvall, Duvall has turned down every offer. Now Francis must write him out of the script.

Uprooted from my friends and familiar life at home, attending to the tedious tasks of getting settled in a foreign place, I find myself fighting a wave of depression. But this is Rome, after all. Deep afternoon shadows fall across the golden autumn light in the courtyard outside the kitchen window. It is still warm enough to sit on the terrace beneath the bougainvillea for lunch. Our street is called Via dei Cappellari, street of the hatmakers. It is a narrow cobblestoned street about ten feet wide where artisans used to live who served wealthy clients in nearby palazzos. Now the interior courtyards are filled with pushcarts and crates of produce for the open-air market. The street is often dirty. Cats dart out from doorways searching for something to eat. Laundry hangs on lines from second-story windows.

We met the local "king of thieves," who lives in our building. He told me to watch out for my purse until I am known in the neighborhood. The Piazza Campo dei Fiori is just a block away with stands selling fresh flowers, fruits, vegetables and fish in the outdoor market each morning. There is a bakery at the corner. Delicious aromas float down the street. Before breakfast I walk out and buy the newspaper, fruit and fresh-baked round flower-shaped "rosette" rolls made only in Rome.

DECEMBER 25, 1989

It is cold. There is a fire in the fireplace. The Christmas tree is shedding needles on the gray carpet.

Francis is in bed listening to news in English on his short-wave radio. Roman and Sofia are asleep on the scruffy leather sofa. I am so completely happy they are here.

Last night, Christmas Eve, we went to Tally's [Francis's sister, Talia Shire's] apartment. It is on the sixth floor of a building nearby and has a huge terrace with views of the city in every direction. She invited Al [Pacino] and Diane [Keaton], Andy [Garcia] and his family, and all of us. Francis's mother made traditional octopus sauce for the spaghetti. It was Tally's son Robert's birthday and all the kids were happy in a chaos of wrappings and presents.

At 10:00 p.m. a group of us walked to the French church for mass. I was anticipating hearing wonderful music resounding within the beautiful space. Instead, thin voices of the congregation evaporated in the arched nave. There were two memorable moments. One was when lights were turned on, dramatically illuminating the vast, elaborately painted ceiling and the extraordinary carvings above the altar. The second was when all the children came to the back where I was sitting; they lit candles and formed a procession to carry a doll of the baby Jesus forward to the altar. As they stood with their cherub faces, holding their candles, fidgeting, waiting for the signal to proceed down the aisle, they looked so beautifully expectant. Diane Keaton's hat bobbed in the row in front of me. Gia fell asleep in her stroller. When a droning sermon began, we left rather conspicuously. The night was not cold and we walked back home through the cobblestoned streets.

Around noon Tally and her family arrived. We were twenty people spending Christmas day together in our two-bedroom apartment. At 1:00 p.m., I put the twelve-kilo [approximately twenty-five-pound] turkey in the oven. There was no baking pan. Our friend Paula told me to set the turkey on the indented floor of the oven. Her advice has been so helpful to me, I decided to cook the turkey in the Italian way. After several hours of roasting, the grease overflowed and caught fire. When Francis lifted the turkey from the flaming oven it slipped out of his hands and slid in a pool of grease across the kitchen floor. I wiped up the grease with paper towels but the floor was still dangerously slippery so I mopped it by hand with a cloth and hot soapy water.

With a bottle of our wine from California under my arm, I went out to a local restaurant and asked the owner to lend me a lasagna pan in exchange for the wine. Finally I got the turkey back in the oven. By four in the afternoon all the sodas had been drunk and the carpet was a sea of nut shells, Christmas candy and wrappings. Members of the family pitched in to clean up a bit now and then, but there was a continuous messy chaos to the day. Somehow everything got done, more guests arrived and twenty-five of us sat down to Christmas dinner.

December 28, 1989

I woke up with little fingers in my hair and the faint acrid smell of wet diapers. Gia was standing next to my bed. She had stayed overnight. Francis left for work early. He seemed relieved to have Christmas over, with all the relatives and guests, and go back to work. I played with Gia for a long time in the bathtub, making desserts with foamy bubbles in her plastic dishes.

Sofia got up late. Around noon the phone rang. She answered it and said it was for me. I took the phone in the kitchen, standing in a patch of sunlight on the tile floor. I was surprised to hear the voice of the assistant director calling in the middle of a shooting day. He is a jovial guy full of fun, and he sounded unusually serious. A little wave of panic flashed across my heart. He said very quickly that the production doctor had just returned from seeing Winona Ryder: "She is too sick to work and is being sent home. Francis has decided to cast Sofia in her part." Winona was cast as Mary, the daughter of Michael Corleone ⟦played by Al Pacino⟧. Francis had read Sofia for the part of Mary. He thought she did well and looked like a real Italian daughter rather than an actress but the studio pushed for a box office name.

The assistant director asked if Sofia could come to the studio immediately because a scene with her character was scheduled to shoot in a few hours and there would be a costume fitting right away. I told Sofia as evenly as I could, but tears of emotion welled in my eyes. She was very excited at first; then as it sank in, she became anxious. I said, "I know Dad would never cast you if he didn't believe you could do the part really well." I could see how worried she was, she didn't want to let him down.

While Sofia got dressed, I tried to feed Gia and find her shoes. The AD had asked us to come the fastest way. The traffic was so bad I thought it would be too slow in a taxi. We took a bus to the subway. Gia's stroller got caught in the bus door. Sofia held Gia while I struggled to get it out. The subway took us to the station in front of Cinecittà and we fast-walked to the costume shop.

JANUARY 1, 1990

All day yesterday firecrackers went off in our neighborhood. Our dog ran barking frantically through the apartment. Paula told me that it was customary for people to throw old things they wanted to get rid of out the window on New Year's Eve and we should be careful in our narrow street. She said that on January first the streets are littered with all sorts of things. "You might even find an old refrigerator."

In the evening we went to a cast and crew party on our piazza in the home of an actor who played one of the members of the board of directors in the stockholders' scene. He said, "I found this apartment in 1960 when everyone wanted to move out of Rome into the new suburbs. The sign advertising it said it had eleven rooms. When I moved in I found it had seventeen. I still pay the same fixed rent." He told us the price, which was lower than what Roman is paying for a studio apartment in our building. The food and drinks were set out in a huge room that had a thirty-foot ceiling. Torn swags of elaborately painted canvas hung from exposed rafters; I could see fittings for elegant draperies long gone.

Francis had a heated exchange with an executive from Paramount who was questioning his wisdom in casting Sofia so quickly in the part of Mary Corleone. It was too uncomfortable for me to witness. I understood the logic of the executive and I knew that Francis's unpopular choices in the past, such as Al Pacino in *The Godfather*, had turned out very well. It was painful for Francis to have his casting decisions second-guessed.

I went out onto the terrace that overlooked the piazza and watched the fireworks. People in nearby buildings were setting off rockets from their windowsills. Several fireballs whizzed within inches of Roman and the kids at the front of the balcony. I heard someone shout through the smoke, "Incoming! Hey, this is like *Apocalypse Now*."

Francis, Sofia and I walked home around 2:00 a.m. I didn't see any major appliances thrown in the street but there were lots of broken bottles, flowerpots, and common garbage. Our entry courtyard was a mass of litter, old shoes, playing cards, broken glass, shards of terra-cotta roof tiles, and a blue plastic dishpan riding a sea of old newspapers and orange peels.

Today is Gia's birthday. We slept late. The maid hasn't been here for four days. She called to tell me there was wet wash in the washer. I hung out the laundry. The lines are attached to the kitchen balcony and extend over a courtyard. One of Francis's socks fell to the roof of the apartment below and I couldn't think of a way to retrieve it. As I was vacuuming the living room Roman arrived. He arranged presents, two cakes, paper plates, glasses and favors on the dining room table. Jacqui and Gia came in the afternoon with all the family. Gia was excited. Francis held her up to blow out the three red candles on her cake. She opened presents on the fat sofa, tearing through the wrapping papers with gusto.

The phone rang intermittently. Helmut Berger called from Switzerland. He said it was very cold where he was, "There is no snow and it's terribly boring." He told Francis that with the front of his head shaved for his part in the film, no one recognized him, and he had to pay overweight charges on his baggage for the first time in years. Milena Canonero called to arrange to have Sofia picked up in the morning and taken to a fitter for body pads to make her look older. She is a thin nineteen-year-old. Winona Ryder called from her family's home in California and spoke to Francis. She apologized for getting sick and having to leave the production. Roman and Sofia talked to friends at home. I could hear in Roman's voice that he was homesick; his friends had gone to Las Vegas for the weekend, having fun without him. Sofia told her boyfriend she is getting tits tomorrow.

In the evening Francis didn't feel like going out. Roman, Sofia and I walked to a restaurant near our piazza. It's been a long time since the three of us had dinner alone; I was happy to be with them but it felt as if something was missing. When the check came, I noticed we were overcharged a few thousand lire for each item, making the bill twelve or fifteen percent higher than it should have been. I knew if I objected the waiter would smile and pretend to not understand what I was saying. Probably if Francis had been with us it wouldn't have happened.

January 2, 1990

Roman went to the studio early with Francis. At 9:30 Sofia went downstairs to a waiting taxi and drove off to get body pads, then to the studio for costume fittings and to have her hair dyed darker. I did the shopping in the piazza. The sky was a clear vivid blue. Wedges of bright morning sun shone between the buildings. I stood in the light in front of a vegetable stall, absorbing the colors of the carrots, crates of shiny eggplant, zucchini, broccoli, dark green spinach, fennel bulbs and long-stemmed artichokes. Shafts of light reached into our narrow street. It looked as if it were a theatrical set. Pink sheets hung from a wrought iron balcony in front of a terra-cotta wall. Green shuttered windows and pots of geraniums appeared to be spotlit. Gray and white cats roamed the shadowy doorways. Even the new year's garbage looked picturesque. I had the day to myself. The first in a long time, a treasure.

January 10, 1990

The early morning light is dove gray with hints of coral appearing behind the jumble of old tile rooftops and TV antennas. A white-haired woman has just opened her shutters across the small courtyard, giving me a momentary glimpse into her simple kitchen with blue walls and wooden table set for breakfast. I am waiting for Sofia to wake up. It is just sinking in that she may not return to college for a year or longer. She attended Mills College last fall but without much enthusiasm. A demanding work experience will no doubt change her.

Francis left early as usual. The last few days have been exhausting. Francis and Sofia are under enormous pressure, which I feel acutely. A number of people on the production think Sofia is too young and inexperienced for her part in the film. They have been very vocal about their opinions. Francis has been shooting a difficult scene with Sofia. Every moment she isn't on the stage she is taken to costume fittings, the hairdresser, or to a diction teacher. Several times she has burst into tears. Well-meaning people tell me I am permitting a form of child abuse, that she is not ready, not trained for what is being asked of her and that in the end she will be fodder for critics' bad reviews that could scar her for years. I am told that Francis can't afford to take a chance on a choice that could weaken his work at this point in his career.

The night before last, Francis went to sleep in a cold sweat and got up at 5:00 in the morning to go to the studio. By the time his new production manager arrived at 8:00, he had made a plan to hire an editor immediately and put a scene with Sofia together and make a final decision based on what was actually on the screen. During the day his lawyer called to tell him that in his contract, he has final artistic control.

Francis avoided being drawn into lengthy discussions with the Paramount executives who have been sent here. He shifted the schedule and shot the rest of the scene which included Sofia's close-up. Roman and I went with her and spent the day at the studio. I didn't hover. I was just there. I took very seriously the accusation that I was being a negligent parent. I could see that at times Sofia felt courageous and excited and wanted to do it and at other times she was tired and utterly miserable. But she wasn't asking me to help her get out of it and I wasn't ignoring her or pushing her on.

January 16, 1990

I am in Francis's office at Cinecittà. It is lunch break. He is at his computer writing a letter to Paramount executives affirming his choice to cast Sofia and reminding them that contractually the decision is his. The day is bright but very cold. I am huddled next to the heater in a thin silk brocade dress. Today I am playing an extra in the party scene set in Michael's New York apartment, in progress on Stage 15. After rehearsing for hours, we are now in a holding pattern while Gordon Willis [the cinematographer] lights the big master shot which involves two cameras covering action moving through several rooms.

This morning there was bumper-to-bumper traffic on our route along the Via Appia Antica, a narrow street leading out of central Rome. We were stopped for a number of minutes at the Porto San Sebastiano where the cobblestoned road goes under the old Roman aqueduct. It still amazes me that we travel over the same roads that were used by chariots so many centuries ago. I arrived at the wardrobe department just after 8:00 a.m. and was taken into a private fitting room. Francis's mother was already there. We talked about what great legs she has, not a vein and she is in her seventies. My costume consists of a short black skirt with a Nehru-style long brocade overblouse with more than three dozen difficult buttons up the front. I buttoned forever but the buttons didn't come out even. Jacqui came in, pulled one off and sent me to hairdressing. Two hairdressers consulted in Italian and then a young man began to curl my hair with a hot iron. His skill was remarkable to watch but I looked very frizzy. When Milena saw me she said, "No, no, the look is all wrong" and they misted it with water and combed it straight back and added a hairpiece swirled at the back of my neck. It was the first time I thought I looked truly grandmotherly.

When Milena returned I could see she didn't like my new style either but there was no time to change it again. I went into makeup where I received a very complete makeover concluding with a lot of powder and bright red lips painted larger than my natural lip line. I went to the set. The rooms of Michael's apartment had been dressed for an elegant party with tables set throughout. The huge buffet table was laden with fancy food and included pheasants, lobsters, shrimp and prime rib. The orchestra was in the main room which had a dais and round tables for guests. There were perhaps a hundred extras and many children.

When I found Francis I could see that he was surprised by my appearance. He thought I looked older and more matronly and reminded him of my mother. He introduced me to my table: "This is Aunt Delphine [my mother's name], Tom Hagen's sister." I had two nephews and a niece at the table and my sister-in-law, Hagen's wife. The actors, led by John Savage playing Tom Hagen's son, stayed in character and spoke to me as their aunt. I could see Francis's mother playing a party guest at a nearby table seated next to Eli Wallach, laughing at his jokes. Sofia was seated on the dais next to

Al; Tally was by her dad, who was conducting the orchestra as he had for *Godfather* and *Godfather II*. The shot was of Tally leading the guests in singing "Eh Cumpari." All of Tally's shots will be done first because she has to leave in a few days to go to work on *Rocky V*.

JANUARY 17, 1990

This morning when I arrived at the studio there was frost, like snow, on the driveways and lawns. I wore the top of my long underwear under my costume but my legs were freezing. I was the last one in makeup. The sign on the door says "Trucco," which in Italian means makeup and also means trick.

The extras and principals are being set for the scene where Mary Corleone gives the archbishop a check for $100 million. Gordy is building the composition person by person for the camera, moving a press person a bit more to the right, Al a half step forward. The camera assistant puts tape X's on the floor to mark the actor's first position and moves. The extras chat and are frequently told to be more quiet. A little boy near me tucks his adult-size tie into his seven-year-old's trousers and carefully buttons his jacket. Several production assistants are wearing tuxedos so they can work in the crowd cueing extras.

Sofia looks lovely with her hair dyed dark and slightly waved. Her chest and hips are padded and in her flattering dress she does look older. I can see hints of her anxiety from time to time but she seems somehow strong enough to handle it. Mary Corleone makes a little speech when she presents the archbishop with the check. She has been practicing for days with a coach, Fret Vreeland [Diana Vreeland's son]. I am noticing how so much of my emotional life is caught up vicariously with Sofia's anxiety and Francis's tension.

I find myself watching Al with fascination. Just moments before the scene begins he shifts his posture, in a way that immediately gives him an appearance of age and ill health.

JANUARY 19, 1990

Today Sofia did the scene where she waltzes with Al. It was so sweet, so reminiscent of when Marlon waltzed with Tally in *Godfather*. She did the rehearsals in her stocking feet, saving her uncomfortable heels until they were shooting. Gia kept running onto the dance floor and grabbing hold of Sofia's skirt during the shot. As I looked out across the set I could see Francis's father conducting the orchestra, Francis's sister in her aging makeup playing Connie, Francis's mother sitting at the table next to Eli Wallach, Gia running among the children and Jacqui at the edge of the set holding a handful of earrings, a necktie and a child's hair ribbon.

MARCH 3, 1990

Last week I returned to Rome after five weeks in California and went straight to the studio. I found Francis on the opera set. We were so happy to see each other. He was working on a scene in *Cavalleria Rusticana* for the final sequence of the film. The set and costumes were absolutely beautiful. After the second take I heard a squeal of delight and Gia ran across the floor over cables, around equipment and into my arms.

The next day I got up with Francis at 5:45 and went with him to the coffee bar as it was opening. The narrow streets looked new to me, so fresh with the scent of bread cooling at the bakery. We ate breakfast and read the *Herald Tribune*. He looked tired, with dark circles around his eyes, and said, "I'm ready to finish out Rome and move on."

Francis left for the studio and I went back to the apartment and started packing for Sicily.

MARCH 4, 1990

Today is Sunday. In the afternoon Anahid Nazarian [Francis's librarian] came over, and she and Francis took their computers out to his favorite restaurant in the piazza and set up on an outdoor table to rewrite a scene. I walked to the French church to see the Caravaggio painting again, to look at the way light rendered folds of blue silk at the top of a sleeve, fell on the boy's face and the man's leg. I stood there for a long time, then went back near the door, lit a candle for Gio and sat on one of the hard wooden benches in the nave to meditate.

In the evening Jacqui, Gia, Sofia, Francis's parents and several friends gathered at the restaurant and we had dinner together at a long table on the sidewalk. Francis was in a bad mood, spoke angrily to his father and concluded by saying that everyone at the table was taking from him and no one was helping him. I tried not to let his dark mood permeate my evening but it was pervasive.

MARCH 6, 1990

I rode to the studio with Francis early in the morning. Sofia was in the first shot. I found her in her dressing room at 7:30, already having been to hairdressing. We talked while the wardrobe assistant hung up her costume and laid out her accessories which included two boxes. Sofia started dressing. The boxes contained her falsies, heavy cold silicone blobs. I warmed them on the radiator before she stuffed them into her padded bra.

I walked over to the stage and found Francis sitting on the big sofa in Michael Corleone's living room. We talked while the crew set up the shot on the main stairway. Francis was very depressed. He spoke so convincingly about all the things wrong in his life: how he hated that he was doing the same thing again that he had done nearly twenty years ago, hated the process of making movies, all the time it took. The only thing he liked about filmmaking was the technology. He talked about his family, he complained about me. I sat there while he ran it all out, not agreeing and not yielding to the temptation to defend anyone, just trying to be there for him. When Francis was called to the camera first position I went for a walk outside. I tried to visualize all his dark words draining out of me, dripping off the ends of my fingers and running out my toes through my shoes. I tried to feel myself filling up with sunlight.

March 8, 1990

It is 6:30 a.m. I can hear Francis's fingers flying over the keys of his computer at the kitchen table. He types faster than a court stenographer. I am still under our down quilt this chilly morning. Today the production moves to Sicily. Yesterday I packed up almost everything and it was picked up to travel by truck. In the late afternoon I walked to the subway savoring a last look at the city. I emerged from the station at Cinecittà just as the sky was turning a deep peach color. I felt the familiar sadness of a location ending, mixed with the excitement of moving to the next place. I passed by the production offices to say goodbye to people who are not going on to Sicily. Packing boxes were stacked in the hallways, all the pictures were off the walls and the bulletin boards were bare. I found Francis in the Silverfish talking to the set over an intercom while the final shot in Rome was being set. It was a close-up of cutting the cake at the party in Michael's New York apartment. When they were ready to shoot we walked out to the stage. Andy Garcia's little girl was the cake cutter with the help of Al's stand-in. Francis was looking forward to having a piece of the cake and celebrating the moment. The cake trolley was moved into position six times before it hit the mark correctly for the camera and the cake was actually cut. Everyone was disappointed to find that under the real icing it was cardboard.

March 14, 1990 Palermo

We took the overnight train from Rome to Palermo. The trip started out rather disastrously when we discovered that Francis's new briefcase was apparently stolen by gypsies who came up to us as we were unloading our luggage in front of the station. Francis was in a fury, his script notes and several books were in it. Finally we went to Sofia and Gia's compartment and we picnicked on caviar, sandwiches, cheese and fruit we had brought and drank champagne, trying to cheer Francis.

We arrived in Palermo at 8 a.m. and were met by the production staff and driven to the hotel with a police escort. The hotel was old, grand and slightly shabby. Francis told me, "Lucky Luciano stayed here when he came to Palermo after World War II."

We spent the day looking at locations that had been selected to shoot in, starting with the Villa Malfitano, chosen to be the house where Michael Corleone stays while he is visiting Sicily. It was a huge, somewhat run-down villa in its own park within the city. The great gardens in the back of the house had been refurbished by the art department. There were new flowers in the flower beds and men were working on the fountain. New lawn furniture and umbrellas were in place. Tables and chairs had been added to the veranda. Gordy, Dean, Francis, the ADs and several other production people walked the premises while it was decided where the first setups would be.

I went inside the house and Gary, a set dresser, showed me a number of rooms upstairs. Bedroom upon bedroom contained an array of personal things on the night stands and chests of drawers, belonging to the owners. He said, "Imagine someone leaving all this stuff here during a shoot." Family photos and paintings covered the walls and faded silk damask spreads were on the beds. Downstairs Gary joined other crew following Francis, Gordy and Dean as they decided where scenes were going to be shot and what furniture would be needed. For a poker game scene in the small library and a reception in the garden room, curtains, round tables, food and flowers would be added. A terrace room had been created by painting solid walls with windows and views out onto a garden. The floors had intricate inlaid marble mosaic patterns in ivory and black. I enjoyed seeing the rooms as they were before the cables were laid, sandbags, light stands and all the equipment were brought in.

We drove to the Teatro Massimo, where scenes will be shot at the entrance, in the lobby and opera boxes. It had been cleaned up a great deal since we were there on the first location scout. The art department had put panels of red damask over the mirrors in the anteroom outside the grand box so that it would be easier to shoot. There were rolls and rolls of red carpet ready to be installed and newly upholstered theater seats were waiting to be bolted in place. A thick gray dust had settled over everything during the twenty years the theater was closed. The art department had vacuumed numerous times but the dust wasn't completely gone. There was still much to do before the location would be ready to shoot. The production manager was looking worriedly at his pages of schedules.

March 16, 1990

On the first day of shooting in Palermo I rode to the set with Francis. We had a police escort to move us through the thick traffic on our way to Michael's villa. I watched the preparations for the first shot. Gary told me that he had spent a day with a flower man working out all the flower arrangements for the different rooms and the man had made samples that were outstanding. Now he had been told that he couldn't use him, he had to use someone sent by the people "sponsoring" the production. A guy had arrived with a load of flowers and just stuck them in vases without the slightest artistry. Gary pointed out the window. I could see a very large man in a black suit and dark sunglasses accompanied by a smaller man dressed identically. They looked as if they were sent by a casting agent to play mafiosi. I asked the production manager about them. I was told, "They are here to 'help' us." Later I heard there were two groups who wanted to "help" the production and there were some difficulties arranging for only one.

As I looked around the set I could see Francis's father rehearsing the band, his mother sitting in the shade chatting with a hairdresser, Tally in costume moving into position with Gia in a velvet dress playing her granddaughter. Francis looked into the monitor as the shot was being set. Sofia was standing next to Andy Garcia waiting to get into the car for the arrival, and Jacqui moved through a group of extras with a clump of tags and safety pins attached to her belt.

March 19, 1990 Villa Malfitano

I can smell fumes from the generators and the trucks starting up. Shooting on this location has been completed and there is a rush to pack up equipment and move to the next location at Teatro Massimo. The owners of the villa served everyone a glass of champagne on the enclosed veranda along the side of the huge villa. Our hosts were startled to see the cast and crew gulp their drinks quickly and return to packing. The sky has turned to pink-gray as evening approaches; trucks turn on their headlights as they pull out onto the gravel drive that surrounds the villa. Al and Francis are in the video van reviewing the footage from two important scenes shot today. Cables are being coiled neatly, the video assist trolley has been rolled out, packing cases are sitting on the marble steps waiting to be loaded. The actor's dressing room campers are driving away. Again the bittersweet feeling of leaving a beautiful location is mixed with the excitement of moving to the next.

March 25, 1990 Palermo

It is Sunday. I went out to get food from a nearby restaurant. We are so tired of the hotel menu. Francis is staying in today to work on the ending of the script. The script originally concluded with Michael Corleone getting gunned down on the opera house steps. Francis changed it to have his daughter, Mary, die from a bullet intended for him. The studio has expressed their doubts about Francis's new ending. Francis feels that worse than a quick death for Michael would be for him to have to live with the pain of what his life has wrought.

March 27, 1990

Last night I walked from the hotel to the set at 1:00 a.m. There was no one on the sidewalk and no traffic. It seemed as if it were a different city. Inside the Teatro Massimo they were working on a wide shot of the Corleone family in the royal box. The red velvet and gold decor glowed in the light of cranberry glass lamps. I watched for a while and then went down into the Silverfish where Francis was giving directions to the set and editing between shots. After the production wrapped at 3:00 a.m., we watched footage on the monitors for quite a while. Today, we got up late and left for the set just after noon. I went to the costume work room to see the progress on the pad for Sofia's dress which is supposed to allow the special effects blood to form a stain in the shape of a rose when she is shot. On the first test, the bloodstain didn't move through the lining fabric, so a patch with different but matching lining material and padding has to be added to each of the three identical dresses. The gold tulle outer layer of the dress has many gathers which had to be sewn again by hand.

I stopped by the hairdressing trailer to say hello to Sofia.

George Hamilton came in to have his hair dyed. He was dressed in an elegant suit and a beautiful overcoat with a fur collar. He wanted us to see the wig that was made for him to use if his hair was back to normal when they do retakes next July. The real-hair wig was neatly pinned to a form. The hair color was quite a good match, only it was wavy and George's hair is quite straight.

Milena and I went across the street to the coffee bar and ate sandwiches standing up at the counter.

John Savage came in and looked carefully at all the Sicilian pastries in the glass cases. He said, "What I really want is a bran muffin." We knew the feeling of being on a long location and wishing for a certain ordinary taste from home.

John was in wardrobe, wearing his priest's black suit. He began talking about how everyone treats him so well when he is in costume. A production assistant came in with a walkie-talkie looking for actors who were supposed to be on the set. John looked sheepish and left.

April 4, 1990

Last night I watched the big shot with 450 extras. The exterior of the theater was lit dramatically. The shot with the extras was rehearsed until 10:00 p.m., then the AD announced the lunch break. After lunch the camera crew worked for several hours to finalize the major camera lighting and the first shot was gotten around 1:30 a.m. It was of the large crowd arriving at the opera house, the Corleone family getting out of fine cars and all ascending the stone steps for the evening performance. It took a long time between shots to get all the cars and people back into their starting positions. By 3:00 a.m. they had completed three takes and everyone was released except the camera crew, who had to move the camera to the starting position for the next day's work.

Today is a perfect spring day. The air is fresh and cool with little warm eddies that greet you as you round a corner or enter a piazza. I walked out to buy fresh milk, fruit, and a wedge of Swiss cheese. We are so tired of the continental breakfast, all that is available at the hotel. I always have a moment of feeling tacky crossing the lobby with my lumpy shopping bags of food.

Francis is feeling great anxiety about the ending, which he shoots tonight. Paramount wants the film to end with Al Pacino dying in a burst of gunfire on the steps of Teatro Massimo. Francis feels intuitively that it should be more unusual, it should end as *King Lear* does: his daughter dies and he is left to live with the horror of his life.

As we were finishing breakfast Sofia came into our room. She was sore from working with Buddy Joe [the stunt coordinator] on her death scene. She has to fall on the steps, and although she will wear body pads under her dress she has to fall correctly in order not to get hurt. She was scared, which scared me. I rubbed her shoulders and hugged her, feeling an echo of deep fear in her movie death. Finally she said, "Oh, Mom" and pushed me gently away.

April 16, 1990 Taormina

Yesterday was Easter. We went to lunch with a group of 25 people that included Dean and his wife, Aurore, Francis, his parents, Jacqui and Gia, Eli Wallach, Gordy Willis, the camera operator, and the owners of the location villa. The restaurant was high on a hill, with a commanding view of the coastline. Several times during the afternoon I took Gia out on the terrace to look at rainbows in the dramatic sky over the sea. We sat down at the table at one-thirty in the afternoon, and left at five. The meal began with delicious fresh sardines dredged in lemon and olive oil, served with round loaves of country bread and spicy green olives. They were followed by platters of tender sliced octopus and cheese breaded and fried. Next we had sautéed wild greens with croutons, then a very good pasta arrived and, finally, roast lamb with potatoes and vegetables served from deep oval dishes brought straight from the oven.

I couldn't remember an Easter without our children. I hid eggs in the hotel room in Trieste during *Godfather II*, in the tropical foliage at our house in Manila during *Apocalypse Now*, in the city park in Tulsa during *The Outsiders*, and in the apartment in NYC during *Cotton Club*.

May 17, 1990 New York City

Today Central Park is shrouded in mist and it is raining intermittently. I feel anxious. Francis is supposed to be shooting outside; a scene in the street with an Italian *festa* and procession culminating in a complicated killing. Two hundred extras were called and over thirty street vendors' stalls with food were rented. Because of the weather they will no doubt have to go to a cover set which is a scene with Sofia. She has been preparing with a coach but I know she is scared. It is an important scene opposite Andy Garcia. I know, rationally, that my anxiety serves no purpose but even here alone in the hotel room my emotions are, as always, inextricably intertwined with their lives.

On Saturday I went to the hotel to get Gia. Jacqui's babysitter wasn't due to arrive until the next day and she had left Gia in Sofia's room when she went to work early. I didn't get there till almost noon and Sofia was cranky. The drapes were drawn and the only light came from the television tuned to cartoons. Gia was in bed with Sofia, wearing only a T-shirt. The clutter, Gia's bare bottom, the darkened room at midday with the TV going made me feel faint. It reminded me of days in the past when the kids were sick on location in a hotel room somewhere with windows that didn't open and the smell of leftover room service and wet diapers in the wastebasket. I would sink into a dark, vicious depression, feeling unable to fight my way out.

Jacqui left clothes for Gia and I dressed her but there was no belt for her tiny jeans and they kept slipping down. She fussed when I tried to brush her tangled hair. Sofia confessed she was depressed because she had read an article in a magazine commenting on the circumstances of her getting her part, which said the other actors hadn't wanted her.

May 27, 1990 In the air

Last night was the wrap party. It was soulful, rather than wild and crazy. Members of the cast and crew had been together for 125 shooting days and were dining for the last time, celebrating the conclusion of shooting and feeling the bittersweet end of a chapter in everyone's life.

June 2, 1990 Napa

This afternoon I walked in the vineyard between rows of vines thick with leaves sheltering spindly clusters of new grapes; I hoped to feel grounded and bring my mind, my memories of all the months in Italy and weeks in NYC back home to my body in Napa. I feel as if parts of myself are still scattered along the way and the terrain of home has shifted too. Sofia is moving to Los Angeles, Roman is on the road with a band traveling in an old VW bus with their instruments, playing from club to club. He called from Kill Devil Hills, North Carolina. His voice was happy and excited. I am trying to be with myself after so many months of reacting to Francis and Sofia making the film, trying to integrate myself into the land and the house. I feel as if I don't yet fit. I bumped my head on the slanted ceiling of my own attic work room. There have been so many airplanes, hotel rooms, days where I had no roots that it feels as if part of me has withered and will take time to grow back into life at home.

July 13, 1990

Last week I went with Francis on the Paramount jet from Napa to L.A. for a screening of *GFIII*. We left in the hottest part of the afternoon and stepped into the cool air-conditioned cabin of the jet.

We were the only passengers and dined all the way on caviar, cold lobster, shrimp and platters of fruits, cheeses and chocolate pastries. A steward attended us, bringing clean plates and filling our glasses. Francis said, "I hope they're not just feeding us well before they hit me with bad news."

In the early evening we drove to Paramount and settled into an upstairs screening room with perhaps a dozen executives. I was the only woman. I noticed the screen had been masked down to a small size. The film started and I was very disappointed to see the image was a video projection of an editing dub and very poor quality. It was very frustrating to be straining to see who the characters were when I knew that the footage was beautiful on film. At the end everyone got up and started talking about what needed to be done. Four men took the tape off to another room to look at it on a different monitor and make notes. I could feel Francis's despair. No one had leapt out of his seat enthusiastically, saying it was great.

July 18, 1990 San Francisco

Two days ago we came to San Francisco to see the first cut of *GFIII* on film. The screening for the executives of Paramount was in the morning at the large North Point theater. The print was clean and perfect. I felt the film's emotional power with an overlay of my own mixed memories woven through it. At the end when Sofia was shot, tears streamed down my face. I had to exit before the lights came up and go to the restroom to compose myself.

We went to a Chinese restaurant for lunch. I was at the table among sixteen men. They clearly had liked what they'd seen and discussed dates that a locked print would have to be ready in order for the sound effects cutters to be able to complete their work, and the prints struck by the opening date. Marketing strategies were discussed. They wanted a new scene to clearly show that Michael Corleone gives over the family to Vincent so there would be a setup for *Godfather IV*, continuing the saga. Francis spoke passionately about why he didn't want to do that, he wanted the focus of the film to be on Michael.

Francis had been up all night getting the last reels of film ready for the screening and fell asleep at 7:00 p.m. I drove to Berkeley to have dinner with a friend. As I drove up University Avenue, I noticed how beautiful the flowers were blooming in the center street divider. I realized I was outrageously happy, so utterly relieved that the film was OK. The tension I was carrying in my body, my mind was draining away revealing normal life around me.

Godfather III opened in the U.S. on December 25, 1990. In February I accompanied Francis and Sofia on the long flight from L.A. to Tokyo; the first leg of a promotional tour of foreign markets for the film.

February 11, 1991 In flight

I am sitting uncomfortably on the footstool of my first-class seat so I can lean closer to Sofia in the row in front of me, hear her above the dull roar of jet engines as she talks softly about decisions that face her now at age nineteen. She is considering changing schools. It would be her third college. "I want to take photography and painting and learn more skills." The school she is attending is strong in conceptual art. She is in her first apartment with her first live-in boyfriend. "Mom, I need to learn to cook some stuff like pasta and roast chicken." I treasured the conversation as she spoke to me as a friend rather than an irritating parent.

Every now and then I lift the window shade to look out. There is a distinct thin horizon line with clear blue sky above and a pattern of white clouds tinged with pink below. It is lasting for hours as we fly in the direction of the setting sun. I remember reading that Georgia O'Keeffe traveled to Japan for the first time in her seventies. She was shown ancient temples and gardens, great museums and cities. She met artists who were designated National Living Treasures. Upon her return she painted her famous cloud series inspired by what she saw out the window during her flight; what I am seeing now.

We drove from the airport into Tokyo through dense traffic. The film distributors put us in a hotel which, we are told, is the newest and most expensive in the city. We are on the top floor. From the bedroom I can see a two-lane section of freeway running by the side of the building a few floors below. There is an enormous blue and white wall of neon attached to the roadway with the word INAX in huge block letters. Our small living room glows with the light from a red and white neon sign entirely covering the side of the building directly across the street. Beyond, giant blocks of neon spelling Fuji Bank, Kawai, Panasonic, Sogo, Dentsu and many logos in Japanese characters are moving and blinking in the cityscape.

Francis and Sofia are having a meeting with the publicity people to go over their schedules. I am in the suite alone. It is surprisingly quiet considering the intensity of the city surrounding me. The furnishings are an elegant mix of clean-lined European and Japanese styles. The sofa and chairs look as if they are pieces you'd find in a contemporary Swiss hotel. There is a small beautiful, traditional Japanese screen, glowing with gold leaf, on the wall at the end of the small living room. Five beautiful bouquets from friends and business associates have been delivered to the room. The most lovely is from Akira Kurosawa. It has light and dark purple long-stemmed tulips, freesias, sweet peas, lilacs and flowering plum branches. There is a tray of confections: spun candy roses surround a chocolate heart filled with chocolate truffles, topped with chocolate ribbons. At the back of the tray a photo of Francis directing *Godfather III* stands upright framed under clear candy. I didn't believe it until I licked the corner. There is champagne in an ice bucket and a platter of perfect fruit.

We haven't been in Tokyo with Sofia since a family trip when she was seven. On Francis's one free day we went to his favorite part of the city, Akihabara, to see all the new gadgets, electronics, cameras and consumer goods. Sofia was interested in a display of little counter-top dishwashers that had porthole windows where you could see water spraying and sloshing over plastic dishes. (Her apartment has a small kitchen, no dishwasher and no place to put one.) Finally she bought a camera in a wide-angle format which had come on the market just two days before.

We stopped for lunch at a stand-up noodle bar that Francis remembered taking Roman and Gio to. After spending a little time in Akihabara's narrow streets packed with stalls displaying so many products I began to feel ill. Every inch on both sides of the street is stacked to overflowing with consumer products with bright signs and whirling, hissing, ringing, steaming demonstration models calling for attention. There are vacuum cleaners in all colors, every size and type of TV set, refrigerators, rice cookers, cameras, radios, tools, humidifiers, washing machines and gadgets of all kinds.

In the afternoon Sofia and I went to a department store in the Ginza where I remembered seeing beautiful rolls of kimono fabric and fine traditional ceramics the last time I was here. I was startled to find only European and American designer products. Sofia wanted some Japanese tea and little sweets that she remembered. We found only French, Italian and Viennese coffee shops. Exhausted, we finally settled for watery cappuccino. Sitting on a little terrace we watched women going by on the street wearing Gucci shoes, and Chanel bags. When we got back to the hotel I phoned my friend Eiko Ishioka. I asked her why foreign fashions and tastes were so predominant in Tokyo. She said, "After war Japanese people so ashamed for losing they decided their way was way of losers. They want to be like the winners and choose everything Western."

Eiko took us to dinner at a restaurant that had been a roadhouse in the countryside frequented by samurai several hundred years ago. It had been brought to Tokyo and reconstructed board by board inside a white marble city building. We went up in an elevator, down a hall and arrived at an ancient wood door. We entered an eighteenth-century room. I thought I could feel the presence of fierce men from the past there in the dark space with its wide uneven floorboards and scent of old wood and smoke.

An attendant in an elegant kimono directed us to take off our shoes and then showed us into a small private room with sliding doors and walls of shoji screens. We sat on tatami mats around a low table. Charcoal glowed on a bed of ash under a small grill in the center. An attendant entered in a kimono with sleeves tied back by a purple cord. Bowing low she presented a hand-painted ceramic platter filled with bamboo skewers of tiny fish wrapped in mint leaves which she grilled over the coals for several minutes and served to us.

There were many courses with ingredients which I couldn't recognize but were very tasty, washed down with frequent servings of sake. One of the guests with us was a film executive from Los Angeles who couldn't manage his chopsticks. Eiko asked our server for a fork. She disappeared and when she returned empty-handed there seemed to be a lengthy explanation followed by much bowing, after which Eiko said, "They have no fork." I found it hard to imagine that there was not even a fork in the kitchen. Finally, with many apologies, they brought bamboo skewers and we laughed as he struggled to spear his food.

The next day I went to the press conference. Sofia was seated on the dais with Francis in front of a huge poster of *GFIII*. Dozens of photographers with flash cameras were shooting at them. Sofia looked so young and thin and vulnerable. I felt how powerless I was to protect her. I had heard the Japanese press would be polite and treat her respectfully, unlike the U.S. press who had harshly, almost cruelly, criticized her screen performance. Francis felt the American press was attacking Sofia as a way of getting at him, just as the character Sofia played was shot by bullets intended for her father.

The questioning lasted for over an hour. "Why did you cast your daughter?" "How was it working for your father?" "Why wasn't Robert Duvall in the film?" "How is it working with Al Pacino?" "Will you make *Godfather IV*?" They were questions that Francis and Sofia had already answered dozens of times for the U.S. press. Finally they were hurried off the stage and out of the main ballroom through another barrage of flashing cameras, into a series of smaller rooms for one-on-one interviews for major Asian TV and magazines.

I left and took a taxi to the National Museum. I looked forward to visiting the long cases of antique kimono which I remembered from a previous trip and had literally taken my breath away. It was a long ride through thick traffic taking nearly an hour instead of the estimated 20 minutes. When I arrived the museum was closed. I couldn't read the sign of explanation. On the ride back I felt a wave of depression settle over me as I sat in Tokyo traffic, immobilized externally as well as internally. My attempt to do something that would interest me failed. I didn't want to go shopping or just back to the hotel, I couldn't communicate with the driver and ask him to bring me to a Shinto shrine or suggest something I'd find interesting. Eiko had gone out of town. I knew no one. Ringing in my ears was the admonition "Get a life!" Once again I was tagging along in Francis's life and now also Sofia's.

Every day here I have been watching CNN, which is unavailable to me in Napa and San Francisco, where we have no TV reception. I've grown to appreciate the lack of TV and the fact that our family has time together that is not in competition with expensive professional entertainment. I think the children benefited from having to develop their imaginations. The news of war is interspersed with commercials and announcements. "February 15, Belgium International Cat Festival; February 18, Bulgaria, Viticulturists Day." I feel a kind of psychic split sitting in my luxury hotel room watching painful and momentous actions in the Gulf War juxtaposed with banal international activities. I feel myself constantly witness to events I am powerless to change, with the underlying echo of Gio's death the ultimate event I was utterly unable to alter.

On a day Sofia was free the two of us went to the Harajuku section of Tokyo, a favorite shopping area of young people. It was a national holiday and the stores were packed with teenagers. We were pushed and jostled about in a way I would never submit to at home. To our continued surprise, we found few Japanese products other than limited designer clothes. When we got hungry Sofia wanted to eat sushi. We looked everywhere; there were no Japanese restaurants on the main street so we headed down several small side streets. We found none and finally settled for dismal fast food in a café called Love Burger.

Yesterday I took a taxi to a small museum of folk art. It was in a traditional old wooden building. There were shelves just inside the door with a sign directing me to leave my shoes and put on the ill-fitting vinyl slippers provided. I went to the right into the first room before I discovered that the entry point and admissions booth were to the left. It has taken me a few days to adjust to the Japanese custom of driving on the left, and the subtler situations still surprise me such as meeting someone on a stairway and veering into them instead of away.

The museum had once been the home of a wealthy lord. The floors were wide polished boards that creaked as I passed through the unheated rooms. Display cases contained exquisite examples of old ceramics, painted wooden paddles, scrolls, lacquer boxes, kimono and unusual objects such as a pair of finely woven quivers. I felt I was having at least a brief glimpse of something that wasn't westernized. It was a relatively small collection, there were only three other visitors.

At 5:00 I was ready to leave and asked the woman at the admissions booth to please call a cab for me. "Rush hour, no taxi now," she said. I walked out along the narrow street and realized I was in an affluent residential neighborhood. It consisted of separate houses, small by our standards, as if they had been built three-quarter scale with tiny garages and with yards that were only a few feet wide. Some were very contemporary, built of concrete and glass. All were neat and well kept which added to the sense that they were more model than real. At the point the narrow road reached a wider street there was a golf driving range encased in green mesh four stories high. A dozen players swung at balls while many more lined up waiting patiently for their turn.

I noticed I was enjoying myself alone in a foreign country, unable to speak the language and having no idea how I was going to cross the vast city to reach our hotel. I felt as if the solitude in the serene small museum with its beautiful objects was a form of nourishment, a conversation within myself, and as a result I was refreshed and curious about everything around me.

When I did finally find a taxi the driver was very friendly and quite frustrated not to be able to communicate. As he drove he tried hard to show me sights. He seemed particularly proud of the Hanae

Mori fashion building in Harajuku, across the street from McDonald's and a few blocks up from Brooks Bros. I managed to convey to him my wish to be dropped off near Ginza Station. He stopped in front of Wako, an elegant department store. The thick crowds on the sidewalk and inside the stores on this unexceptional February evening were similar to what we encounter at the height of our Christmas season in midtown New York City, except that it is a strange experience as an American to be in a dense crowd with no ethnic diversity.

I stopped at a café for tea. Entering the restroom first, I washed my hands in the elegant marble sink but found no towels. I noticed a Japanese woman take something from her purse that appeared to be a large compact. Inside was a small thin handkerchief. She dried her hands, folded the cloth neatly and put it back in the container. I marveled at such a common ordinary human task addressed from such a different point of view.

Walking the few blocks to the hotel I enjoyed a last look at the Tokyo cityscape. I felt as if I were in a vortex, Eastern and Western forces hurtled together, not quite fitting but causing great creative energy. We were to leave the next day to continue the press tour in Europe.

February 17, 1991 Berlin

The plane landed at Charles de Gaulle airport. There was new snow on the ground and flurries of flakes swirled around the windows. Baggage cart tires cut patterns on the tarmac. Bad weather delayed flights all over northern Europe and we waited four hours for our flight to Berlin. The lounge was crowded and smoky. We were tired and irritable; Francis's mood grew blacker. There is nothing he enjoys about a press junket. His life is on hold while he endures the repetitive promotion of a film that he has completed. *Godfather III* is over for him. He is anxious to begin work on a new project filled with creative possibilities and adventure into the unknown. His frustration is palpable; similar to bad weather, it's affecting us all.

We arrived in Berlin after midnight, and eventually reached the hotel. A dense crowd of photographers and autograph hunters waited in flurries of snow.

The next morning it was a free day and we were driven through west and east Berlin to see famous sites such as the Brandenburg Gate. We were shown where the Berlin wall had been taken down. Thick snow covered the city creating a dreamy patina belying the painful events that had taken place there.

We spent the afternoon in the Einstein coffee house, which had been recommended to Sofia. It had pale yellow walls with white trim around tall French windows. There was burgundy velvet, Bauhaus-print upholstery on the banquettes where we sat and looked out through the black trunks of trees into the snow-covered garden and at the reflections on the glass of the room with people drinking cappuccinos, reading newspapers and talking together. I wished we were at home with a fire in the fireplace and the smell of chicken roasting in the oven.

Wim Wenders took us to dinner. He spoke with concern about his film *Until the End of the World*, which is six hours long. "The distributors insist it can't go over three." Francis offered to go to the editing room, see the film and give Wim his ideas. Francis wants to help his fellow director, but also to spend the day in the editing room, be in a familiar work environment instead of the marketplace of the film festival.

Out the hotel window isolated snowflakes float erratically in the air. I see people walking along snowy sidewalks. Cars are buried in hip-deep drifts at the curb. In the distance there is a canal and a path next to it where parents pull brightly bundled children on wooden sleds. Francis is downstairs outside the front door smoking a little Italian cigar while he waits for Wim to pick him up. Sofia is on her way to the airport to meet her boyfriend, who is coming to visit. I have to decide what to do with myself this Sunday afternoon. I should jump at the chance to go to a museum but I am tired of traveling, saturated with sightseeing.

FEBRUARY 19, 1991

Yesterday *GFIII* was screened in the early afternoon for the international press, followed by a press conference at 5:00 p.m. At the entrance, Francis and Sofia were mobbed by autograph seekers. Once inside the conference room there was a long salvo of flash bulbs. It was standing room only. The press at the back of the room were on ladders, some with video news cameras and some with still cameras that had huge telephoto lenses that looked as if they could photograph Sofia's eyelash.

Eventually Sofia's boyfriend and I were led through a maze of ladders, photo equipment and densely packed journalists to folding chairs cleared for us at the far corner of the room.

Francis fielded the questions masterfully. I am continually amazed at how easily, articulately and intelligently he speaks to a crowd. The questions were the same ones asked everywhere. I'd think a professional in the field would have read the foreign press and ask something different. "Mr. Coppola, did you have any contact with the Mafia?" "Sofia, how was it to work with your father?" "Francis, what are your thoughts on family and on power?" One person asked Francis what his feelings were regarding the Gulf War. "I hope a true United Nations peace-keeping ability will be an outcome and that the legitimate grievances of the Arab nations will be heard." He concluded with "A taxi driver in L.A. told me 'There should be a Geneva convention that doesn't allow anyone under the age of fifty to go to war. The guys who order it should fight it. Then see how many wars there'd be.' "

After an hour the press conference was concluded and there was another round of photos. Marina, a film producer standing next to me, said, "What do they do with all those pictures? No one ever sees them." We were pushed and shoved along into a side reception room. Champagne was served while we waited for the press to clear.

We had an hour at the hotel before going down to the lobby to meet our hosts for the evening. At dinner we were in the company of the director of the festival and his wife, the executive staff of UIP [the company distributing *Godfather III*], and a Swiss woman exhibitor and manager of the film market. Sofia was seated several places away from me. I could see her laughing with her boyfriend. She passed me a message written on a folded paper napkin. It said, "Pretend you have to run off with one of the men at the table, who would it be? And not Dad, of course." I learned she had a bet with her boyfriend as to who I would choose. It was a tough decision. Sofia laughed hard at my answer and said she won. She passed me a paper to draw a head on and fold it over so she could draw the next part of a body without knowing what I'd drawn. I enjoyed playing with her while conversations about newly discovered Romanian documentaries and various films at the festival swirled around me.

The dinner lasted three hours. The festival officials wanted to keep us occupied until the evening screening of *GFIII* finished. Francis and Sofia were to be introduced onstage at the end and Francis was to receive a lifetime achievement award. We arrived at the theater during the last ten minutes of the film. I was ushered into a box. It was painful to see the final scenes with Sofia, in the part of Mary Corleone, shot to death. Even though I've seen it many times, I couldn't remain calm. The echoes of a child of mine dying jolted me upright in my seat. There was loud clapping as the film ended and a few scattered shouts of "Booo." We had been told that the festival crowd was very vocal. A staff woman from UIP assured me, "The screening went very well."

Part Five

October 15, 2002 Napa

I am drinking green tea from a Japanese teacup that is one half of a traditional "husband and wife set," the husband's cup being about a third larger than the wife's. The cups are delicate and beautifully hand-painted. We brought them home from a family Christmas trip to Tokyo in 1978. Japan has been on my mind. Sofia is directing her second feature film, *Lost in Translation*, shooting in Tokyo and Kyoto. I plan to visit her and take Gia, who has never been across the Pacific. I'm looking forward to seeing Sofia and traveling with Gia in a country that always intrigues me.

October 20, 2002 Japan

After an eleven-hour flight from Los Angeles (crossing the international date line) and a two-and-a-half-hour bus ride from the airport, Gia and I arrived at the Tokyo Park Hyatt hotel in the early evening. She asked me what time it was in California. My approach to travel is to immediately accept the local time and not think about what time it is at home. I didn't want to tell her. She insisted. "It is 8:00 in the morning yesterday."

The hotel lobby was on the 41st floor with commercial office space below. Our room was on the 47th floor. Through big windows we could see the dense city, sparkling with lights, spread out to the horizon. Gia ordered a pizza from room service. As she ate she was falling asleep. I asked her if she would be OK if I left her alone to sleep while I went to see Sofia. She said, "OK." Now at age fifteen, she is willing to stay by herself. As a younger child she never liked to sleep alone. When she visited Francis and me in Napa, she preferred to have a sleeping bag on the floor next to us rather than spend the night in her own room.

I hadn't seen Sofia for two months; Roman was with her and I was anxious to see them. I knew they were shooting nights so I called the production office and an assistant sent a fax with directions to the location. A map emerged tonguelike from the fax machine in our room. I went down to street level and showed the map to the taxi driver. We drove for half an hour before arriving on a dark street; he opened the car door, spoke rapidly in Japanese and pointed animatedly, indicating we were near and I should get out and walk the rest of the way. I wouldn't. In Japan I feel as if I'm on another planet where I'm completely helpless, I can't read a sign or ask a question. Reluctantly the driver negotiated numerous one-way streets and only when I could see the familiar sight of grip trucks and crew with walkie-talkies was I willing to pay, get out and walk.

A production assistant took me down three flights of stairs in a narrow building to a small bar disco where the shot was being set up. I stepped over cables and in and out of the light until I realized Sofia wasn't there. I found her upstairs next door having tea with Roman, Stephanie [Sofia's childhood friend working with her] and Brian [Stephanie's boyfriend and the film's music producer] at a small café. As we hugged I could feel her thin arms and shoulders. I was glad I'd brought her a Tupperware container of homemade chocolate chip cookies. With a big grin she opened the top, took three and passed them around. There wasn't room for me to sit down so, seeing a small empty table nearby, I started to pull it over. Sofia said, "No, we can't do that. In Japan they don't move tables around. I've gotten in trouble for trying. Here tables have their place and they stay there." Roman got up, gave me his chair and went back to the set.

Stephanie and Sofia discussed casting extras for a scene to be shot later that night. Stephanie had a list. "How about Nobu's friend George?" A production assistant came to the table and told Sofia she was needed on the set. I stayed and watched her work. I could see she had a lot on her mind but she seemed to have a clear vision of what she intended to accomplish and worked with a kind of excited ease.

Gia woke up at four the next morning and couldn't go back to sleep. Around five we took a taxi to the legendary fish market. We were too late to see the auction of huge tuna sold for sushi but walked through the narrow lanes of stalls looking at the displays of urchins, crabs, sea cucumbers, snails, spiny rockfish, blowfish, all types of exotic sea creatures we'd never seen before, many still moving. We watched a butcher cut up a several-hundred-pound tuna; he worked as if he were a performance artist.

There were numerous sushi bars open, I let Gia pick one. Eating raw fish at 6:30 a.m. doesn't sound appealing but it was delicious! We sat at the long bar among men in business suits and fish market workers eating sweet raw shrimp, tuna, yellowtail, clams and sea urchins.

Around noon I called the production office to see how Sofia's shooting went. "They worked from 8:00 last night till 10:00 this morning and got everything that was scheduled." I could feel my chest tighten with concern for how tired Sofia must be.

Our friend Phillis Lehmer and her nine-year-old daughter, Grace, joined us at the hotel. The four of us decided to take the Tokyo subway and asked the hotel concierge the way to the station and how to find the line that would carry us to Shibuya, a center for shopping. We found our way to the station but we couldn't find the gray line train we were told to use. At one in the afternoon the station was as filled with people as Grand Central in New York City during rush hour. Phillis is tall and blond. Grace is pale, delicate and angelic-looking. It wasn't hard to keep track of them in the crowd. With people brushing against us from every direction we stopped a man in a business suit and asked for help. He could barely speak English but understood where we wanted to go and led us through the dense sea of people to a bank of vending machines selling train tickets, and then directed us to the right track.

We arrived in Shibuya and walked many blocks so Gia and Grace could visit Kiddy Land, a six-story toy store. Sofia and Roman met us at the front door. Roman put his arm around Gia, tickled and teased her as he led her inside and up the crowded stairs. She had an expression of utter happiness being with him.

I stayed on the ground floor with Sofia. I was curious to see what she was drawn to. She was buying baby presents for friends' new babies. Sofia is focused on her career. She and her husband are pursuing their creative lives and seem in no hurry to start a family. When I was her age I already had two little boys and was frustrated that I was expected to be a traditional homemaker wife and mother.

I began to feel all the cute things in the store pressing in around me, smiley faces on twenty varieties of soft toy mushrooms, lady bugs in frilly hats, frog furniture, mouse tea sets, lavender butterfly music boxes, pink velour piglets; cartoon eyes looked at me from every direction. There were literally thousands of things and I was just inside the front door. After shopping in Tokyo, when I'm in New York City and step into Barneys it will seem as spare as a Zen temple. I went outside to a bench on the crowded sidewalk to wait.

Sunday afternoon Gia and I took a taxi to Sofia's apartment. I wanted to see where she lived and it was her only day off. We found the address, an apartment complex set back from the street. There was a lobby with lounge chairs and a flat-screen TV where I was told Sofia watches rushes with her producer and cinematographer. Everything seemed miniaturized. The scale of the chairs and tables was smaller than we are accustomed to. I thought of Francis, who would not be comfortable here. Sofia's apartment was at the end of a hall. When she opened the door the first thing Gia and I saw was a row of perhaps fifteen pairs of shoes. Some we had seen in Tokyo stores. She was in her stocking feet so we took off our shoes too. I was surprised to see she looked rested after the week's long night shoots.

Sofia showed us her small white rooms. In the bedroom there were several chaotic mounds of clothes piled on the floor. She stood next to one smiling and said, "Do you like my sculpture?" The living room table and floor had shopping bags, books, tapes, gift packages, art supplies, cups, glasses, notebooks, pens, magazines and more. In the small kitchen I opened the tiny refrigerator. She said, "Oh, don't look in there." I was relieved to see it was full of food.

This evening another map was faxed to our room and Gia and I took a taxi to the shooting location. We arrived at a one-lane street lined with little noodle shops and bars; there were noisy video game and pachinko parlors. We found the crew setting up a shot in which Bill Murray and Scarlett Johansson run out of a bar and down the street ducking into a pachinko parlor to escape an angry bartender with a BB gun chasing a customer. Sofia was conferring with her cinematographer near the main camera. Roman was reloading the second camera. Gia and I stood aside and watched a rehearsal with the stand-ins. Then the cast was called and we saw Bill Murray ambling up the street.

Sofia had written the leading male role for Bill but then found it impossible to contact him; he neither returned calls from his agent nor from her. Many frustrating months passed. People began saying, "Sofia, you have a good script, cast someone else, get on with it." She had envisioned Bill in the part and was determined not to make the film without him. Eventually a mutual friend called her with a tip that he was at a particular restaurant and she hurried there. They hit it off.

Bill towered over the Japanese crew. We were introduced. I told him how much I appreciated his taking the leading role in Sofia's film. He grinned and said, "Well, if it's a disaster I'll tell people I just did it for her mom." He had a Japanese phrase book and was approaching crew members making them laugh with renditions of his Japanese for "May I have a cup of tea, please" or "Where is the toilet?" While the crew finished setting up the shot Roman took Gia to play pachinko.

Assistant directors and production assistants were assigned to control the pedestrians, bicycles, motorcycles and occasional cars that came down the lane. As the evening wore on, drunken businessmen wandered into shots paying no attention to the crew's directions.

At one point I noticed where I was, out in a Tokyo street at night with Sofia directing her second feature film. She had drafted Gia to be an extra and placed her with several other people outside the door of the bar Bill Murray and Scarlett Johansson run out of. Roman was in position behind the second camera and I'd been handed a video camera to shoot for the documentary. Moviemaking, which as I grew up seemed so exotic, was now a way my family spent an evening together.

By 1:00 a.m. Gia was tired, cold and hungry. The crew wasn't going to break for lunch till 3:00 so I took her to eat in a little café on the street that served Korean barbecue. We warmed our hands on the small brazier in the center of the table.

OCTOBER 28, 2002

Phillis, Grace, Gia and I are on the bullet train traveling to Kyoto. We are seated in large plush seats on the right side of the car so we will have the best view of Mount Fuji. Small fields punctuate the densely built suburbs on the outskirts of Tokyo. Sheaves of stalks artfully tied in bundles are drying against buildings. There are row after row of unattractive Western-style houses, each the same, only their pastel colors vary. Very few of the traditional buildings with blue tile or slate roofs remain. During all the days in Tokyo I only saw five or six women wearing kimono. The bombardment of advertising signs and sounds seemed more intense than the last time I was in Japan, twelve years ago. When I was young I swore I wouldn't be one of those people talking about the "good old days." But now I see it is a natural progression. I notice things I appreciated that are missing, which of course no young person would be aware of. The women in patterned kimono gave the crowds of pedestrians exotic beauty.

Once on a trip to Japan years ago, I was taken to visit an artist in his home. It was so appealing to me with its traditional architecture and uncluttered spaces. Then our host opened a sliding door to retrieve something and behind the door I could see utter chaos; a jumble of boxes, assorted textiles, ceramics, papers, vases, paintbrushes, lacquer bowls, rolls of scrolls all piled on top of one another. Maybe empty spaces as I desire them are not attainable in real life.

October 29, 2002

Kyoto schoolboys in navy blue suits and caps stood in groups of three or four at the entrance to the Golden Pavilion shrine. They approached and read from a card in halting English: "We are students on a school outing. We are practicing English conversation. May we take a photo with you please?" They were especially excited by tall blond Phillis and very pale, pigtailed Grace. Three boys stood with us while a fourth took our picture. One boy presented a notebook and pointed to a carefully ruled space where he wanted our names and country of origin.

We passed through wooden gates, walked up the path and found the Golden Pavilion shining in the morning sunlight with its double shimmering on the surface of the pond before it. I took photos of Gia with the pavilion in the background. She was acting like a bored teenager with a grandmother taking yet another picture of her, or was she uncomfortable because she sensed my emotion? I was remembering the last time I stood in this spot and took a family photo, Gio was in it.

January 6, 2003 Napa

I knew Francis would be home around 7:30 in the evening expecting to find me preparing dinner. At 8:00 I was still in my studio standing at my table in the midst of working on a large watercolor. I put the piece up on the wall, hoping the wet places wouldn't drip, and stood back to look. It was very different at a distance. I saw where more work was needed and quickly applied a wash of pale gray. I hurriedly put on my hiking boots as I took a last look at the piece. I felt a little ripple in my boot and thought it was the leather tongue unfurling but my attention was on painting a few more brush strokes. Then I noticed another odd tiny ripple but no time to unlace my boot and investigate.

I walked back in the darkness with the double circle of light from the old flashlight trained on the steep rocky trail. When I reached the dirt road I felt tension release from my back, relieved to be on flat ground. I knew if I stepped in a rabbit hole or tripped over a rock on the hill and twisted my ankle, it could be a long, cold time before anyone found me. The old road curved between fragrant bay, eucalyptus and pine trees and emerged next to the vineyard. Out from under the tree's black canopy the sky was clear and the stars brilliant in the dark country night. Looking up, the sky appeared as I imagined it in a folk tale I liked as a child. In the tale the night sky was velvet indigo cloth that separated the earth world from the world of the gods. All the points of light we call stars are really peepholes where the gods look down at us and watch what we are doing. If you climbed the highest tree you could look through a hole and see them. As a child I worried that if I climbed up and looked through a hole, I might see a huge scary eye staring back at me.

I reached the apartment and found Francis hungrily smashing walnuts with a veal pounder and eating pieces of nuts picked from the broken shells. I stepped into the tiny bedroom and pulled off my boots. A small limp lizard fell off my sock. I sat down on the bed, heartsick. Francis heard me sigh and came to see what was wrong. He scooped the little lizard up on a subscription card from *Newsweek* magazine, carried it outside the door and laid it gently under an oregano plant with the remote hope that it would revive.

January 14, 2003

My Parisian friend Aurore insists that American towels are better than French ones and often arrives in California with an empty suitcase to fill before she returns home. I bought several sets of towels to take to our Paris apartment the next time one of us goes. The box is sitting on the floor next to my desk. Every time my foot bumps it I wonder if I am an utter fool.

May 9, 1997 Paris

Rain is hitting the windowpanes. I can hear pigeons cooing, huddled on a protected ledge. There are rumbling sounds as the Métro trains pass underground. Next to my left wrist the big faucet drips. I am lying in the long tub in the bathroom of our apartment in Paris. The foam of bubbles has disappeared but a faint floral scent rises from the orange-tinted water. I am soaking my sore shoulder, trying to relieve an agonizing pain. The doctor tells me I have a frozen shoulder that will probably take a year to heal. It has made me very aware of my physical fragility and given me new compassion for people in pain. I always chastise myself for living a life out of balance when a physical problem arises; believing it to be a message concerning something I'm not paying attention to, such as shouldering a burden I'm not telling myself the truth about. So far I have been unable to give my affliction any meaning and my mind is wandering away to the events of the last few days.

Saturday I celebrated my birthday with women friends; we had lunch on our wide porch in Napa. I sat next to Paula. She began telling me about her backstage experiences directing a concert of mariachi bands. I clinked my glass and asked to go around the table and each tell a highlight of their year. Barlow told about the foundation she heads, funding vegetable gardens in public schools. Carol, Chris, and Moira each spoke about their books being published this year. Rita recently spent three weeks living in the Alaskan wilderness. Pat told about being bitten by a rattlesnake, almost dying from the anti-venom treatment, and how it changed her attitude toward living. Virginia talked about becoming president of their winery and the vicissitudes of being in a man's business world. Margrit said she was creating an art studio in a structure that formerly housed her husband's pet llamas. Mary said, "I didn't do anything this year. I just ran the winery, worked in the garden and took a walking tour around Sicily."

Francis and I flew to Paris on Sunday. As we drove in from the airport the city looked freshly washed by the rain. The trees had leafed out. The sky was alternately cloudy and sunny. The dramatic light gave buildings the look of theatrical sets. Our little apartment was clean and cozy with views out the tall windows across the busy street where people walk, browsing at the bookstalls and postcard vendors along the quay next to the river. On the opposite side of the river we can see a large elegant stone building, the police station, with the spire of Sainte-Chapelle beyond, pointing into the changing sky.

The days have been rainy and unseasonably cold. I've stayed in reading a galley copy of the book my friend Moira talked about at my birthday lunch called *Spectral Evidence*, which covers a sensational recent trial that took place in Napa. A high-profile, highly paid executive at the Mondavi winery and father of three girls was accused by his oldest daughter of having molested her when she was a child. The mother believed the daughter and divorced her husband. The father vehemently denied the accusation. He lost his job, his family and finally sued his daughter's therapist for malpractice.

In the course of the trial every intimate detail of the family's life and the parents' sex life was brought to public attention. A family was destroyed beyond healing. A number of the people written about are people I know in the community. I found myself made very uncomfortable by the intimacies revealed. Aware that I am engaged in writing about private thoughts and moments in my own family's lives; nothing so intimate, but questioning myself with new vigor. Why do I have the continuing urge to observe and write about my family and myself?

The night before last I was reading in the apartment while Francis went down to smoke a cigar in the little bar on the ground floor. When he came up around 11:30 he wanted me to go out with him to a Cuban club he had heard about. I was comfortable, engrossed in my book with no inclination to move. His enthusiasm won me over. I got dressed and we walked through the narrow streets of the Left Bank for perhaps fifteen minutes until we arrived at the address and found a small crowded bar playing Latin music and serving Cuban drinks. We ordered mojitos and took our glasses down narrow stairs to a small smoke-filled room where perhaps a dozen couples were dancing. We put our drinks down and began to dance.

At first I thought I might faint from the dense smoke in the air and the acrid smell of perspiration; but I was able to switch to my "good traveler" mode of observing different customs and not comparing everything to home. My shoulder aching, I left the dance floor before Francis and sat down near our drinks. A man leaned toward me and very drunkenly shouted something to me in slurred French with his thick alcohol breath. I couldn't understand him at all so he just kept repeating it. When I thought enough time had elapsed to qualify me as a good sport I asked Francis to leave. We stepped into the street. With cool air, the quaint buildings and Francis's large, warm hand holding mine I felt very happy. I was glad he got me up from my comfortable chair to go on an adventure in the Paris night.

There were a surprising number of people out at one in the morning. At an intersection we saw a long line that extended around a corner and down the block. Investigating, we found a movie theater showing the opening day of *The Fifth Element*, a science fiction/action film starring Bruce Willis. The first French production with a $90 million budget, written and directed by a young Frenchman in English. We decided to buy tickets and get in line. While I held our place, Francis went back to the corner and bought us crepes from a street vendor.

The line moved slowly forward and we finally found ourselves in a large clean theater. It was nearly filled. We sat down on the aisle. A young man entered our row to take the single empty seat next to me. He turned and said to Francis, "You look like the director Francis Ford Coppola." Francis replied, "Thank you." The lights dimmed and the film started. I was immediately aware of the high-quality sound in the theater. I noticed in the titles that the costumes were designed by Jean-Paul Gaultier and felt reassured that even if the movie didn't especially interest me the apparel would be visually arresting.

The film was a big comic book of a movie: three parts *Star Wars*, one part *Indiana Jones*, one part *Batman*, all flavored with Peter Greenaway and enhanced by our receptivity to mindless entertainment at that late hour. We sat through the long end credits so I could see my brother Bill Neil's name listed as "Director of Photography for Visual Effects." As we left the theater, several young people came up to Francis and one said, "We are film students. I want to be a director. Your films have influenced me the most of any director. I see them over and over, but why did you make *Jack*?" As we crossed the street near our apartment at 3:00 a.m., we noticed a young man following us. He approached and said to Francis, "My favorite film of yours is *Rusty James*." [The French name of Francis's film *Rumble Fish*.] Then he said accusingly, "Why did you do *Jack*?"

Francis has been brooding about the student's comments. Thinking about his career, asking himself why he did so many commercial films, why he didn't do more original writing, why he hasn't written an original script since *The Conversation* in 1973. He is aware that there are very few directors his age that get the big fee he gets for a Hollywood project. He knows that he won't be able to get it forever so there is always the seduction of doing it one more time. He tells me Hollywood has changed. "More and more films are concept films with a big star attached. They don't care who the director is. The big companies can just as well hire some young guy from MTV. It doesn't matter to them."

He wants to write an original work and has started character development for a script he began years ago and set aside to take films to pay old debts and, in 1995, to buy the vineyards and château which became our winery. He was still talking about his personal writing when we went to dinner the next night at Brasserie Lipp. I was preoccupied; I could see Charlotte Rampling at a nearby table and Lauren Bacall across the room. When Francis talked about what the students had said, I repeated one of Brando's lines from *Apocalypse Now*, ". . . to be free from the opinions of others." He said sadly, "But it's my opinion too. I've let them down; worse, I've let myself down. I should have been writing original work all along." He said in the book he is reading the author says if you are not making the film you want to be making right now, you never will. "Not doing the work you want to be doing the author calls 'having your heart on ice.' "

February 19, 1998

Francis directed the film *The Rainmaker*, from John Grisham's book. It is opening in Europe in April. I traveled with Francis to Paris for his publicity junket. Journalists from France, Germany, Italy and England have scheduled interviews with him for five days at the Plaza-Athénée hotel. Every twenty minutes a new person is seated in front of him or he is moved to a new camera and interview setup. When he left the apartment this morning he was tired. He said, "I have to work but you are free." The words made me flinch, a flush of heat spread across my chest.

The weather is unseasonably mild for February. It is sunny and the temperature is in the 60s. Out the window I can see a couple walking with their arms around each other, they stop to kiss under a bare tree. A man and woman sit in the winter sunlight leaning against the stone wall next to the river in an embrace. I feel depressed. I straightened our small apartment and then sat in the blue club chair reading Phyllis Rose's book *The Year of Reading Proust: A Memoir in Real Time*. At one point she says, "My senses, lagging behind my body, were still in New York. I was suffering jet lag of the soul." Part of me is still in Napa where daffodils are blooming around the pond and the delicious solitude of my new barn studio is waiting with a project half finished. I greedily accepted the trip to Paris with Francis, yet I don't seem to be wholly here. My inner self is clinging to my life at home.

I enjoy the way Phyllis Rose weaves many aspects of her life together with references from her reading. She abruptly shifts from Proust to tell the reader what she watches on TV, experiences with her elderly mother, early years of marriage, her son, her second husband, estrogen or what she cooked for dinner but when she writes that her husband is allergic to garlic and she doesn't use any, she loses me.

I threw on my coat and left the apartment, walking fast through the picturesque streets of Saint-Germain-des-Prés, barely noticing where I was going. I stopped only to look in the windows of the shop that creates custom-made wedding gowns, to admire lavender French lace, thick creamy silk satin, and a bouquet of miniature calla lilies. Crossing the Pont-Neuf I looked down at the river moving swiftly under the bridge. It was dark green-black and looked very cold. For a moment I thought about jumping, wondered if in the water I would try to get out of my black winter coat, imagined the shape it would make as it sank. As I stepped away from the railing I was furious at myself for lacking the imagination, the character, to find contentment and joy in my privileged circumstances.

In the evening we went to dinner with Paul Rassam, an old friend who has distributed Francis's films in France starting with *Apocalypse Now*. Between the foie gras and the fresh asparagus the conversation turned to Saddam Hussein. Paul said, "You know, my mother was a friend of his wife. Years ago Madame Hussein used to come to Paris with two bodyguards accompanying her, each carrying a briefcase filled with cash; rows of bills in stacks. My mother would take her shopping." The waiter brought a platter of sliced Parma ham. As we helped ourselves Paul continued, "You know, when Saddam used to go to Russia he brought all his own food and heated it. He wasn't comfortable wearing shoes; it was always a big effort for him to wear European shoes to those meetings. Part of the reason Saddam is so dangerous now is that he hasn't left his country for twenty years. Imagine how isolated he is. He has no idea what's going on in the rest of the world. It's got to make him crazy."

On the drive home Paul took the road along the river. As he drove down into a tunnel it felt eerily familiar; I recognized the image engraved in my mind from news coverage: the site of Princess Diana's fatal accident.

February 20, 1998

Today Francis had a day off with no interviews and stayed home in the apartment happy to have an opportunity to continue writing on a project of his own. The concierge, Monsieur David, is proud to have Francis in his building, proud to be seen with him, proud to introduce him to his friends in the neighborhood. He wants to hang out with him. He rang the bell this morning and asked importantly to come in, he had the mail. It was a postcard. A little later he was back, he asked to come in. I could already smell alcohol on his breath. He told us the cleaning lady was ill and would not be coming.

As soon as Francis was working at his computer and I was in the shower, the bell rang again. Monsieur David was at the door with cleaning supplies. He said he would do a little cleaning himself. Francis said, "*Non, merci.*" Francis called our Canadian neighbor Marilee who speaks English and French and asked her to call Monsieur David and tell him that he didn't want to be rude but he needs his privacy, he is writing and needs to be undisturbed.

After lunch Francis was settled again in front of his computer. Monsieur David arrived, his alcohol breath was stronger. He had a hammer in his hand ready to hang a picture that has been on the floor leaning against the wall for a week. He said proudly in broken English, "I not disturb." I said, "Thank you but not now."

Around 3:00 we went out for a walk. Monsieur David was in front of our building. He told us he had the car and would drive us around Paris sightseeing. Francis said, "*Non, merci.*" He invited us to his home for dinner. We said we already had plans. At 6:00 we were back in the apartment. The bell rang. Monsieur David had Francis's jacket from the dry cleaner. I had given him two suits; I wondered if he would bring each piece separately. It was Friday. We all said, "*Bon week-end.*" I closed our heavy blue door. We sighed with relief. Francis slumped on the sofa. He said, "There is no resort without mosquitoes."

February 26, 1998

Eiko Ishioka was commissioned to design the costumes for the four operas of Wagner's Ring Cycle produced by the National Theater Company in Amsterdam. The first opera, *Rheingold*, was performed in September 1997. The second opera, *Die Walküre*, was produced in February 1998. Francis and I flew from Paris to Amsterdam to see Eiko and attend a performance.

We arrived on Saturday. Eiko met us at the airport. I saw her first, her long black hair and the distinctive silhouette of her black Issey Miyake coat in the distance. We hugged hard. The taxi took us to the hotel to leave our bags and then on to an Indonesian restaurant. After a late lunch we walked to the Van Gogh Museum. Francis wanted to see his favorite painting *The Zouave.* After he looked at it carefully, he left to go back to the hotel and read.

Eiko and I stayed and looked at all the paintings. I could feel my heart beating rapidly, I wanted to race home and paint big swirling brush loads of paint. I can hear my art teacher, Sister Magdalene Mary: "You go to see art because it makes you want to do your own." We walked up one floor and found an exhibit of block prints by the Japanese artist Kuniyoshi that had been collected by van Gogh and his brother Theo. We marveled at the way Kuniyoshi was able to show such dynamic action through carving wood blocks. Black, white, red and indigo blue images of warriors, women and animals gripped my mind. Eiko told me the artist was particularly known for rendering cats wearing clothing and participating in political events.

At precisely five minutes before 5:00 p.m. a large matronly guard whom I had noticed looking frequently at her watch announced firmly in English, "The museum is closed!"

Because the weather was so unexpectedly warm and sunny people and bicycles crowded the sidewalks and bike lanes, trams and cars clattered along cobbled streets. Eiko and I walked the dozen or so blocks to her apartment. It was in a narrow building on a picturesque canal. We went up three flights of steep steps; her apartment was on the top floor under the roof. She apologized, "So sorry, big mess." There were stacks of art books on the floor and piles of file folders and sketch pads. It looked very appealing to me. She was separating her possessions to take home to New York City the following week or store until she returned in three months to work on the next opera. In the small open kitchen she heated water and made green tea. She apologized for serving it in Western-style cups. We sat in her small living room with the window open above the canal.

She said, "How is Mom?" I said, "She's getting frail but for eighty-nine she's amazing. She still walks a mile every day. How is your mother?" She said, "Mom is well. Eighty-two now. She came to see me. She liked Amsterdam very much but she worried about me walking in narrow streets. She has friend whose son, ten years ago, took his bride honeymoon in Paris. They walked in narrow street, found small boutique, went in. Bride found dress she want to try on. Man took her in back to dressing room. Told husband to wait. Bride didn't come out, didn't come out. Finally husband went to look. No one there. He went to police and to embassy. Never found her, suspect she in harem somewhere Middle East now. . . . Embassy never tell public these thing."

We walked to our hotel. When we came to a particularly narrow street we linked arms and walked rapidly, glancing furtively into doorways. I imagined a long octopus-like arm reaching out to grab Eiko.

We arrived at our hotel room and found Francis working at his computer. While we sat on the sofa waiting for him to finish I asked Eiko how she came up with her ideas for the opera costumes. She told me that before a big meeting about a particularly difficult character's costume for *Rheingold* she stayed in her hotel room for three days to create a concept. "Three days pass, I couldn't come up with any genius idea. I gave up. I was lying on my bed very depressed. I saw a fly going round and round by the ceiling. I got furious. What is fly doing in my room this expensive hotel. I think call reception, tell them send somebody get rid of fly. Then I get idea to make character looks like fly. I meet with director, tell him my idea, tell him think about it for two days. Maybe Eiko's idea too crazy. In one day he call. Say, 'OK.' It was one of best costumes."

After dinner the three of us rode the tram to the town center. It was surrounded with movie theaters, coffee houses and beer halls. There were Peruvian musicians and a fire-eating juggler performing in the square. The streets were closed to cars. Crowds of people were out walking in the temperate evening. Coming out of a café in a group of people was a film executive who recognized Francis. Kevin Costner was behind him and came over to say hello. Francis introduced him to me and to Eiko.

While Francis and Kevin talked I visited with a young man in the group who excitedly told me they were on an international publicity tour for Costner's film *The Postman.* "We've been to Rome, Munich, Paris, and after Amsterdam we're going to Tokyo." As they left to go back to their hotel Kevin came over to me and said good night, "I am very glad to have met you." It was such a specific gesture in the casual gathering, it felt as if he had been trained by a wife who told him how uncomfortable it is to be the invisible person and that he should always acknowledge celebrities' wives. When he left Eiko said, "Oh such a handsome man, such a skinny face. Not like in the movies."

The next day, Sunday, we went to a matinee performance of the opera. I am not an opera lover and it was a four-and-a-half-hour performance, in German, with Dutch surtitles. I went for the visual experience. As we took our seats I noticed every seat was filled. I was pleased to see a sold-out audience for an avant-garde production. The San Francisco Opera is so conservative I rarely go. I once sat through the entire Ring Cycle because I thought it would be an educational experience I should have. All I can remember is trying hard not to fall asleep and jerking awake on a crescendo of music to see great craggy fake rocks with Valkyries in long blond braided wigs, heavy, dull Norse helmets and big brown dreary dresses.

In the Amsterdam production there was no curtain covering the stage; a huge circular slanted ramp made of curved strips of pale wood extended from deep backstage, down and out over the apron to the edge of the audience. The orchestra was seated onstage left, in full view inside the circular ramp. Two huge wooden troughlike structures hung suspended from cables along the ceiling on both sides of the stage. I could see part of the audience seated high up looking down. There was a small sign near the stage with an arrow and words in Dutch and English which said, "This way to adventure seating."

The second act was the most memorable. The music swelled into "The Ride of the Valkyries," which is the music Francis used for the helicopter attack in *Apocalypse Now*. In the ceiling of the stage a long spear shape rotated as if it were a helicopter blade, in homage to the film. Fire emanated in dramatic sequences from between the curved slats of the circular ramp.

The Valkyrie women had short angular black hair and wore sleek, glossy, silver helmets with a skull impression in front. They were dressed in tight-waisted black wool coats that had points standing up on the shoulders and four deep points at the hem. They carried two molded shiny silver wings which they held from the back as if they were shields and moved to flash and glisten in the blue and gold light.

Wotan wore a great red silk kimono; red on the outside and black inside. It hung just above the floor with sleeves that were longer and trailed beside him. He had a white tunic shirt, black pants and boots. He used the robe dramatically, opening it to expose the black inside and swooping as if he were a bat, then closing it imperiously, showing only a slit of white down the front in the folds of heavy red silk, thrusting a sleeve in a gesture that implied a warlord's armor.

At the intermission I met Eiko at the bar in the lobby. We drank coffee and ate miniature ham sandwiches. I told her I thought her costumes were remarkable, but I admitted that I was expecting something even more far out after hearing about her fly costume. She laughed and said, "First opera I was soooo over budget, producer tell me this one have to be on budget, so Eiko's costumes not so crazy." She grinned and whispered, "Next one go over budget."

January 21, 2003 Napa

Yesterday morning Francis left for Belize to work on the resorts. I stayed home and walked up to my studio along the narrow deer trail through the wet gray grass. Scents of bay and eucalyptus from nearby trees rode the crisp air to greet me. I opened the tall doors of my studio, got my clippers and headed downhill, stepping around the muddy ruts in the dirt road to arrive at the old olive grove. I cut long thin flexible branches. A few olives still hung like small dark ornaments among the smooth boat-shaped leaves. I carried an armload back up the hill with the unruly branches pressed to my jacket and bouncing against my knees. I spent hours clipping, editing leaves, bending thin branches and wiring them together in evocative shapes. I arranged them above paper where, under a light, I painted their intricate shadows in gray, watery, watercolor washes.

All day and into the early evening I was utterly alone. Occasionally I could hear a coyote barking in the distance. Squirrels rustled in the dry leaves under the oak, a woodpecker tapped high in a nearby pine, a horsefly buzzed against the window. I watched afternoon shadows cross the floor and the pale winter sun slip early behind the rim of hills. I walked home in the dark with the flashlight casting long, slightly scary shadows across the road and into the trees.

The embrace of yesterday, working in solitude surrounded by nature, lingered with me today as I drove into San Francisco. Now I am in the Gold Room, an ornate old banquet hall of the Palace Hotel. I am attending a California Historical Society luncheon: "A Tribute to Alice Waters." I pretend to read the program, but I am observing my surroundings seated here at a round table for ten. An accordion-folded napkin fanned out from the rental wine glass, two forks, two knives, a dessert spoon and fork frame my menu with its distinctive Chez Panisse radish design. When I raise my eyes slightly I can see a centerpiece made of three fat Chinese cabbages standing upright with a red plaid ribbon tied around them and a small painted bird perched in the leaves. I am quiet, trying to hold on to the solitude I felt yesterday in my studio for a few moments longer. Fingers of conversation reach toward me. "She was the maid of honor at my first wedding and he was my first boyfriend, the first one, I'm talking the real one, from seventh grade." "When your kids become adolescents you go from being a dog owner to being a cat owner." "Don't you think romantic love has replaced religion in our culture?"

I drove into the city to be here for Alice; I feel deeply happy that she is receiving this award. I met her in the late sixties when she was a Montessori schoolteacher and have watched her passionately and relentlessly pursue her beliefs. She thinks it is possible to effect positive change by the food we eat, by supporting sustainable agriculture, by teaching children to grow gardens and learn to nourish themselves and ultimately the planet, to bring family, friends and community together around the table to pass on our culture. Alice is the only person I know who held revolutionary beliefs as a college student in Berkeley and is just as passionately working toward her ideals today. She has had a life of remarkable accomplishment.

As I sit here in my banquet chair reflecting, I notice that under my pleasure for Alice, I feel aching regret. I have two women friends with children and long marriages to successful creative husbands who are receiving honorary doctorates this year. I am happy and proud they are being recognized. But it has caused me to question my own life. My path carried me off in so many directions: documentary films and videos, drawings, sculpture, photographs, installations, to design costumes, write, travel to remote places in search of ethnic textiles and more, but never to create a long consistent body of work. I am continually drawn to follow some inner directive, curious, slightly afraid, yet relentlessly compelled toward the adventure of trying something new, just as I was in my studio yesterday. Over the years I stopped whatever it was I was doing to go on location with Francis and the children. I sincerely tried to be a good wife and mother to my family. For a variety of reasons, I haven't created a body of notable work in my life when many around me have, and I haven't yet made peace with that truth.

I stop my wandering mind. Alice is at the lectern. She tells about having to conquer her fears of public speaking. "My speech coach said, 'Look out at the audience and imagine they are all little lettuces and make a salad.' " She talks about food preparation as only Alice would: "Chop that shallot the way you would want to be chopped if you were a shallot." She speaks with infectious passion. "Food is an enormous part of our culture and our culture is our history."

January 26, 2003

At lunchtime I went to Francis's library in the coach house. He has nearly 60,000 volumes attended by Anahid Nazarian. Sometimes when Francis is out of town, Anahid and I eat lunch together and play cards, moving aside the incoming and outgoing books and reference materials on the central wood table. We play a game called Machiavelli which encourages wily, competitive strategy and taking advantage of your opponent. These are not characteristics generally associated with either of us but when we play cards we indulge in them with abandon and claim that the strategic aspects of the game are healthily exercising our brains. Today while we played, I noticed in a stack of books near me a biography of Anne Morrow Lindbergh. I began thinking about how the place I've read certain books is a vivid part of the memory of the book. When I looked back at the cards on the table, Anahid was winning.

February 2, 2000 New York City

Yesterday was a perfect early spring day in Napa, clear and cool. The tips of daffodils poked up around the pond, wild mustard was beginning to bloom in the vineyard, buds were swelling on bare peony stems, two gray squirrels scampered along branches in the magnolia tree. Last night I arrived in New York City to join Francis. The apartment in the Sherry-Netherland hotel has been sold and while he looks for a property downtown we are staying in a small rented apartment in Little Italy. Francis left for work early. His office is in the MGM Building in midtown, where he directs a small team working on his short-story magazine and another developing a slate of low-budget independent films.

I can hear a screech and expulsion of air as a big truck brakes at the corner, then the knocking of the idling engine followed by the guttural sound of acceleration as the light changes. Traffic rattles on the cross street, hitting potholes filled with dirty ice. A siren screams in the distance. There is the sound of a metal grate being rolled up in front of a store across the street, the slam of a delivery-truck door and a horn honking impatiently. In the room I hear the water trickling in the radiator and the refrigerator exhaust fan in the small kitchen. The light coming in the windows is gray. More snow is expected. I am in bed under a down quilt, wearing pajamas, sweater and socks; reading the biography of Anne Morrow Lindbergh. The book tries to explain her complicated emotions: a son dead, a celebrity husband who demands she fly with him to distant locations, her desire to write, to have a life independent from his at a time when the world was in depression and the culture was praising domestic life, saying the place for women was in the home, leaving the few jobs that were available for men.

My mother is from that era. When she became a widow she went back to school and studied library science. When she graduated and found a job, her financial adviser told her that it wasn't worth taking; the money she would earn would put her in a higher tax bracket. He told her she would be taking a job from someone who really needed it. She couldn't bear the thought of depriving someone of work that could feed his family. She fought depression all her life. My friend Lynn Hershman once told me, "Life is like knitting an argyle sock. You can't see the pattern until you're nearly finished." Now I can see how I've struggled with the same depression my mother did. In recent years I am happier than I've ever been. I can see the pattern in the sock I am knitting. Francis can too and it's OK when I walk out the door onto the dirt road leading to my studio.

February 9, 2000 Flying to California

I spent a week with Francis in New York City. The afternoon I left for home, I went to his office in the MGM Building to say goodbye, then stood on the curb and hailed a taxi to take me to the airport.

As I fastened my seat belt and leaned back the taxi driver said, "Once I picked up Francis Ford Coppola right where you were standing." A crackling radio voice interrupted. The driver's supervisor asked where he was. "I'm heavy and rollin'!"

As we left the city I looked out the window into a long underpass. The high concrete walls were blackened with dark sagging stains. Bold stripes of light passed through thick overhead girders. It looked like a theater set. The car was moving very slowly, then I saw flashing lights of emergency vehicles a quarter of a mile ahead and we came to a halt on a long bridge with a chest-high barrier wall of thick dirty concrete posts and heavy square rail. At the edge of the roadway I could see an array of debris. It had a strange beauty. If a twenty-foot section of the road, just as it was, were put down in a pristine art gallery, it would have its appeal. There were seven blades of green grass standing up intrepidly from a crack in the concrete next to a flattened plastic bottle; five cigarette filter tips huddled together as if in conversation. There was an oil-stained deteriorating glove with most of the thumb missing, shards of flat orange reflector glass, a wad of cassette tape caught on a balustrade, two scraps of black rubber tire, a used emergency flare with its faded pink paper nibbled away exposing gray cardboard. Slowly the car began to move again. As we picked up speed my roadside view became a textured blur. The art show was over.

February 15, 2003 Napa

I joined Francis at Turtle Inn in Belize to celebrate our 40th wedding anniversary. I brought two photos I'd put in a double silver frame, one taken of us during our wedding dinner at a Las Vegas supper club and another taken recently. In the first, Francis is dressed in a dark suit with narrow tie, his young face is clean shaven and he is wearing thick black-rimmed glasses. His head is turned, looking at me sweetly. I am wearing a little hat with bows perched on my long dark hair swept up in a French twist. I am looking shyly, tentatively toward the camera. I had learned a week earlier that I was pregnant. In the second photo we are sitting on a wicker sofa on the front porch of the big house in Napa. Francis has a full beard, nearly white. The rims of his glasses are thinner, his body heavier. He is wearing a vintage Hawaiian shirt and looking into the camera with his arm around me. My hair is short, dyed light brown to cover the gray. I am sitting a little forward leaning into the strength of his chest, traces of a bemused smile on my face as if I am slightly surprised to find us still together through all the ups and downs of our lives.

I realize now how my life was shaped by pregnancy. In 1963 abortion was illegal and I had neither the courage nor the knowledge of how to have an illegal abortion. When I found out I was pregnant Francis was on location working on a Roger Corman film.

I had several days to consider my situation before he returned. For me there were only two options, go away somewhere to have the baby and let it be adopted or get married. I tried to use my calmest voice when I told Francis so he would not feel pressured. He was overjoyed! "I've always wanted a family." We got married the next weekend.

Before I left for Belize, Sofia called from her editing room in New York where she is working on *Lost in Translation*. She said, "Mom, I'm so glad you and Dad stuck it out." I was reminded of a woman I know who weathered many rocky years of marriage. When her kids left home her friends thought she would get a divorce. She said, "Hell, no. I'm sticking around for the good years." It feels as if we've arrived.

While Francis and I were away our family assistant, with help from the maintenance men, moved us from the little two-room apartment next to the clotheslines into the newly refurbished guest cottage. Jonathan Barnett, the designer who is doing the main house, supervised remodeling the old cottage, adding a second bathroom, new heating, air-conditioning, a bay window which overlooks the pond, and new furnishings, everything down to new soap in decorative soap dishes. Our personal things, such as a Clarice Cliff vase, a carved wooden box, a silver pin dish and a clutter of family photographs, were placed on new dressers and end tables, our books put on the new shelves. A painting that used to hang in the entry hall of the big house is here above the telephone table. It feels a bit unreal; there is a kind of decorative order as if it were a set for a theater piece and an actor might walk out of the bedroom at any moment delivering well-rehearsed lines.

As I stepped out of the new marble shower wrapped in a thick new towel I noticed diagonal stripes of morning sunlight on the bathroom wall slicing across a lithograph that used to hang in our upstairs hall. It is an artist's proof by Akira Kurosawa, one of the great Japanese director's costume designs for his film *Kagemusha*.

The image is of a peasant figure dancing; the fabric is drawn in exquisite colorful detail. The lithograph was a gift from the director. This morning I have been thinking about a trip I took with Francis to visit Kurosawa on location while he was shooting *Kagemusha.*

November 11, 1979 Tokyo

It was raining in Tokyo as we were driven to the airport in bumper-to-bumper traffic. At the terminal we were crowded into an orange bus and taken out to the plane on the tarmac. The flight to Hokkaido was full, every seat occupied. Out the window the visibility was low, hangars and buildings in the distance were gray shadow shapes. Mexican music played over the PA system as the plane waited on the runway a long time before it was cleared to take off in heavy rain. During the hour-and-twenty-minute flight, two stewardesses hurried to serve passengers a paper cup of orange juice or green tea.

My thoughts were of Napa, the fall and the children. I was unhappy leaving eight-year-old Sofia again. She was upset the night before I departed. I made a calendar for her with each day marked with her activities and colored on the days that she would stay overnight with a friend. When I put her to bed she said, "Why are you gone so much? Why aren't you home more?" She said, "Why can't we just be normal? Why do we live in this big house?" She began weeping. She said, "I wish we could just be normal."

I got into bed with her and rubbed her back until she fell asleep. The next morning I drove her to the bus stop. When she saw her friend through the car window, she hugged me and jumped out. I sat watching her until the bus came. She seemed to be OK.

On the plane, I closed my eyes and just felt the conflict run through me: wanting to go with Francis and wanting to be home with Sofia, and noticing that when the trip was tiring, or boring, I longed desperately to be home.

The plane landed at 6:00 p.m. It was already dark. We hadn't had any lunch. Francis wanted to stop at a little noodle shop in the airport but the people who met us said we had to hurry, Kurosawa had invited us to the set and wanted us to arrive in time to see the last shot of the day. A production assistant quickly bought us a box lunch with egg salad sandwiches and orange soda and escorted us to a waiting car. We were irritable. Francis doesn't like mayonnaise, I don't care for orange soda. We rode for over an hour in the darkness. Our driver spoke no English.

I thought we were passing through flat farm land. We finally came to a lighted intersection and could see shops with strips of small fish drying, hung outside like curtains. I opened the window and could smell damp sea air. The car turned off the highway onto a sandy rutted road. As the car bounced along, the headlights shone on sand dunes. Finally, in the distance, we saw lights on a hill. As we got closer I could see scaffolding towers with huge arc lights creating a circle of illumination in the darkness. The car stopped in a flat area where buses and horse trailers were parked. We stepped out into cold damp wind.

A production assistant directed us to walk about a quarter of a mile to the bottom of an enormous sand dune and into a lit area. As we left the shadows, I could see cables, supply boxes and equipment. Crew members spoke over walkie-talkies. We walked up a steep road through sand. I was watching where I stepped, trying not to stumble and stopping frequently to shake sand out of my open-toed shoes. At the crest of the hill, I looked up. I felt a rush of excitement, the way I felt going on the set during a big night shot for *Apocalypse Now*, as if my every cell was suddenly, acutely awake. In front of me I saw a samurai army in full sixteenth-century armor; hundreds of foot soldiers were in formation around an elaborately costumed shogun. Lines of mounted samurai sat on horses that snorted and pawed the sand. The lead riders carried tall poles bearing colorful banners flapping hard in the wind. Orange scaffolding towers supported huge lights with green gels which cast a tint over the whole scene. Fine sand whipped in the air.

A short woman in a fur hat, seal boots and a down jacket hurried toward us. It was Nogami, Kurosawa's producer. She greeted us and led us through the samurai to a place by the B camera. The last shot of the evening was about to begin. I leaned against a fir tree pole used to brace the scaffolding of a lighting tower. I could hear a conversation about a shot the previous week that had two hundred dead horses on the field after a battle. "Over 40 veterinarians were hired to tranquilize all the horses at the same time." "Hey, the horses on this picture are costing more than the extras." "Yeah, because it took over a year to train those horses to get used to the armor and swords."

I looked at the intricate costumes of the samurai; each had a colored banner on a thin bamboo pole attached to his back. I could hear someone say that the black banners represented the mountains, mounted troops who protected the shogun. Green banners represented the forest, the foot soldiers who mopped up. Red banners for fire and silver-gray banners representing the wind were the attack forces.

The horses were restless, everyone was still, waiting for word that the cameras were rolling. Voices crackled over walkie-talkies, a signal was given and directions went out over the PA system. A charge of mounted samurai I hadn't seen came out of the dark shadows at the bottom of the hill and rode up the side of the huge dune in clouds of sand to attack the forces defending the hilltop and protecting the shogun. There was a flurry of swords, sand and samurai in military maneuvers. The charge was apparently rebuffed. The shot ended and everyone around us immediately began packing equipment and preparing to leave for the evening.

In a few minutes Nogami appeared with Kurosawa. He had been by the A camera at the foot of the hill with the angle up on the attacking forces. He was bundled in a heavy parka, scarf and ski cap and wearing his signature dark glasses. Through an interpreter he said he was glad to see us but wasn't feeling well and would meet us the following afternoon. He hurried away and we began to walk back to the car. I suddenly noticed how cold it was. I had been so absorbed I hadn't realized my body was shaking. When we got to the parking area I hurried into the car out of the wind. I could see samurai still in their armor board waiting buses and horses being loaded into trailers.

November 12, 1979

Francis and Kurosawa are seated at a small table. White tissue reflectors, lights, photographers and journalists surround them. The room is hot. Kurosawa is wiping his face with a cloth and writing in a book of his drawings with a brush. He dries the ink in front of one of the lights and gives the book to Francis, pointing out certain drawings. Francis tells him, "It reminds me of the way Eisenstein drew. I draw sometimes, but not as well as Sofia." The translator interprets for Kurosawa and he smiles. Francis says, "I was a theater director, Kurosawa was an artist. We each work in our individual ways to achieve the results we want." Through the interpreter Kurosawa says he remembered that Francis carried a copy of *Heart of Darkness* in his pocket while making *Apocalypse Now*. He said that he is carrying a copy of *War and Peace* in his pocket while he is making *Kagemusha*.

March 2, 2003 Napa

It's been exactly one year since my mother was moved to a nursing home. Today I am making a little altar with her picture and some shells I gathered from the beach in front of her house the last day she was there. I feared moving her at age ninety-three could cause her rapid decline. She seems to be OK, maintaining a health plateau and always glad to see her children. I frequently send her pictures and cards and visit every month, but I miss calling her as she can no longer answer her phone.

MARCH 2, 2002 SOUTHERN CALIFORNIA

I went to my mother's house in Sunset Beach, arriving at 5:00 in the winter evening as the light was fading to gray and a pale orange glow was forming over the ocean. My mother was sitting in her chair in the living room with a pillow supporting each arm. She looked frail and gazed vacantly at the small TV on top of the piano. When she heard me she turned slowly and smiled in delight. "Oh, I'm so glad to see you," she said. The TV was tuned to a rerun of a sitcom. She never cared much for TV. I switched it off, sat down next to her and took her hand, stroking it gently almost as if I were petting her. She said, "My, that feels good. It's so relaxing." I thought about old people with caretakers being touched only to dress or be moved. I spoke to her about the family, what we were all doing. She listened distantly. After a while I asked her if she would mind if I took a little walk on the beach before it got dark. She said, "That would be nice."

I walked out on the beach and turned back to look at the house. When I was growing up it had been the tallest house on the block, now it was the shortest. The houses on both sides had built up three stories, packing every inch of their small lot with generic blocky construction. My mother's house was built in 1930, a quaint beach cottage artistically designed by a local builder. As I looked up and down at the beach-front houses, I could see four other houses by the same builder; all had large additions and little remained of the original design. Over the past 70 years the value of the small beach-front lots has gone from several thousand dollars to over a million. My mother has lived in her house continuously since she arrived on her wedding night 71 years ago. I am here this evening to tell her it is no longer safe for her to stay in her home; her sweet Filipino caretakers can no longer manage her care. It will be the last evening she will spend in her house; the last time I will see her in my childhood home. The wind from the ocean blew my tears flat across my cheeks as I walked down to the water's edge. A dead seal was marooned on the wet sand in the receding tide; two sea gulls stood near it facing out to sea. Sandpipers raced along just out of reach of the waves. I could smell the familiar damp air and remembered childhood evenings when I knew any minute I would be called into the house for supper and have to leave the world on the beach where I played. My mother would stand on the front porch and briskly shake a cowbell. It was so embarrassing. That rusty misshapen bell is still on a shelf near the front door.

My brothers arrived with their wives. We ate supper at the dented redwood table in the living room where we had every childhood Thanksgiving and Christmas dinner. My brothers and I gently told my mother we would be moving her the next day. We said, "Just try it for a few weeks, we believe you will get better care, you won't be so isolated. And you will be closer to us, we'll get to see you much more often." She didn't seem convinced. With more coaxing she finally said, "I guess it sounds reasonable," in her reserved English way. We knew the next morning she would not remember where she was going. When I tucked her into bed I rubbed her shoulders and gave her many little kisses on her soft cheek.

The next day I arrived at the nursing home just as she finished an examination by the house doctor. Her familiar caregiver was putting her clothes away. Every garment had a tag sewn in with her name as if she were going to summer camp. I asked her if she would care to lie down and rest after her long drive. She looked at the bed and said, "No. That's not my bed." I wheeled her out into a sunny patio where my brothers were talking with the head nurse.

All day family members took turns coming and going so someone would be with her. I went to a nearby mall and bought a thick fuzzy blanket to supplement the thin bedcover provided. I had supper, and returned at 8:00 p.m. My mother was already in bed. I was relieved to see she wasn't agitated. I tucked the new blanket around her and asked if she was comfortable. She said, "Of course. I brought my own bed."

March 5, 2003 Napa

A cold wind is rattling the window. I've put on a maroon cashmere sweater I always used to take to New York in the winter. Recently I discovered it had four moth holes so I have been only wearing it here at home. In my mind's eye I can see the sweater thrown over the back of a sofa in the apartment we used to own in New York City.

March 3, 1998 New York City

It was our last day in New York. We were having guests for lunch. I wanted to see a show of ancient Chinese textiles so I made a 1:30 p.m. reservation for our guests at the restaurant downstairs and dashed out to the Metropolitan Museum. The plan was to all meet at the restaurant but when I hurried back to the hotel at 1:20 to drop off a shopping bag of books and my winter coat, Francis told me he had invited the guests up to our apartment. The doorbell rang and as he answered it I quickly closed the double doors to our messy private rooms and then joined him to greet Carole Bouquet, Gérard Depardieu, Jean-Paul Scarpitta and Isabella Rossellini with the traditional European kiss on both cheeks. Francis immediately flung open the double doors and took them on a tour of all the rooms. I could feel embarrassment curl in my stomach. The dining room table was covered with three days of newspapers, coffee cups, cereal bowls, and banana peels. Packing materials spilled from two boxes of camera equipment. The credenza had an assortment of mail, crumpled messages, piles of magazines, scripts, books, an empty vase, packing tape, and pencils with broken leads. Roman's girlfriend's red high-heeled shoes were lying on the floor next to the couch. A navy overcoat, a gray jacket, two scarves and a sweater were flung over the back of the sofa. The kitchen door was open with a view of cereal boxes on the sink among dirty dishes. Coffee grounds were scattered along the counter. In the bedroom a tangle of Roman's socks, underwear and jeans lay on the floor in front of the closet.

This week we all were busy doing things in the city and no one took the time to straighten up. Everyone is grown. A maid comes every day to dust and make the beds. I didn't want to stay in and be the clean-up martyr but in my heart I felt responsible.

Finally we went down to the restaurant. It was very crowded; six of us were pressed around a table for four. I was sitting between Jean-Paul and Isabella. We had all gone to the premiere of *The Man in the Iron Mask* the night before. Gérard played one of the three musketeers. He had a scene in which he runs across a courtyard in the nude. Now, sitting across from him, I felt as if I could see through his Armani suit, see the exact shape of his shoulders, his buttocks. Jean-Paul flung his fringed cashmere scarf over his shoulder, leaned close to me and whispered extravagantly, "Oh, my god! How the film was terrible! Oh, my god!" He gestured toward Gérard, continuing: "Oh, I told him. And such terrible photography, such flat lighting! Oh, my god, the costumes! And the story! Such a silly story. No one in France will go to see that. Gérard is good, though. He's so talented."

The conversation at the table switched back and forth from English to French to Italian. When I couldn't understand what was being said I looked at the precise line of Isabella's short hair, the cut of her very plain gray suit with a pink lavender shirt buttoned to the neck. I stared at the diamond in Carole's ring, the largest I've ever seen a civilian actually wear. It was $^{3}/_{4}$ inch across and startling as she waved her slender hand. Isabella spoke about how she had been madly in love with David Lynch for seven years; how he always said he didn't want to be tied down, couldn't commit, kept their affair very private. Then one year he won at the Cannes Film Festival and kissed her in public in front of all the cameras. She was sure that meant he had finally accepted their relationship. "A week later he broke up with me and went off with his editing assistant, who was pregnant!" I asked about her children. She said, "I don't know what I would do without my children, they balance my life." I said, "With kids you get to experience things over again; celebrate Halloween." She said, "Yes, when my daughter and her friend were at the age when they stopped believing in Santa Claus and were just pretending to believe for my sake, I had my brother-in-law dress up in a cheap Santa Claus suit with cotton balls for a beard and come to the house. The kids pretended to believe it was Santa, but I'd hired an actor with a real white beard and well dressed as Santa. He arrived at the house and bawled out my brother-in-law Santa for trying to trick the children. After that they believed for another two years."

April 3, 2003 Napa

A folder of miscellaneous snapshots arrived from Francis's research library. I was asked to sort and date the photos, select those to keep and discard the rest. The one on top was of Francis leaning on a black Volkswagen Rabbit with a Japanese flag decal on the back window. He looked almost too big for the car. The car was kept in the garage of our bungalow in Los Angeles and eventually it became mine to drive when I was in L.A.

February 28, 1995 Los Angeles

I've been to catacombs in Italy, mountain villages in southern China, the Safari Club at the base of Mount Kenya but never to Pep Boys at the corner of Hollywood Boulevard and Gower. I walked down one of the long aisles past thirty feet of black fan belts, silvery chrome exhaust extensions, red and white bottles of brake fluid, yellow fog lights, coils of purple, orange and green bungee cords. At the back of the huge store I found handsome Latino men standing on risers leaning imposingly across a wide counter in front of computers, working on orders. A machine displayed a ticket tongue; I took a number. I heard no English spoken. Three Latino laborers with brown weathered faces and worn, stained, thrift-store clothing were ahead of me buying carburetor parts. I was touched by their dignity, and the concern etched in their expressions. I thought of times I had tried to buy an appliance part in a foreign country.

When it was my turn I stepped up a bit uncomfortably. I was greeted by an exuberant young man. He introduced himself with a flirtatious smile: "I am Fernando, how can I help you?" I felt a flush of remembering being noticed just for being female. "I'm looking for a new battery for a 1981 Volkswagen," I said. He grinned and attacked his computer. In seconds the screen showed the stock number, the model, the price with and without service plan and the number in inventory. He grinned broadly while explaining the optional service contract, answering a phone and checking an item on a second computer. He seemed delighted to be tending the phone line, two computers and me. "I've only been working here two months," he said with amazement. I wondered if this was a new improved generation taught by computer games to quickly multitask. He took two more calls, dispatched them rapidly, then dashed into the rows of stock shelves and returned just as the computer was printing out my invoice. He strode jauntily down the aisle carrying my battery as if it were a melon, toward the cashier at the front of the store, waving for me to follow. He directed me to pay while he took my purchase ahead to the service center for installation. Before my credit card receipt had appeared, he returned for a cheerful goodbye; then he was on his way back to the order counter. I watched Fernando as his head bobbed above the stacks of blue gallon bottles of antifreeze, passed the air filters and swivel radiator caps and disappeared by the safety flares.

Part Six

August 20, 2003 Napa

All morning I spent answering intercompany e-mail, preparing fifteen pieces of snail mail to go out, speaking to my mother's doctors, making appointments. Suddenly I was hungry for lunch and wanted to go to the garden and pick ripe tomatoes and sprigs of basil. I put on my sun hat and walked rapidly, my head down, thinking of phone calls I still needed to return. On the path a covey of quail startled me and I stopped to watch them. The adults were in the lead followed by their family, no longer fuzzy chicks, now slim teenagers. They ran rapidly out from under rosebushes and crossed the gravel path chirping noisily. Behind them the head of a brown snake emerged from the foliage; I watched it move out across the path to its full length. Four pale yellow rattles at the end of its tail angled up toward the sky. It was so elegant, so silent, so at ease in its surroundings. It reminded me of seeing elephants in Africa, regal and relaxed, in harmony with the plains of Kenya, so different from the same animals with agitated eyes we see in circuses and zoos.

I was surprised to find myself more fascinated by the snake than afraid. It was exhilarating to see a creature so perfectly at one with its environment, its colors blending with the tones of the earth and the gravel, its alert smooth body gliding toward me with grace. I stood still, it didn't seem to notice me. I looked out across the hedges for one of the gardeners; they had gone to lunch. I backed up slowly, returned to the house and called the winery maintenance department: no answer. By the time I returned to the garden the snake had disappeared. I felt sad, knowing that if one of the gardeners finds it when I'm not around, they'll kill it, even though I repeatedly ask them to use a rake to pick up any snakes they find, put them in a plastic trash bin, drive up our canyon and release them.

September 15, 2003 Belize

Cays outlined by fringes of palm trees dot the gray-green horizon. The sky is dark and turbulent to the east and clear pale blue to the north. A pelican is diving down in the choppy sea near the shore. Hopefully last night's storm is blowing past. We slept with the doors open. I was awakened several times by the noise of cracking thunder, warm tropical wind whipping the sheets and great bolts of lightning illuminating the bedroom before crashing into the sea.

Francis and I are at Turtle Inn. It is closed for six weeks while work is being done before the season opens in mid-October. So many things were not completed when the resort opened last December. We are a crew of 18 who have come down from the States, plus perhaps thirty locals. While I tack new upholstery onto the bar stools, rub furniture oil on carved wooden doors, secure textile wall hangings, my mind is elsewhere. Each day we have received phone calls and e-mails with the latest news about the release of Sofia's film *Lost in Translation:* "Mom, we heard we're getting a good review from the *New York Times!*" Francis calls out from his computer, "The *Wall Street Journal* gave it a terrific review." An e-mail from the West Coast says, "Did you know the *SF Chronicle* gave it a little man clapping, falling out of his chair! It's the best you can get." "Ebert and Roper gave it two thumbs up!" "The opening weekend's grosses were higher than we thought they'd be."

I am so excited for Sofia. She has gone to a spa to recuperate. I am picturing her lounging in her robe, eating well, having massages and walking in the countryside to regain her balance of body and spirit after the heady reception as the darling of the Venice Film Festival, having the cover story of the *New York Times Magazine*, success at the Toronto Film Festival and all the extraordinarily good reviews. I think about her having this moment of triumph and all that it means for her future, especially the freedom to do the next project of her choice. It is thrilling that her success is coming from a film she wrote and directed herself, her personal vision drawn from her inner and outer life. This success will give her courage to stay on her own path, have confidence in her voice; there are few women's voices in the film industry. A man would never have made *Lost in Translation*.

I noticed that many articles refer to Sofia's influences from her filmmaker father. I am not mentioned although there are references to her "lack of pretension," "her quiet strength," qualities that have been ascribed to me. I remember Francis's mother once saying loudly to a journalist, "Don't forget, Francis got half his talent from me!"

Last week Francis and I attended Sofia's screening of *Lost in Translation* at the Toronto Film Festival. As we entered Francis stopped to sign autographs for a waiting crowd while I walked ahead into the theater. The next day there was a photo in the newspaper. It showed Francis standing next to a fat, elderly lady with glasses. The caption said, "Francis Coppola and his wife." We all laughed.

January 5, 2004 Napa

The family went on a holiday vacation in the Caribbean after Christmas. Francis and I came home to Napa two days ago. It is sunny but cold. Memories of warm tropical air and flowering dense vegetation are quickly melting away. This afternoon I walked through the garden surrounding the main house. It was transformed in the ten days we were gone. There were still fall leaves when I left but a major storm over the New Year dropped the canopy completely. Now there are views of the winter sky through webs of branches. I looked for flowers to put on an altar for the new year. I found white narcissus and, surprisingly, a few pale pink roses with brown-spotted petals that had a kind of beauty like old ladies. Carrying my bouquet, I hiked up the hill to my studio.

In the altar niche in the wall I cleared away things left from last year. I read each prayer rolled in a scroll and tied with red thread. Prayers for a friend who died, prayers for family members, prayers for world peace. I unrolled the list of my intentions for 2003 to see which ones I had achieved and which will remain on the list for 2004. I dusted a rock I brought from a retreat with a friend on a pristine lake, two sea shells from the beach in front of my mother's house, a dime-sized sand dollar from a walk on a winter day at Stinson Beach last year, and a small pink shell with a hole in it I found on the beach in Belize on our 40th anniversary last February.

My studio sits on a knoll. The large barn doors face a clearing where new green wild grasses have pushed up through fallen leaves and around unruly gray tufts of last year's growth. On the far side, live oak trees are backlit; ribbons of glowing bright green moss run along their dark branches. The day is piercingly sunny after days of stormy rains. I am reviewing the year in my mind. I was too busy the last months to digest my experiences. It's as if I need to take time now to sort and integrate all that happened.

Today I am putting away several boxes of messages that were gathered from a collaborative art installation I have worked on intermittently for nearly five years. The installation is called "Circle of Memory, a public space that inspires visitors to remember and commemorate children who are lost or have died." It is in the shape of a cairn and constructed of straw bales. Small pencils and paper are provided for visitors to leave messages to loved ones tucked in the walls. By the closing date thousands upon thousands of messages were wedged into the straw. I read some:

> "*It has been nineteen months since you were stabbed by the parking meter, we miss you so much. —Mom and Dad*"
> "*I feel blessed that I have no child's name to place here and thought of those who did.*"
> "*This is my fourth visit. I wish the exhibit was permanent.*"

"Davey, it's been 45 years and I still miss you."
"Now I know that art can heal."

In the mid-nineties I visited my friend Jean McMann in Ireland, where she was studying an ancient cairn for a book she was writing. She led me and several others over stiles, across pastures, through flocks of sheep, to the top of a hill where we saw a mound of stones. She told us this was a prehistoric site called a cairn or passage tomb. She located the crumbling entrance and led us through a low passageway that emerged into a dark round stone chamber with a high-domed ceiling. Jean took candles from her backpack and lit half a dozen, setting them on stone ledges.

We could see the corbeled ceiling and marveled at the engineering and technology it took to build such a structure long before modern tools. "Cairns were built about 5,000 years ago," Jean said. "Bones were found and perfectly round stones. It is thought that rituals pertaining to death and renewal were performed here." We could see small round holes carved into the large stones that looked as if they would fit a marble and also complex patterns of spirals cut into the rock. Jean suggested we create a ceremony ourselves to commemorate people who had died that were important to us. We stood in the semi-darkness and took turns saying names of loved ones. We named grandparents and favorite authors but when I finally said, "My son Gian-Carlo Coppola," I felt unexpected intense emotion, as if I were connected to all the mothers who had lost children down through the ages.

Later I thought about how we don't have a place in our culture to evoke this connection and commemorate our children. I wondered if it was the shape of the space that affected me, if the Ancients had developed a spiritual technology for celebrating the lives of those who died and healing those who remained that we no longer have. Jean told me, "Passage tombs of this shape, consisting of a low passage leading into a round chamber with a high ceiling, are found in Africa, central Europe, ancient China and other parts of the world." The experience in that Irish cairn remained with me.

Five years later my barn/studio was built of straw bales. When the walls were up I found the aroma of the straw, its color and texture so appealing I wished it wasn't necessary to plaster over them.

A year or two later the thought came to me: if a cairn were made out of straw bales, would it have evocative qualities such as the ones of stone I visited in Ireland? Straw bales are cheap, readily available and simple to build with, unlike the process of moving huge stones. It could potentially be easily built in any community and be a universal space without religious, political or ethnic overtones; a space for anyone to commemorate the loss of a child, whether their own or the tragedies we confront almost daily through the media.

I consulted with Jean about the possibility of creating a straw-bale cairn as an art installation, thinking that people come to art venues with a curious and reflective attitude. We decided to form a collaboration with another artist as well as an architect, a designer of stage lighting and sets and a sound designer. The six of us developed the concept over several years, meeting when we found time in everyone's busy schedule. We made a mock-up of the piece on our ranch in an old barn which Francis uses as a rehearsal space. The day came when Francis said he needed to use the barn and we should dismantle our construction. He had heard me talk about the project but hadn't seen what we'd made. I called him in his writing bungalow and said, "I'd really like you to see what we're working on before we take it down." I could hear by his voice I'd interrupted him. He said reluctantly, "All right."

He appeared at the barn door with an expression of "OK, I don't have much time, let's get this over with." When he smelled the straw and saw the form he visibly slowed down; his body seemed to melt as he moved along the passageway into the darkened chamber and sat down on a straw bale facing the thin stream of falling salt. We six collaborators were there and waited quietly for him to give his critique. He was silent. I looked over and saw a tear roll down his cheek. He said quietly, "It works."

Richard Beggs, the Academy Award–winning sound designer, created a tapestry of children's voices reciting the alphabet and counting in over a dozen languages. The sound is low and evocative and comes in and out of the audience's awareness from four unseen speakers inside the round chamber.

Set and lighting designer Alex Nichols created the structural design and a machine set in the dark ceiling which releases a thin stream of salt that falls continuously onto the floor, forming a glowing mound that grows over the course of the installation. The falling salt refers to the passage of time, to tears and is an essential element that we need for life. Alex created beautiful evocative lighting.

Artist Robilee Frederick directed us in making a translucent, organic curtain of hog gut that hangs at the end of the passageway. The visitors see it as they proceed down the passage and walk around it to enter the interior chamber. It suggests the demarcation between the outer world and the inner world of reflection and contemplation; it also symbolizes the separation between life and death.

Elizabeth Macdonald, a PhD in urban planning, created the way the structure is oriented in a space in relation to its architecture, windows and doors. She designed the flow for visitors entering and exiting and where they would sit. Jean created a series of photographs, life-size portraits of the stones that ring the cairn in Ireland I originally visited with her. These five-foot-square photographs are mounted on the wall surrounding our straw-bale cairn, creating a setting and connecting our installation with the original site of its inspiration.

The structure was quickly covered with heartfelt notes and from the response we knew it had a profound visual and emotional impact on visitors, making all the time and work we'd invested feel worthwhile. I found the experience of collaborating with other artists very gratifying.

The installation opened to the public on October 30, 2003, in the Oakland Art Gallery. Over Thanksgiving weekend the family drove to visit Circle of Memory. We sat together on sweet-smelling straw bales in the semi-dark, circular chamber. I could see Francis, Roman, Sofia and Gia near me. I felt I'd created a connection between us and Gio.

The work was so well received it was held over an extra month and has been invited to museums in San Diego, California, and Santa Fe, New Mexico. It felt strange to see myself in newspaper articles and on TV for something I'd initiated.

I also had a show of my olive-branch pieces in a gallery in San Francisco last month. The walls were painted a pale gray-green to set off the work, which was unframed on ivory paper. The pieces were lit to feature the natural branch shapes, the watercolor-painted shadows and the real cast shadows. I got a good review and several major collectors bought pieces. But I was surprised to notice that the most satisfying aspect of the experience were personal responses such as a note from a woman I barely know: "Elegant, intelligent, amazingly beautiful. I had no idea you did this work." Telling me that I had managed to make visible part of a world that is vivid inside me.

JANUARY 12, 2004

We are all wild with happiness over Sofia's nomination by the Screen Directors Guild! Only five women have been nominated in the history of the guild. No woman in a decade. I checked myself to find out if I had passed through the dark painful jealousy that haunted me last year. I am buoyant with happiness for her and deeply thrilled.

January 25, 2004 Los Angeles

Whenever I come to L.A. I feel as though I have left my real world and stepped into a parallel universe. It is familiar the way a movie is but the lawns look greener, the colors of the bougainvillea more intense, the sun glinting off windshields seems brighter and people wear clothes I've only seen on TV.

Last night we attended a Hollywood party for cast and crew to celebrate the five Golden Globe nominations *Lost in Translation* received. I learned about the party at the last minute. Frequently Francis makes plans that are familiar to him from multiple e-mails but forgets to mention them to me. I've learned to be flexible. I felt superficial, but asked him what people would be wearing. "I'm sure it's casual. They'll be wearing jeans." I tried to call Sofia but couldn't reach her. As the mother of the director, I thought I ought to be a bit dignified so wore slacks, a cashmere sweater and a Japanese scarf.

The party was held at the home of screenwriter/producer Mitch Glazer and his wife, actress Kelly Lynch. I could see from the address it would require a complicated drive into the Hollywood Hills. I drove Francis along steep narrow roads that appeared to dead-end then continued in tight hairpin turns. I was relieved to finally arrive and see a "Valet Parking" sign and give our car to an attendant whose broad smile displayed his irregular white teeth. A man holding a clipboard with a list of names saw Francis and directed us to walk up a steep driveway lit by tall votive candles.

The intricately carved large front door of the house was open. We were met by a waiter holding a tray with glasses of champagne. The house was built on a hilltop in a dramatic semicircle with a view of what appeared to be all of Los Angeles sparkling below. I looked around quickly and realized that the men were dressed casually but all the women were wearing cocktail dresses; especially beautiful ones. A childhood memory of being eight years old and arriving in white shorts at what I thought was a beach party and finding all the girls in pastel party dresses flooded over me. I walked over to the window and pretended to be looking at the view as I told myself, "Hey, you are in your sixties. It's OK. You can wear anything you want." I was amazed at how tenaciously a childhood experience still influenced me.

I found Sofia in the crowd and gave her a lingering hug as I congratulated her. She received my words with a delighted grin. She was wearing a mint green, very short, ruffled chiffon silk Marc Jacobs dress and high pointy heels. I apologized to her for not dressing for the occasion. She said, "Oh, Mom, you look fine." I knew in her voice that it really was OK with her.

People were crowding around Sofia. Everyone appeared to be in their thirties, glamorous with tan shoulders, long sparkling earrings, spaghetti-strap dresses, deep décolletages, bare legs and high spike heels. The men wore open-collared shirts and sports coats with jeans. Some had a look of purposefully not shaving for a day or two. They looked as if they were people in magazines.

I felt a little tug at my arm and heard a familiar voice say, "Hey." Zoe Cassavetes came into focus. As the daughters of film directors she and Sofia have always been comfortable together, done things together. Zoe treats me as if I were a favorite aunt. I've been out with her and Sofia in New York City and Paris and she's opened the car door for me, offered to lend me her coat when it's cold or if we're in some offbeat place she might say, "Oh, you're so cool. My mother would never come to a place like this." I thought about her mother, Gena Rowlands, the remarkable actress. She always looks so perfectly coifed and elegant. Living in Northern California has saved me from constantly comparing myself to a fantasy of how the "director's wife" is supposed to look, but when I come to L.A. I am jolted by reminders.

Leslie Hayman pushed her way toward me. An attractive, blond beauty in a skimpy black dress. She and her sister are Sofia's childhood friends from St. Helena. Leslie was the star of Sofia's first film when she was four and Sofia was perhaps eleven. The title was *Doughmain*. Leslie was nude and covered in biscuit dough. The quintessential blond California girl, she played one of the sisters in *The Virgin Suicides* and was the model for Sofia's clothing company.

Leslie's sister Stephanie joined us. Stephanie was Sofia's partner in her clothing company. Last year the company sold to a Japanese firm so her responsibilities for production ended. She said, "Guess what? I'm going to Beijing in March to study Chinese medicine." I remembered that she had been studying at night school for several years while she worked with Sofia. I thought about Stephanie's life path. One of nine children in a rural family growing up in the Napa Valley; a good student in subjects Sofia was weak in, such as chemistry and math. Now she was preparing to go to China to become a practitioner of alternative medicine. I was glad to learn that her life was moving forward toward goals of her own after all the years of working on Sofia's.

As I began to relax I could see beyond the ring of people around Sofia and found familiar faces. Francis was sitting on a sofa with Fred Roos, his casting director since *Godfather* who helped cast several parts in *Lost in Translation*. Fred's wife, Nancy, called me over. She had on a hand-painted silk kimono jacket I admired. I felt a twinge as I saw her notice what I was wearing.

Nancy said, "Look at this," as she lifted up an object from the coffee table. It was a narrow bronze sculpture of a thin nude woman standing on a long pedestal. "It's an award for Sofia. Bob and Anjelica have a family film festival and they are brutal, they rip the films apart. Well, they just gave this year's award for Best Picture to Sofia!" I realized she was talking about Robert Graham and Anjelica Huston. "You know Dana and Ed Ruscha, don't you?" I looked at the couple sitting next to her; I've met them from time to time but was not sure they would remember me. They did. I am such a fan of Ed's work and have several pieces from the '70s but I have no way to express to him how much his work has meant to me over the years. Next to Ed was the artist Elizabeth Peyton. Sofia recently sat for a portrait and she gave us one of the sketches as a Christmas present. I was pleased that the crowd gathered to celebrate Sofia's film consisted of so many artists and friends among the agents and film company executives.

I walked over to Anjelica Huston. She was easy to see, she is tall with beautiful posture and was wearing a dramatic floor-length Chinese coat. I've always liked her. She gave Sofia wise counsel when Sofia was brutalized by the press for her performance in *Godfather III*, just as Anjelica had been for a role she played as a teenager in a film her father directed.

Lance Acord, the cinematographer of *Lost in Translation*, was in the crowd. I thanked him again for all he did for Sofia. Not only did he shoot the film with artistry on a brutal schedule of only 27 days, but he wasn't a prima donna; he constantly resolved difficulties between the American and Japanese crew and he kept a fast pace, avoiding costly delays. I congratulated him on his nomination from BAFTA [British Academy of Film and Television Arts]. "Are you going to London?" His answer was a modest but excited "Yeah," and he asked me, "So, how's your new house coming along?" I had to confess, "It's stuck. The foundation is in but we can't find the right builder."

Lance is a fan of contemporary architecture and began pointing out details of the house we were standing in. "It's a Lautner house from the fifties. He used natural materials, wood and stone. They've completely restored it." Lance is a friend of the owners, and showed me into several side rooms. I appreciated the sparseness of the design, but found the wood veneer walls oppressive. Hanging art on the wood grain created a visual conflict for me. There was a perfection about the house as if it were a museum; except their daughter's room, where posters and photos were casually Scotch-taped to the handsome wood walls.

When I asked Lance what film he was going to do next, he said, "I've been shooting commercials here in town. I want to do a film but it's hard, I don't want to go off on a long location and leave the kids. George [his three-year-old boy] just wouldn't understand. I can't leave him." Lance's wife, Rema, joined us. As we talked about the difficulties of balancing family life with the film business I noticed how openly they talked about it. Rema said she didn't want to leave her friends and home, live in a hotel with the kids and see Lance only an hour or two each day. When I was her age I thought it was my duty to go and never imagined I could openly consider doing otherwise. I told her, "Clive Owen recently came to see Francis in Napa. He said his solution was to rent a huge house on location for his wife and kids and invite family and friends to come visit."

At midnight there was a stir as Bill Murray and his wife arrived directly from a European flight. Bill is in Wes Anderson's film *The Life Aquatic*, shooting in Rome. When I greeted Bill I'd forgotten how tall he is, how far he had to bend down to kiss me on the cheek, and I stumbled backwards. It was the first time I'd seen him with gray hair and a beard. He introduced me to his wife. I'd heard he was very devoted to his family. I asked her about her children. She said, "We have six boys. Two boys seventeen and nineteen from Bill's previous, ah, earlier marriage and four ages two to ten." Her eyes grew dark and I thought I saw pain in them as she took a big gulp of wine. I imagined how difficult it could be, home with four school-aged children while your charismatic actor husband is being catered to on a movie location in Rome.

As the evening wound down and we walked out through the big carved door I was glad to be alone with just Francis.

February 7, 2004

We are sitting at French wicker tables under umbrellas, on a sunny terrace by the pool of the Chateau Marmont. Around me looks as if it could be a magazine layout. My chair faces an azure pool. On the other side a young man, a James Dean look-alike in jeans, white T-shirt, and aviator glasses, leans back in his lounge chair into the sun. To the side behind me two men in business suits with open-collared dark shirts and sunglasses sit eating tuna carpaccio and talking on cell phones.

At our table Sofia is seated at one end and Francis at the other. Bart Walker [Sofia's agent] and Ross Katz [Sofia's producer] sit on one side, and Gia and I on the other. We have just come from a symposium at the Directors Guild of America where the five nominated directors for the Guild award sat before a large packed auditorium answering a moderator's questions. It lasted from 10:00 a.m. to 1:00 p.m., three intense hours of dense information about the directors and how they work. Sofia sat onstage with Gary Ross, the director of *Seabiscuit*, and Peter Jackson, the director of *Lord of the Rings;* next to Peter was Clint Eastwood, director of *Million Dollar Baby*, and next to him, Peter Weir, director of *Master and Commander*. Sofia, in a soft sweater and jeans, looked so tiny and young; sunk in a canyon of large men's shoulders.

Long clips from each director's film were shown and the questioning began. The moderator addressed Peter Weir first. "How did you prepare for your film?" He answered very eloquently in his Australian-accented English about the research he'd done reading hundreds of books and how he spent days on a ship that was a replica of a sailing vessel from the period. He worked as a deck hand in rough seas and slept in a hammock to have the physical experience as if he were on board a sailing ship in the 1600s. I was worried for Sofia among these older, seasoned male directors but when the moderator turned to her she was articulate and graceful.

Francis, Gia and I were seated at the side of the auditorium down close to the front and when the symposium ended a production assistant directed us up onto the stage and out into an atrium to join Sofia, the other panel members and their guests for a private reception. Francis introduced me and Gia to people who came up to congratulate him on Sofia's success. Clint Eastwood asked Gia, "So are you going to be a director?" She shyly looked down at the floor and smiled nervously. Three other people asked her the same question. Gia is seventeen, a lovely, gawky teenager. I imagine she is feeling pressure about what she is going to do or be in her family of high achievers. The two cousins she is closest to are Tally's sons. Robert at age twenty last year signed a major recording contract and his brother Jason just starred in a film opposite Dustin Hoffman. With luck the family legacy will be constructive, give direction to her life, spur her on, but I worry it could be a crushing burden. Later I asked Francis what Gia should say. "She should just say, 'I haven't decided yet.' "

Lunch was served. We discussed the symposium. Sofia was asked about her shooting technique and she responded that she shot with two cameras. Now she remarked, "Clint Eastwood said he shoots with one camera, that if you shoot with two, one is always compromised." Francis replied, "Kurosawa always shot with two cameras." Sofia grinned: "Yeah!"

When we finished lunch, Gia and I went up to Sofia's room with her because Sofia planned to loan Gia a dress to wear to the black-tie Directors Guild awards ceremony that evening. An open suitcase on the floor overflowed with sweaters and underwear. In front of the sofa on a low table there was a wide clear vase filled with exquisite pale pink roses in full, fragile, swirling bloom.

Sofia saw me looking at it. "Mom, I got so many flowers [after she won the Golden Globes], my room looked like a funeral parlor."

Sofia opened a garment bag hanging from the top of a door. It contained two beautiful designer cocktail dresses. She took one out that was sheer, black with bands of paillettes that shimmered in the afternoon light. She turned to Gia: "You can wear this, but you have to bring it back. I have to return it. Do you have something to wear under it?" Gia nodded. Her face was alight. I realized the clothes were all sent by designers hoping Sofia would wear theirs in front of the press cameras. Tonight there will be a red carpet with densely packed press. Sofia chose a cocktail-length dress for herself that had a dramatic open back with a hint of fullness below, the suggestion of a bustle. The front was straight and almost tailored. The back will flounce as she walks across the stage.

Sofia looked utterly exhausted. I knew she had to leave soon to speak to the line of press people at 5:00 p.m. before the 6:30 dinner and 8:00 awards ceremony. "Mom, I have to practice my speech and a makeup person is coming in twenty minutes. I'm so tired. I don't know how I can talk to another person." I gave Sofia a long hug and hurried out of the room before I found myself saying things such as "Take a hot bath, breathe deeply." She has been going to film festivals and awards events all over the world for months.

February 16, 2004 San Francisco

It was Saturday, both of our husbands were out of town; my friend Robbie and I drove into San Francisco for the night. We had an early dinner and attended a performance of the ODC Dance Company. Afterwards we talked excitedly about what we had seen and were in no mood to go to our apartment. I called Jeannette at Tosca bar and asked if her reserved parking space was available. She said, "I'll make room. Come on over."

I drove up Columbus Avenue; traffic was slow, lots of people were out. When we arrived outside Tosca, the doorman saw me and removed two orange cones from the passenger loading zone so I could park. Robbie and I entered the long narrow barroom filled with a noisy Saturday night crowd. Jeannette was at the end, where she was watching both the front door and the tables in back. She slid off her high stool in jeans and floppy sweater to hug us. She looked around shrugging her shoulders and flapping her arms in a gesture toward the loud, young crowd and said, "I'm gettin' too old for this."

I laughed: "Hey, you love it. Your place is full, you're making a ton of money. Come on, I'll buy you a drink." She grinned. We sat down in old chrome chairs with red vinyl seats at a front table. The waitress came over and asked for our order. Jeannette said, "I'll have the usual."

"Three usuals," I said, knowing that would be a bottle of water for each of us. Jeannette talked about the upcoming Academy Awards. "I'm renting a big flat-screen TV and the guys from your husband's office are going to set it up for me. We're going to watch the awards right here and have pizzas run over from your café." (Francis's office building with café are a block away.) I said, "Sorry I won't be in my jeans sitting here with you. I'll be walking up that red carpet. So are you going to loan me your mother's earrings to wear?"

"Yeah, I brought them from home. They're here in the safe."

Jeannette's mother, Armen [[Baliantz]], was a wealthy young Russian Armenian woman living in China with her businessman husband and three-year-old Jeannette when the Japanese invaded. They were incarcerated in a Japanese prison camp and lost all their possessions except a trunk of belongings and the jewelry that she hid. I've heard a story that when Armen was pregnant with Jeannette's brother she traded a pearl pin to a prison guard for an apple and then agonized over whether to give it to Jeannette or eat it herself to nourish her unborn child. Armen has beautiful, valuable, old jewelry. She gave a pair of antique Russian earrings to Sofia when she got married. I have never been drawn to jewelry. I'm sure it has been a disappointment to Francis, who has given me fine pieces over the years that I rarely wear. I don't happen to have the right earrings to go with my dress for the Academy Awards.

We went into Jeannette's tiny office next to the jukebox. The three of us barely fit. I was pressed against the desk facing the wall. I never tire of looking at the snapshots she has pinned up. There is one of three-year-old Sofia sitting on Santa's lap, next to one of Jeannette and Rudolf Nureyev wearing snow caps, and photos of her lounging by a pool with Lauren Hutton, standing by her jukebox with Marc Jacobs, sitting in a booth with Sean Penn next to a signed eight-by-ten glossy of Robert Mitchum. The wall is crammed with photos. She opened the big old-fashioned safe and took out a small red leather box with embossed gold designs. "So here they are," she said, opening the box. Resting on a tiny velvet cushion were two earrings; each had a huge cluster of diamonds and a large dangling pearl. She lifted one up and handed it to me. "Look, my mother had special guards put on the back so you don't have to worry about losing them." I laughed nervously and tried them on, looking in her small wall mirror. "Let's face it, they're great!" she said. The diamonds sparkled brilliantly. I said, "I bet your mother will be able to see these on TV they're so bright. You know, I'm really afraid of losing one."

Jeannette told a story about Joan Crawford saying to Irene Dunne, who never wore much jewelry, that she should borrow a pair of her beautiful earrings for a special event. Joan said to Irene, "People expect movie stars to look glamorous." Irene borrowed the earrings and accidentally lost one. She didn't want Joan to know so she just had it replaced. "And it cost her twelve thousand dollars!" "Now you're really making me nervous!" I said, thinking that would be at least fifty thousand today.

I put the small red leather box with earrings in my purse and as we left the bar I had the strap around my shoulder and the purse tucked tightly under my arm. When we got to the apartment I looked around carefully to see if anyone had followed us and then chided myself for my paranoia.

The next morning Robbie and I had breakfast at Caffè Greco, where Francis thinks they make the best Italian coffee. The Hispanic cappuccino maker behind the bar asked me, "Where is El Grande?" I told him, "Francis is in New York." He said, "Oh, so what would you like, Tía?" I wonder about him calling me "Tía"—was it better or worse than "Señora"? He served me a double cappuccino in a cup the size of a soup bowl.

After breakfast we walked two blocks to the edge of Chinatown. I wanted to look for things to buy cheaply to resell at the winery store or at our resorts in Belize. We entered my favorite place for bargains, a run-down store that has no tourist appeal whatsoever. Merchandise is stacked haphazardly on shelves and overflows from torn cardboard boxes in the long narrow aisles. Everything looks dusty and the color is slightly off under the dim fluorescent bulbs. There are cooking pots, plastic wash tubs, rows of plates and bowls of all sizes, thermos bottles, flashlights, underwear, pajamas, flower vases, funeral papers and much more.

I approach the cavernous room like a treasure hunt. I find an open carton of denim beach hats for $1.49 each. Out of this context they will look fine and sell well at our store in Belize for $8. I put Robbie to work sorting out four dozen of the best ones in several colors. She laughs as she comes across girls' underpants and Chinese music cassettes mixed in with the hats. I get on my knees to sort through a shelf near the floor for ceramic bowls with frogs perched on the edge that I will put with merchandise at the winery store when we do a garden theme this spring. I like to add occasional quirky items so the store's selection doesn't look like it was chosen by a corporate buying committee. I take a stack of 99-cent straw hats, and cellophane packages of orange candles on sticks.

We bring our selections to the cash register near the front door. The owner is sitting to one side on a box eating his lunch from a battered aluminum bowl and giving orders to his employees. He is talking with his mouth open, grains of rice flicking into the air. No one is speaking English. The disheveled man behind the counter sees we have five plastic baskets of items. He looks at us warily and points emphatically at a scrap of brown paper Scotch-taped to the register with wobbly hand-printed letters: "Cash only." I nod my head. He looks to the owner, who gets up and comes over to us carrying his bowl of food which, up close, smells strongly of fish. The owner looks at us sharply. He points to the sign and I nod again. He says something and his employee begins to ring up the sale.

Everything is counted twice in Chinese, then the numbers are entered reverently on the old cash register keys. Each time he reaches a subtotal he looks to me for agreement. When the final total is tallied, $217.58, the man turns to me with an expression of grief as if he is thinking, after all his work, we surely won't have that much cash. To his surprise I produce bills, fresh twenties from the ATM. He counts the money carefully, then turns the bills over and counts them again from the back before pressing the key consummating the sale and creating a ribbon of receipt. He grins showing his brown stained teeth and lifts his feet in a joyous little step. He begins putting our purchases into thin, rumpled pink plastic bags.

We point and gesture that we want him to hold our many bags behind the counter until we return with the car. He doesn't understand. We try to speak to the owner but he is uncomprehending and unconcerned. Robbie calls out loudly to the other customers, "Does anybody here speak English?" An old Chinese woman in a plum-colored sweat suit responds. She translates for us and we see our bags piled in a corner behind the counter. Our clerk grins broadly; he counts to ten hesitantly in English and bows as we leave.

Out on the sidewalk Robbie laughs at me. "I never saw this side of you before. Last night it was diamond earrings and today it's three-dollar frog dishes. You do both."

March 1, 2004 Los Angeles

In the split second between sleeping and waking, before my eyes were open, I sensed I wasn't at home and felt deep undefined emotions. It was similar to the way I felt for months in 1986 waking up on location in Washington, D.C., each morning, away from home and disoriented, waking after the escape of sleep to the first moment of realizing that Gio was dead. This morning I realized I was in Los Angeles and when I was awake enough to define the emotion it was not pain I remember but happiness. Sofia won an Oscar last night.

After an event at the winery in Napa Friday evening, Francis and I flew to Los Angeles, arriving at our little house at 1:30 in the morning. Francis and Sofia were to rehearse their part as presenters of the Oscar for Best Adapted Screenplay. At 8:30 the next morning a car took us to the Kodak Theatre, where the Academy Awards are held. We were directed into the green room where guests who were scheduled to rehearse were waiting. The chairs and sofas were black lacquer with white silk upholstery in a style reminiscent of a glamorous 1930s hotel lobby. The numerous sconces and chandeliers were made of globules of glass surrounding bright bare bulbs which cast an unflattering harsh light.

Across the room I could see Catherine Zeta-Jones enter. She was wearing skin-tight black leather pants and high heels. Her hair was down and looked perfect. A few minutes later Sofia arrived. She was wearing jeans, tennis shoes and a soft sweater of unusual design. She looked tired. There was a big party for *Lost in Translation* last night, she had also just traveled from London, where she attended the British Academy Awards and accepted the Best Actor award for Bill Murray. I watched as Sofia and Francis practiced their lines, getting acclimated to the teleprompter. A camera operator with a large hand-held television camera practiced getting into position and shooting the cardboard pictures of Sofia and Francis in their seats which the director would cut to for reaction shots on awards night. After Sofia and Francis rehearsed their entrance and speeches several times the stage manager was satisfied and released them. We went back into the green room. Sofia and Francis talked with the show writer. There was a joke in her dialogue that Sofia thought was lame and she didn't want to say it. The writer finally said, "OK, let's cut it" and penciled out a line in the pages on his clipboard.

As we made our way out through the security check I was given a tote bag for Francis containing an Oscar-logo sweatshirt and baseball cap while he and Sofia were escorted to a table to sign a dozen posters for the Academy archives. As an afterthought, the woman reached into a box and pulled out an extra baseball cap and gave it to me. "I bet you'd like one, too." I felt I was being treated like a kid at a birthday party who didn't win any prizes.

Our limousine was backed up into place and the trunk sprung open. A production assistant lifted in a large piece of leather luggage tied with a huge bow and card with Francis's name. It held gifts given to each presenter, rumored to be worth seventy thousand dollars.

Sofia was in a hurry because she was already late for an appointment in her hotel room to have her hair and makeup done for the Independent Spirit Awards that were to begin at 1:00 in Santa Monica. The awards are given by the Independent Film Producers organization to honor films that are made for under $15 million, worthy works which are usually overlooked by the Academy Awards. The IFP awards are presented in a large tent on the beach in Santa Monica during the early afternoon over lunch. They are televised on Bravo in the evening. We had decided to attend and went back to our bungalow so I could change. These awards pride themselves on being antiestablishment and casual. Although Sofia had been nominated in three categories, I didn't have any expectations she would win because I felt Sofia was perceived as a filmmaker of privilege and they tend to reward the offbeat artist rather than the mainstream. I thought the fact that Sofia was also nominated for three Academy Awards worked against her.

As Francis and I stepped out of the limo at the entrance to the Spirit Awards shouts went up: "Mr. Coppola," "Mr. Coppola," "Over here, Francis." A crowd restrained behind a fence called for him to autograph books and photos they held. I waited at the entrance to the long red carpet with photographers lined up for fifty yards. I realized I'd forgotten our tickets and spoke to the guard. He said, "You with that man over there?" He gestured toward Francis. I nodded. "I think we can let you in." I stood in the wind a long time while Francis was interviewed by reporters and smiled for the cameras before we entered the tent. Midway through the ceremony Sofia won the award for Best Screenplay. I was surprised and really happy. As the afternoon went on she won for Best Director, and when Bill won for Best Actor everyone at our table jumped up in unison. He loped up onto the stage and gave a rambling, deadpan, funny speech. Then *Lost in Translation* won for Best Film! I was stunned!

Sunday morning Francis and I had a late breakfast with Roman in the Polo Lounge of the Beverly Hills Hotel. It was so nice to spend time with him alone. He has been working in Rome for six weeks directing the second unit for Wes Anderson's *The Life Aquatic*, and it was the first we'd seen him other than for a hug at the party the night before. We ate heartily as we knew we wouldn't be eating again until the Academy Awards show ended around 10:00 in the evening.

That afternoon as we approached the Kodak Theatre I could

hear helicopters overhead. Spectators lined barricades along both sides of the street. All the limos had tinted glass. We could see out but people outside couldn't see us with the late afternoon sunlight reflecting off the car windows. When I'd attended years ago, at times Francis was nominated, there was little security and the public called out from the packed sidewalks as we drove, with windows open, to the red carpet. Now it felt disconcerting to be surrounded by a huge crowd yet be completely isolated. Finally we arrived at a line of stopped cars and waited our turn to move into position to open our doors. We stepped out onto the red carpet lined with photographers and press calling out to Francis. He moved from microphone to microphone. The questions were the same. "You must be very proud of your daughter." "How does it feel to have your daughter nominated?" "I'm sure you're very proud tonight, tell me how it feels." "What advice did you give your daughter this evening?" I stayed with him part of the way but then stepped aside and watched the spectacle of the parade moving along the red carpet, hoping to see Sofia yet knowing she would probably be one of the last to arrive. Finally Francis reached the end of the press line and I joined him to enter the theater lobby. Drinks were being served and waiters carried silver platters with small slices of pizza and miniature bruschetta toast rounds into the crowd. Most of the women weren't eating. No one wanted to disturb her lip gloss. A PA system made frequent announcements: "Please take your seats in the theater. The show will begin in 18 minutes . . . in 15 minutes, in 12 minutes." Francis and I walked up the ramp into the auditorium. We passed the section where the people who had worked on *Cold Mountain* were seated. Renée Zellweger was standing next to her front-row seat as if trying to calculate how to sit down in her dress without ruining its enormous bustle.

We found our row and I was happy to see our nephew Nicolas [Cage] already there a few seats away. Sofia's producer, Ross, was next to me and I asked him to switch so I could sit with Nicolas.

He works so steadily that we see each other infrequently. I could see Clint Eastwood sitting with his mother at the end of our row and Sandra Bullock in front of Nicolas a few seats to the left. Diane Keaton, wearing a tuxedo and black bowler hat, was in the front row. Roman slipped into the seat next to Francis, and Sofia sat on the aisle just as the house lights went down. Billy Crystal stepped out onstage and came to the edge right in front of Sofia; he sang to her humorously, about being nominated for Best Picture. I was startled, in a daze, realizing the show for those moments was focused on Sofia and being watched around the world. I could see she was amused and smiling.

About midway into the program, well before it was time for Francis and Sofia to be called backstage to present, Francis and I went out to the lobby. It was filled with people drinking at the bar and watching the show on monitors.

At the next commercial break a production assistant came to escort Francis and Sofia backstage. We shifted our seats so that Nicolas, Roman and I were together to watch them present the award for Best Adapted Screenplay. Sofia and Francis stepped out onstage. When they spoke I could hear an edge of nervousness in their voices. I felt my elbows pressing my sides hard as I worried about them getting through their lines without mistakes. Francis looked handsome in his tuxedo and Sofia lovely in a gown Marc Jacobs designed for her. They spoke with charm and grace. I sucked in my breath audibly seeing them onstage together, father and daughter, both nominated over the years in the same industry, in the same categories, best writer, best director, best picture.

As soon as the winners, Peter Jackson and his co-writers, who included his wife, completed their acceptance speeches, the lights dimmed. There was a commercial break and Francis and Sofia came quickly down the stairs off the front of the stage and back to their seats.

The next award was Best Original Screenplay. When Sofia's

name was read as the winner I felt literally a flood of relief, a sensation of something at the top of my head flowing down over my shoulders and along my arms. A deep guttural sound escaped my lips as I felt jerked up and back. I desperately hoped the noisy clapping crowd around me concealed my involuntary response. I had told myself that being nominated was reward enough for Sofia, that the actual Oscar wasn't important; it was after all just a metal statuette voted by a small, fickle Academy membership. I hadn't realized I was just a mom, wanting my child not to have to bear the disappointment of losing.

Francis and I simultaneously rose out of our seats hugging each other and Roman and Nicolas, then hurriedly sat down to hear Sofia's acceptance speech. Although I was aware of a slight tremor in her voice Sofia spoke eloquently as she stood onstage, poised in her exquisite silk gown, and thanked everyone without using notes. When she thanked "my mom for always encouraging me to make art," tears flowed out of the corners of my eyes streaking through my makeup. It is what I most wanted to be appreciated for. She spoke with grace and a kind of authenticity. I often told her growing up, "Everyone is going to expect you to be a spoiled brat. Please surprise them." I think she did.

Part Seven

April 2, 2004 On a flight

Sofia, Roman, Francis and I are flying to Europe on Francis's new seven-passenger jet. It reminds me of a road trip. We've packed food, books and games. The first leg of our journey is a flight from New York City to Reykjavik, Iceland, where we will spend the night and fly on to Italy the following day. We are traveling to Milan where Sofia and Francis will present an award for the best feature film made for Italian television. The awards program, the Telegatto, is similar to our Oscars, red carpet and all. We've heard it is watched ardently throughout Italy. Francis and Sofia, Sidney Poitier, Harvey Keitel and Eric Roberts will attend from the U.S. The show has paid the expenses for Francis's plane to fly to Europe. After a day and a half of obligations we will travel on to celebrate Francis's sixty-fifth birthday in the south of France.

White light is passing through the oval windows of the plane illuminating us and the remains of our home-cooked Armenian lunch Anahid made. Crumbs of flat bread, a plate with three remaining *sarmas*, small bowls of hummus, olives and red pepper spread litter the two fold-out tables.

We have only been together a few hours and I can already feel the family dynamic starting to set as if it were Jell-O. Francis, Roman and Sofia are directors, each used to being the center of their worlds. Roman just finishing directing a huge commercial, responsible for telling the cinematographer, art director, location scout, everyone what to do and how to achieve every detail. Sofia is just back from film festivals and awards shows honoring her for her writing and directing. Francis always the consummate writer/director/producer presiding over films and companies and the family. Their success is due in great part to their attention to controlling all the details.

In the tight capsule of the plane's cabin, there is the subtle strain of each of them, used to directing the action, having to hold themselves in check. Who will have the final say, even about how the food is laid out or whether it will be on a paper or plastic plate. It's subtle but I can feel it. I become the audience, maneuvering ever so slightly to keep things smooth. I wonder, as others have I'm sure, if the natural instinct and experience of women negotiating with their children to stop fighting, share things, and urging their husbands to be more forgiving, would come to the fore if women were world leaders. Would we naturally be inclined to negotiate peaceful solutions, or would our cat-fighting qualities emerge? Recently I attended a fund-raiser for the Global Fund for Women at which a speaker said, "Women are the world's greatest undeveloped resource."

Out the window I can see the shadow of our plane crossing the tip of Greenland. Fingers of snow-covered mountains cut deeply by fjords reach into the sea giving the white land the shape of enormous fern leaves. The pilot says, "This is a rare moment. Ordinarily it's hidden by cloud cover and you can't see anything down there." The sun on the ice is searingly bright. I can see glaciers flowing to the edge of the land and great icebergs floating in the blue-black water.

When we arrived over Iceland, the coast appeared brown and flat. The plane landed in the early evening in the bleak landscape. The rocky surface was covered with lichen in ten thousand shades of brown; no plants, no trees, just rocks with edges softened by a thick mat of the strange vegetation. As we drove from the airport the sun slowly set into the brown horizon. Streaks of radiant orange spread across the sky in the window behind Sofia's head as she made calls on her cell phone trying to find a musician friend in Los Angeles who had recently been to Reykjavik. When she reached him she asked him to recommend a restaurant for dinner. I was thinking about the age we live in when it is easy to speak from a car driving through desolate tundra in Iceland to pals in California. I know a couple who took many car trips around the U.S. in the '70s. They had someone they would call from wherever they ended up, a remote town in Nebraska, a back road in Louisiana, a gas station in the Arizona desert, and their friend could always tell them a good place to eat.

Reykjavik reminded me of a medium-sized city in Scandinavia but starker, with fewer old buildings. It was cold, even though it was April. Few pedestrians were on the streets and there was no traffic in the center of the city.

The name of our hotel is "101." The style is minimal; no flowered bedspreads or bad art, just white walls, sheer white curtains, white down-filled duvets and unadorned wood floors. It soothes me.

At 10:00 in the evening, in the pale light of northern dusk, we walked through the icy air to the recommended restaurant. The Lobster House was in an old Victorian home with tables clustered in all the small rooms. We were shown upstairs and seated at a table with a comfortable sofa on one side and two chairs on the other.

We had the local "lobster," which turned out to be a type of large crayfish. As we ate dessert, a large man came out of an adjoining room and seeing Sofia he grinned excitedly and patted her on the shoulder, congratulating her on winning an Oscar and telling Francis he was a fan of the *Godfather* films.

The next morning we flew for three and a half hours and arrived in Milan. The plane touched down smoothly and came to a stop on the tarmac. Out the window I could see our welcoming committee, five people wearing perfectly tailored suits and sunglasses. We were such a contrast, Roman with his thick hair smoothed only slightly with his hands, his shirt worn two days, Sofia in sneakers, sweatpants, hooded sweater and dark glasses; although even jet-lagged and without makeup, her beauty is evident. Francis was wearing a rumpled suit and I was in pants and a sweater. Our host, whose name is Pupi, wore a perfectly pressed navy blazer with striped silk breast-pocket handkerchief.

Francesco from the Telegatto and two government officials quickly whisked us through customs. We drove to the hotel in three cars. The first car was filled with security guards, followed by Pupi, Francis and me in a car, then Sofia, Roman, Pupi's wife, Wendy, and another security guard.

As we drove, Pupi told us excitedly, "The suite you are staying in is the second-largest hotel suite in Europe. There are three bedrooms and an indoor swimming pool!" I thought I knew the largest suite, the one where we stayed in Cannes. The just-finished one with the pool on the private terrace and the new floor that buckled our first night there. Pupi talked enthusiastically about his business interests. "I have licensing rights to sell Cuban cigars in Brazil." "I owned 27 percent of Donna Karan but I sold my share in 1991 when her husband came on. I didn't agree with his business ideas." "We have an apartment in New York City where we lived for five years." "I met my wife there, she was a model for Chanel." "I am Italy's ambassador to Belize."

At the hotel we were directed into a private elevator which opened onto a private foyer with a handsome inlaid design in the antique marble floor. Two security guards were positioned next to the door leading into the "Presidential Suite." Inside there was a long hall. Three bedrooms opened off the hall, each with hand-carved furniture upholstered in silk brocades, Oriental carpets and large marble bathrooms. The master bedroom has a king-sized bed with a red velvet canopy trimmed with thick red and gold fringe and tied back with enormous tassels. There is a real fireplace and a cabinet filled with perfectly cut pieces of wood stacked with such precision they resemble a work of art. Antique oil paintings of fruit and flowers with old cracked glaze are grouped on the walls in burnished gold frames. Tall French doors lead out to a handsome terrace connecting all the rooms. Thick vines pour over the balcony and large pots overflow with flowering plants.

Off the hall there is a small room with video monitors where security guards can keep a watchful eye over the suite. I imagined some head of state's Secret Service men in there. The large butler's pantry is followed by a second entry area with doors to the dining room where an enormous Murano glass chandelier presides over the long, gleaming table. The vast living room is furnished with a grand piano, heavy damask draperies, chairs and sofas upholstered in velvets. A well-stocked bar occupies a large corner of the room. Tall windows provide views of the terrace and the city beyond. In the entry area a third set of double doors open to the indoor swimming pool with sauna and steam room. The large pool and lounge area is adorned with frescoes as if it were inside a noble home in Pompeii. The bottom of the pool has an intricate mosaic design of two swirling dolphins. There is perhaps 8,000 square feet of space. The cottage where we are living in Napa is under 1,000.

Our suite's butler, Fabio, wears black tie with tails. He asks each of us what we would like to drink, then steps behind the bar or into his pantry. A large silver coffee urn is on a side table in the dining room with ten bone china cups and saucers arranged in diagonal rows. On the bar are silver dishes of olives, roasted almonds and pistachios. On the grand piano are crystal platters of small fancy cookies and chocolates.

Pupi and Wendy and Francesco tell us to have lunch and they will return later for the press conference. After Fabio takes our order he sets the table in the dining room with linens and fine china. When we finally retire to our rooms, I notice there are gifts. For Francis an expensive leather travel bag from Fendi, a T-shirt and Montblanc fountain pen. For me a watch, a T-shirt and a card inviting me to choose a Fendi dress to wear to the black-tie awards show.

At five-thirty I enter the living room and find eight reporters sitting in a line opposite the sofa and two chairs. Francis, Sofia and Roman are in the midst of a televised interview on the terrace. A woman comes forward and I introduce myself; she tells me, "I am the producer of the publicity." She is nervously waiting to begin the interviews with the gathered reporters.

Finally Sofia, Roman and Francis come from the terrace and settle into the sofa and a chair. The questioning begins. It is quickly apparent that there are no questions directed to Roman and he gets up, leaves the room and returns with his 16mm camera. He starts shooting Sofia being interviewed for a documentary he is making. I recognized this familiar survival strategy, having used it myself.

Around 9:00 p.m. Wendy and Pupi arrived at the door of our suite to escort us to a restaurant. Downstairs we found three waiting cars and I realized we were going to have security guards with us all the time. They were silent and polite, but just the idea felt unsettling.

I was happy to see that there were only eight of us at our table in the very elegant restaurant, including Francesco from the Telegatto and a man who we were told was the "head of an important bank." The conversation turned to politics. The prime minister of Italy, Mr. Berlusconi, owns or controls 90 percent of the television stations in Italy and we were his guests, as Francis and Sofia will enhance the awards broadcast.

Pupi talked about his cigar business and his trips to Cuba. "Fidel is a nice guy." Francis talked about traveling there, teaching at the film school and meeting Fidel. "He treated me well, he gave us a house with two Mercedes." Pupi said, "Yes, and you know where he got those Mercedes? Saddam gave them to him. You know who is a nice guy is Arafat. He's my friend. Would you like to talk to him?" Francis said, "Well, ah, sure." Pupi dialed on his cell phone and spoke rapidly in Italian. We went on with dinner.

Fifteen minutes passed and Pupi's cell phone rang. He picked it up and said, "Yes, yes, Mr. President," and handed the phone to Francis. Francis was in a conversation with Wendy and thought Mr. Berlusconi was on the phone so he said, "Thank you, Mr. President, for inviting me to your beautiful country." Pupi waved his arms frantically. "No, no, no, on the phone is Arafat." Francis looked startled but recovered quickly and after a short conversation concluded with "I wish you wisdom and courage."

The next evening we attended the awards event, held in a huge tent. There was a red carpet with a bank of photographers and TV cameras along one side. Francis held my hand as we made our way through the volley of flash bulbs; we tried to stay together, walking with Sofia and Roman so we would appear in the photos as a family. (The picture I saw in the paper the next day was of Sofia, Roman, Francis and part of my left arm.)

Inside the huge hall, people milled around. Francis and Sofia made their presentation early in the show. Sofia had been told the winner in advance so she could practice pronouncing the rather complicated Italian title of the movie. She opened the envelope and did a convincing job of appearing surprised as she read the winning title with ease.

It was not similar to the Oscars with a lobby where you could go out, walk around and have a drink during a commercial break. The tent was very warm from the bright TV lighting; no water was served. The program was all in Italian, of course, and started at 8:00 p.m. After an hour or so, jet lag hit me and I dozed when I thought the roving cameras covering the audience weren't on us. The show ended at 12:30. We were taken back to the hotel for dinner in the grand banquet room. Under the table I pinched my leg to stay awake.

Around noon the next day we were escorted back to the airport and said our goodbyes to Pupi, Wendy and the entourage. The security guards wanted to have their pictures taken with Francis. He is generous about requests for autographs and pictures and stood on the tarmac with them, squinting into the sun.

We flew to Nice, France, and drove in two taxis to the small mountain town of Saint-Paul-de-Vence. Just at the edge of the old stone walls that surround the ancient fortress is the Colombe d'Or, a wonderful country inn that has historically been frequented by artists, writers, musicians and actors. It consists of a cluster of old comfortable buildings with a swimming pool in the courtyard and a huge Calder mobile standing next to it. There is a large terrace with planters and pots overflowing with mixes of herbs and flowers. Several old fig trees growing up through the uneven worn tiles provide shade for the guests. Every meal is served outside, weather permitting. Throughout the rooms and hallways there are works of art. An original Calder drawing is next to the reception desk. There are paintings in the dining room by Picasso, Braque, Gris and the many artist friends of the owners. Now, after a theft, the valuable paintings are behind glass and wired for security.

We arrived in the late afternoon, were shown our rooms and then sat down at a table on the terrace. A smiling, plump, older waitress told us we were too late for lunch but she would go to the kitchen and see what she could bring us. She returned with a basket of fresh bread, a platter of prosciutto, four melon halves and a bottle of rosé wine in an ice bucket. I let my deep contentment seep through my body as I sat in the last of the afternoon sun on the old terrace, just the four of us relaxed, alone together, each of us between projects, not stressed, at ease. A rare moment.

Sofia left for New York City and Roman flew home to Los Angeles. Francis wanted to drive through the southeastern region of Italy.

April 12, 2004 Italy

We are traveling in Puglia and Basilicata. Francis is looking for possible hotel properties. He is thinking of developing a small chain of international boutique hotels, adding other properties to the three resorts in Central America. I am enjoying the food and the spectacular wildflowers. Francis enjoys traveling most when he has a purpose. Looking for real estate opportunities is perfect for him. He is practicing speaking Italian with Andrea and his wife, Laura, who are guiding us while he envisions beautiful, crumbling old farm buildings restored into fine small hotels. I marvel at our oppositeness. The idea of starting a new business from the ground up in a foreign country is not appealing to me; still I admire his ability to dream big and imagine building something where there was nothing before.

April 23, 2004 Rome

Francis and I have arrived in Rome. It is the first day of sun after nearly three months of rain and everyone is outside. The streets are uncomfortably crowded. Large groups of school children on spring holidays fidget in front of lecturing teachers in the Piazza di Spagna. There are hordes of tourists with backpacks, maps and cameras. Even the small Piazza Farnese is swarming with groups and their guides holding up purple paddles with white numbers. There is a cluster of Asians with umbrellas shielding them from the sun, Scandinavians in shorts and hiking boots and many other foreign visitors, including me. A few local women can be seen weaving through the tourists on their way to the even more crowded Piazza Campo dei Fiori. Italian women can always be identified by their shoes. They glide elegantly along over the uneven cobblestones in fine leather high-heeled boots and shoes while the tourists wear thick-soled sneakers.

I haven't been in Rome since the making of *Godfather III* in 1989. As I walk through Piazza Campo dei Fiori, I see that the shops where I bought cheese and meats have been turned into *gelaterias* and bars with outdoor cafés. Now the piazza is lined on both sides with tables and chairs filled with young people. Last night the police came when a rowdy group began breaking beer bottles. Today there is a ban on selling glass bottled drinks after 10:00 p.m. Still, golden light slants down the narrow side streets that look as if they are opera sets and craftsmen repair furniture in small shops, fix motor scooters and gild mirror frames. The appealing smells of varnish and sawdust mix with the perfume of vegetables stored for the morning market. Best of all, the old *forno* on the corner is still baking fine bread.

April 30, 2004 Barcelona

Francis is enjoying the freedom of having his plane in Europe, where major cities in different countries seem to be less than two hours' flight apart and he can hop from place to place at the slightest provocation.

Yesterday I visited a store specializing in antique fabrics. The shelves are stacked with extraordinary shawls, table linens and bedcovers; its drawers are full of laces, linen and silk clothing; there are racks with baptismal dresses, capes and curtains; stacks of old silks are piled on chairs. Every item is from the mid-1800s to about 1940. I opened and refolded pieces with the shop owner, Pilar, as she told me the story of each one, her dark eyes sparkling with excitement. "Look at this bobbin lace. You'll never see a finer example, it belongs in a museum, don't you think? You know this exquisite openwork will never be done again. No one knows how to do it. No one has the time anymore. Look at this astonishing shawl! It was ordered by a rich woman in Madrid in the 1800s and made in Manila. Did you know all this dense embroidery was done by men?"

When I left the store I hurried to find a taxi to take me to meet Francis and friends for lunch scheduled at 2:30 in the afternoon at an outdoor restaurant next to the harbor. I arrived after 3:00 and made my apologies. Francis said, "You look happy."

Joan, our host, owns a restaurant where we would dine that evening. During lunch he made cell phone calls checking orders for special seafood he planned to serve us. His phone rang frequently and he shouted excitedly, "We got them, huge crabs, the best!" "The barnacles arrived! They come only from one place in the north." All the while we were eating paella served from a huge round pan straight from the oven accompanied by rice cooked in squid ink.

After more than four weeks of travel with Francis in Europe I was eager to come home, walk in the vineyards, eat just salad from our garden and spend time in my studio. Francis wanted to settle into a friend's apartment in Rome and focus on a writing session so it seemed right to both of us that he stay and I come home.

May 9, 2004 Napa

Early Mother's Day morning I flew down to Los Angeles to see my ninety-five-year-old mother at her nursing home. I hadn't seen her for two months and felt anxious, preparing myself to find her in further decline. She is wheelchair-bound and suffering from dementia. I worry that she will not recognize me. She noticed my arrival from across the room and as I approached said, "Oh my, what a surprise!" Her face glowed with good health and she was much more alert than the last time I saw her. She said, "I hope Francis enjoyed his birthday trip." She mentioned her best friend whom she had known since eighth grade and had recently died. "I always thought I'd go before her." Then as if she were traveling down a different hallway in her mind she said, "I walked to the post office yesterday but the fish food I ordered hasn't arrived."

I pushed her wheelchair outside along the walkways of the well-kept garden. The raised planter beds were in full bloom. She looked at specific flowers carefully with interest. "Just look at that deep yellow color." "See these tiny white ones." She listened intently to the birds. "Doesn't it sound as if that bird is saying Peter, Peter, Peter?" In a way it was as if she were a Zen master living completely in the moment. At times I have aspired to that state with little success. My mind is constantly making "to do" lists and thinking about the past or what I'm doing next, such as driving across town.

It was nearly noon when I arrived at Jacqui's house. Gia had just gotten dressed; as we hugged, her hair still wet from a shower smelled of peach shampoo. Her Chihuahua jumped and danced with excitement at our feet. Jacqui said, "See, Merlin remembers you. You always feed him."

Roman arrived. He made Mother's Day pancakes in exotic shapes. I scrambled eggs with avocado and served Merlin on a saucer. We lingered over the Sunday papers and then all drove to the Los Angeles County Museum of Art, which was featuring an exhibition of the work of photographer Diane Arbus. I'd given Gia the catalogue for Christmas and promised to take her to see the show.

Roman, Jacqui and her husband, Peter, walked through all the galleries in about twenty minutes, then went out to the bookstore and café. Gia and I walked arm in arm slowly through the crowded rooms. I was surprised how attentive she was. She observed that some of the early prints were grainy and noticed marks near the edges of others. "Those look like chemical streaks." She remarked about a photo that had areas in sharp focus and areas out of focus. "She probably used a lens with a short depth of field."

I said, "Diane Arbus often photographed people who we consider freaks but she shot them in their own environment where they were not out of place. Look at this photograph of Russian midgets at home together in their apartment." Looking at a photo of a couple sitting on a bench in Washington Square Park staring toward the camera, Gia said, "It looks like those people think Diane Arbus is the freak." And it did. Something I had never thought of.

I was happy to see Gia so interested and thoughtful about photography. Perhaps it will be an avenue of expression for her. She has had three photos published in recent issues of a teen arts magazine.

May 18, 2004

I was home a short time exploring the spring green hills, cleaning spider webs out of my studio and attacking a four-foot-high stack of mail when my friend Yoshiko Wada called. She invited me to travel with her to China to see ethnic textiles. Three other people would be along, all textile professionals. I was at once so eager to stay at home and yet not wanting to pass up a unique opportunity. When I went to India with Yoshiko, she took me off the beaten track to places where there were no tourist accommodations. We slept on the floor of a government guesthouse, were eaten alive by fleas and saw women riding camels across the barren desert in clouds of dust wearing some of the most beautiful textiles I've ever seen.

I sat down quietly to meditate and ask myself what the right decision was. I closed my eyes but before I could ask the question, an inner voice shouted, "Go!"

May–June 2004 Southwest China

Rice terraces extend down thousands of feet on both sides of a deep valley with the Pearl River flowing at the bottom. Each terrace is outlined with a stone wall built by hand. We are being jostled in a small bus over unpaved roads full of potholes filled with muddy rain water. I can hear Yoshiko and my travel mates Torimaru-san, a professor of textiles, and Mr. Shindo, a textile artist and teacher, conversing in Japanese. Our two young men guides are chatting in Mandarin Chinese. The other traveler is Christina Kim. Christina sits in the front, and when I want to have a conversation, I move up to a seat beside her. She is Korean by birth, and lives in Los Angeles. She designs clothing and home furnishings and is the head of her own international company called Dosa.

We have stopped along the roadside next to a rice terrace. Women in small groups stand bent over in calf-deep muddy water, inserting bright green seedlings in neat rows. They appear to be gossiping amiably together and stop to look up at us quizzically. We look back with interest, as they are wearing finely pleated indigo skirts and indigo jackets decorated with batik and turquoise patterns of exquisite embroidery. They have indigo and white head wraps and large silver earrings. These are Miao women (an ethnic minority) wearing the traditional clothing of their nearby village. We smile and wave. They seem shy; curious about us, they smile and giggle but don't move from their tasks, continue working unselfconsciously in their handsome handmade clothing and jewelry.

Men work alone in half-drained terraces, guiding wooden plows behind water buffalo. We can hear them shouting commands and swatting the animals with bamboo switches as they turn them to till slowly back and forth through the thick mud. They wear indigo trousers rolled up to their thighs; most are bare-chested, some wear a simple indigo jacket. The terraces are in various states of production: some planted for several weeks are a lush blanket of green, other paddies recently flooded glisten and reflect the sky with fast-moving clouds. The surrounding hills are divided by red dirt paths that are steep, rocky and muddy. I see a woman high up who appears to be about my age, hoeing a tiny terrace perhaps four feet wide containing a dozen cabbages.

Our two young Chinese guides are Mr. Kuma, who speaks fluent Japanese, and Mr. Xiao, who speaks English. Mr. Xiao tells us the English spelling of his name would be Shiau. "Pronounce it like 'shower,' then leave off the 'er.' " He wears American sport clothes, gifts he has gotten from visitors he has guided. He tells me he is watching the NBA play-offs. "The Lakers are playing the Pistons. I'm getting up at 4:00 a.m. to see the game live." He treats me politely but when I tell him I've seen the Sacramento Kings play and sat on the floor right behind the coach's bench, his eyes sparkle with excitement and his attitude toward me changes dramatically.

In the distant mist I see jagged rock forms and layers of mountains in deepening shades of gray, as if they were watercolor washes like those in scroll paintings. I'd always thought the rather mystical images in Chinese paintings were creative inventions of the artists; now I see they are drawn directly from nature. The view travels past the bus window as if it were a movie.

We left our bus and walked up a steep rocky, muddy path, watching out to avoid water buffalo dung, while a band of small children trailed us or ran ahead laughing at our graceless, panting ascent. We arrived at a small village of weathered wooden houses high above the road with no access except the trail. There were only young children and old people to be seen. All who were able were working in the rice terraces. An old lady came out from a low doorway and greeted Torimaru-san familiarly. Torimaru-san has written three books about textiles from this area and I recognized the woman as one who had been photographed for a section on indigo dyeing. She showed us the crock of dye she kept on the corner of her front porch. Torimaru-san suggested we visit the village to see the way of life, then return to the little house. This would give time for the word to spread that foreigners had arrived and villagers would bring their textiles for us to see.

We walked along what appeared to be the main street, a dirt path the width of an oxcart. Pigs lolled in pens next to houses, their noses protruding between wooden slats. Traditional indigo skirts and jackets hung on clotheslines next to T-shirts and bright-colored polar fleece jackets. Through an open doorway I could see a dirt floor swept clean, an iron tripod and ring holding a boiling pot over a small wood fire.

When we returned to the first house there were a dozen women and one man crowded onto the narrow path in front of the small porch. As they moved toward us the humid air filled with the strong smell of garlic, wood smoke and body odor. In everyone's arms were bundles of textiles they wished to sell. They unwrapped festival jackets unique to the village, pleated skirts and aprons along with rolls of hand-dyed indigo fabric and pieces of batik. Torimaru-san had not gone on our walk; she had stayed behind and bought several excellent examples of the house owner's work for her research collection. Little children surrounded us pressing in against our legs. I opened my backpack and took out glitter stickers of stars and kittens and I stuck them on the hands of each child; while they were absorbed in looking at each other's stickers we were able to stand on the porch and see the textiles the women held out to us.

The women grabbed at our sleeves aggressively and waved fingers in our faces to indicate price. When we got into a negotiation for a particular piece our guides helped us translate. I bought a woman's jacket with fine embroidery and batik designs appliquéd on hand-woven, hand-dyed indigo fabric. It took time to make a purchase as I had to feign lack of interest and consider other pieces proffered in arms reaching toward me before my offer of 200 and her asking price of 800 was settled at 400 yuan [$48]. I think about what the woman earned for her hundreds of hours of handwork. Although in her economy, perhaps she can retile the roof of her house from the sale.

We are traveling off the main routes, so there are no tourist accommodations. Tonight our hotel is a businessmen's worn lodging: the Hotel Miracle Express with a loud karaoke bar on the first floor.

Xiao warned us that the bathroom would be "stinky." He was right. It has an Asian squat-style toilet in the floor. When I turned on the sink faucet I got my feet wet before I realized the basin drains onto the sloping floor and flows into the toilet. There is a hissing fluorescent bulb over a fly-specked mirror and a small hot water tank attached to the wall. The shower spray head is at the end of a thin, pink plastic hose hanging from a hook. The bedroom carpet is old and lies in uneven stained ripples. I have taken out my flip-flops to wear, not wanting to put my bare feet on the floor. There are plastic curtains covering the windows which I have slid open hoping to catch the slightest movement in the humid night air, as the room smells strongly of cigarettes; there is no such thing as a "nonsmoking" room. I learned that in order to stop the opium trade, farmers were encouraged to grow large amounts of tobacco, and they did. All the men in China appear to smoke. One of the doors is missing on the cabinet that holds the ancient-looking TV. Standing next to the TV is a tall yellow spray can with black lettering in Chinese and one large red word in English: "Insecticide." I am imagining what might crawl out from cracks in the walls and gaps in the carpet when I turn out the lights.

We drove to a village outside the city of Kaili. A friend of our guide had grown up there and came along. He explained, "When I lived here all the houses were wood, now as you can see, it is changing." About half the buildings were made of concrete block. We parked at the edge of the village and walked through unpaved narrow lanes to a weathered wooden house. A red motorcycle stood in front of the door. An old lady peeked out and grinned. She was expecting us. A middle-aged man in his undershirt came out from a side door and moved the motorcycle to one side so the family could step out the front door to greet us. The old woman was perhaps in her seventies; she had a husband who looked quite a bit older, their son (who had moved the motorcycle), his wife and a five-year-old grandson. We had come to see a process of creating a distinctive dark, glossy green-gold fabric used in the traditional hats and jackets of the village. The son's wife, an expert in the technique, was documented in one of Torimaru-san's books. She brought out several small paper packets and laid them on the floor of the cement porch. She unwrapped each with care to show us the dark, metallic, powdery dye.

I am less interested in specific details of technique; I enjoy the visual thrill of seeing the handwork, and the ways the textiles are used. I took out my video camera and as I bent down to capture details of the wife stirring dye in the bottom of her chipped crockery pot I could hear runny noses sniffling by my ears as children peered over my shoulder to look into the camera monitor. I turned the camera toward them and rotated the monitor so they could see themselves on the screen. They laughed excitedly, pushing and shoving each other into the picture.

The children stayed nearby playing cat's cradle with pieces of worn, knotted string. I was pleased to see they were more interested in their own games than in us. Two of the boys climbed a tree and picked small ripe plums which they threw down to the others, who offered the fruit to us. I feigned being busy with my camera so they passed me by. I am passing up certain delicacies in an effort to stay well.

The husband had left the house, and now he returned holding several chunks of pork meat in a piece of paper. Yoshiko told me the guides had given the family money from our tour expenses to buy the meat, that it is traditional to serve pork to guests and was a special treat for the family. Lunch preparations began in the dark kitchen under the light of one small dangling bulb. I stood near the door and watched. The old grandfather made numerous slow shuffling trips outside to the back of the house, returning with handfuls of small branches he fed to the fire under the wok. I was surprised to see the husband and our guide, rather than the women, chopping the pork and vegetables and beginning to cook. The husband put the pork fat into the wok and when it had been rendered, he cooked pieces of meat in the sizzling grease. He removed the meat and stir-fried several combinations of vegetables in the hot fat, then the cooked meat was added back in. I thought about eating all that fat, but no one in the family was overweight. I could see a large cauldron of cooked rice sitting in the shadows.

The old lady pointed and waved to us as her special guests to sit on stools around a very low table in the house. Our knees poked up awkwardly around the table. She set bowls of vegetables with pork and a large bowl of rice in the middle of the table. Then she took two worn beer bottles down from a wall altar and grinned as she filled teacups with clear liquid for each of us. It was her home-brewed moonshine and tasted as if it were a cross between sake and grappa. I was hopeful it would sanitize the cup which came straight from a tub of dirty dishes soaking in cold water in a corner of the kitchen. When I thought no one was looking, I stuck the tips of my chopsticks in the brew too. The food, containing lots of hot spicy green chilies and pork fat, was delicious! The husband bragged that he ate three large bowls of rice at each meal. He was slim and muscular.

When we got up from our table the old man sat down. He looked so at ease compared to us; his knees flexible and relaxed. The old woman served her husband and then she sat down. They both ate heartily. I wondered why they hadn't eaten with the others at the outside table. When the old woman finished eating, she stood up agilely and hurried outside to a pen in the yard where she opened the worn wooden gate and released a water buffalo. Waving to us cheerily she herded it briskly down a path toward the rice fields. Her son remained at the outdoor table drinking and growing more boisterous.

After lunch the dyed fabric left in the sun was dry and brought to the porch along with a large clay bowl. The wife brought coals from the kitchen and started a small fire in the bowl which she fed with branches of green pine needles, creating a cloud of thick smoke. She draped the piece of dyed cloth on twigs and held it over the fragrant fire and literally smoked it. The fabric slowly took on a dark burnished gold color. When this step was complete she folded the fabric into a rectangle of layers and sat down at a low stool. She placed the fabric on the smooth end of a block of wood which she set between her knees and began to beat the cloth with a wooden mallet. The husband came over and took the mallet but after a few swings that missed he stepped away and the wife patiently continued. Yoshiko said, "It takes several hours of pounding to achieve the gloss on the fabrics they use in their festival clothes."

Before we left, I asked to use the restroom. Our guide pointed to a wooden door between the pig stalls so I knew it would be "rustic." I imagined an outhouse. In the dim light inside I could see two huge pigs, slightly agitated by my presence, just inches away on either side of me held back by waist-high slatted boards, their backs bulging above the top. A thick wooden stick stood in the corner. It appeared to be to use for beating the pigs back if they became too aggressive. The facilities consisted of a board removed from the floor with a trough below that slanted into the pigs' stall. It was an ecologically perfect design.

We are flying back to Shanghai. Our travel in rural China is over. My last vivid memory was of being in a small village, standing on worn wooden floor boards in a house perched high above rice terraces. I watched a woman with a sleeping baby in a wrap on her back painting with hot wax, forming an intricate batik design on a narrow strip of cloth. She used a delicate brush made of five hairs from her head bound to the quill of a feather.

June 26, 2004 Napa

"New blank document"
white rectangle on my blue screen
anything is possible

I woke up at dawn with light turning to pale gray through layers of branches in silhouette, their thick dark patterns of summer leaves fluttering. The screened window is open and the faint scent of magnolia blossoms is carried into the room on the fresh morning air. There is the sound of a wild duck flapping hard as it lifts off the pond. I am so deeply happy to be at home in my exquisitely comfortable bed with Francis breathing rhythmically beside me.

Having been out of the country most of the last two and a half months, my calendar is nearly empty. I've been forgotten about or given up on. Before the calls come from friends we've met everywhere in the world who are visiting the Napa Valley, before the winery staff has noticed that I am back and schedules meetings to approve new products for the tasting room or staff uniform changes and before I must tend to shipping arrangements for my artwork going to a gallery in Chicago or the details for the Circle of Memory installation in San Diego, the day is free and clear.

Yesterday I walked in the garden. New peony roses with swirls of chiffon-like petals in palest shades of pink are in bloom; there are multicolored hydrangeas, begonias, lavender and fuchsias. In the greenhouse I found new baby lettuce, bushy Italian parsley and young basil. In the vegetable garden I saw I had missed the fava beans entirely, the plants were lying on their sides with pods of beans molding against the ground, but there were still a few potatoes and beets, some strawberries, new green peppers and tiny green beans. Five torpedo onions, their stalks bent over, are still in the ground. The artichokes were in bright purple flower, nothing edible left. Nectarines on a tree near the fence were beginning to color.

I walked to my studio along the shaded dirt road sniffing the air hungrily for the familiar scents of eucalyptus and bay. When I reached the open hillside I could see the lush spring-green grass was gone along with the wildflowers; only a few California poppies and small magenta vetch blossoms could be seen in the tan dry grass. I climbed up the narrow deer path along the hillside, panting hard, remembering women my age in China walking agilely up to high rice terraces carrying heavy loads. When I opened my studio door it smelled of heat trapped in the space. Dozens of daddy longlegs had made webs on the rungs of the ladder, under table corners, around the window frames and in the niche of my altar; dark crumbs of their catch of flies scattered beneath the constructions. I picked the spiders up on the feather duster and carried them outside only to see them walk determinedly back toward my door.

Now as I lie in bed thinking of the day ahead, I remember that the clothes in the closet here in the guest cottage where we are staying are winterwear, and the season changed while I was away. I need to lug sweaters, coats and wool trousers down to the caretaker's cottage, a vacant bungalow next to the small apartment where we stayed, as my summer clothes are stored there and my temporary office is set up on its porch. I expected to be moving into our new contemporary house about this time, but it is still long delayed. The main house is supposed to be finished in six months and Francis tells me he would be content to just move back there and forget about the new house. But the main house has not been designed for our daily living. It is intended for guests and only occasional use by the family. The closets are for two suitcases full of clothes and there is no space for an office for me. Now it looks as if we will be living there while we wait for the new house. I see at least another year of interim living. Our home base has been disrupted for four years and my Taurus nature longs to be settled. My studio has become my stable point.

Francis and I are both delighted with the design of our contemporary house and the way the architect has situated it on the site. The foundation was finished last October. We have had contractor after contractor bid the building and the cost has been estimated at three times the budget.

Perhaps it is a result of the Coppola name on the project, or the high cost of building in the Napa Valley, or the nature of the stark, board-formed concrete and glass design, or all three. Francis, the architect and the contractors are fighting it out, pointing fingers. It is man's work. I have no power to move things forward. I am trying to make peace with the idea that I will be living in temporary circumstances for several more years. When the main house is finished I will be surrounded by beauty that is not my aesthetic, beauty I find exhausting to look at on a daily basis, as if opera were playing constantly and too loud: all the intricate inlaid woodwork, elegant patterned carpets and fabrics, marble with dramatic veining in the kitchen and bathrooms, complex stained glass windows and decorative moldings. It seems to be one of my life's cosmic jokes that my very beautiful home is baroque and I long for simple, spare spaces.

July 10, 2004

Marlon Brando died last week. Random memories of him have been coming to mind.

When Francis started shooting *Godfather* in the spring of 1971, I didn't meet the film's fabled star right away. There were major production difficulties with rumors that Francis would be fired or Marlon would be. I was occupied with our two young boys Roman [five] and Gio [seven] and very pregnant with Sofia. We were living in a small, cramped apartment in New York City. It belonged to a relative and we were there rather than leasing a place in case Francis lost his job and we suddenly returned to California.

One evening during the second week of May, George Lucas and his wife, Marcia, were visiting, waiting for a night flight to London to begin a backpacking trip through Europe. Francis was still at work. We were sitting around the kitchen table. Looking at my huge belly George said, "You could have it on my birthday, you know, it's tomorrow." We laughed. They left around 8:00 p.m. and about an hour later I began having labor pains. I called the production office. Someone was sent to find Francis; he was in the screening room watching dailies. I called the doctor. He said, "Well, come in after midnight. If you come in before, you'll have to pay for a full day today." It sounded right; we didn't have much money. When Francis got home around 10:00 p.m. and saw me experience a few pains he said, "We're going." Sofia was born at 2:00 a.m. on George's birthday.

When she was about three weeks old I took her to the *Godfather* set. The production was shooting in the garden of a big house on Staten Island. It was the wedding party scene. Marlon was waiting in one of the upstairs bedrooms. His makeup man and hair stylist were with him. Francis introduced me. It was the first time I really understood what charisma was. Marlon took my hand and looked at me with such charm. He spoke with "that" voice. I felt as if I were standing in a special beam of light and he found me utterly fascinating. It was a fleeting moment as I imagine a hit of heroin to be: stunning, short-lived and dangerously seductive. Then Marlon turned to Sofia. He lifted her out of my arms so tenderly, holding her with an ease that only comes from experience. He looked at her with intense interest, examining her long fingers and tiny toes.

A few days later a little gold bracelet arrived. The card said, "Dear Sofia, Welcome to the world. Love, Marlon." Somewhere over the years the card and bracelet have been lost but I still write "Welcome to the world" on baby gifts I give.

⚜

I am thinking of a time in the Philippines during *Apocalypse Now* when I asked Marlon to do an interview for the documentary film I was shooting. I waited for a moment when he was not working, and relaxed. We were at the production designer's house together for Sunday lunch, Marlon was sitting by the window. He had been talking intently about the life and habits of ants, as he could do in a spellbinding way. When there was a lull in the conversation I hesitantly asked him for an interview. He said, "What do you want to make a documentary for?" I felt as if a giant school principal were grilling tiny me. Whatever my answer was, it seemed insufficient. As the documentary filmmaker I felt as if I was a nuisance, in the way of the main production, asking for favors. Marlon reluctantly agreed to let me film an interview with him after he completed shooting his part in the movie. As soon as he finished I arranged a time to do the interview. He didn't show up. When I called to set a new date I discovered he'd already left the Philippines.

From my perspective he treated Francis badly on *Apocalypse Now*. Marlon received three million dollars for three weeks' work. (I watched Francis labor on the film for three years and saw our family go completely into debt.) Marlon spent the first week of his contract sitting in his trailer engaging Francis in endless conversations about his character and avoiding going to the set. He hadn't lost weight to play the part of a Green Beret as he promised he would, forcing Francis to create a way to change the part to accommodate his girth. Work stopped for an entire expensive week. It felt to me as if Marlon was torturing Francis. Nonetheless he was an extraordinary talent and as it turned out, his remarkable work helped support our family over many years.

JULY 22, 2004

Joe Cohn was our next-door neighbor for many years. According to the papers he lived to be 100 but his family told us he was 103. He was fiercely proud of his property, a beautiful ranch with vineyards and a once-grand old home. I remember hearing that in the past a wide porch surrounded the house and one day Joe, annoyed with its sagging, got out his tractor, attached it to the porch and pulled it off. He always said he would never sell any part of his land the several times we gently asked. Last year we bought most of the vineyards adjoining our property from his grandson.

Recently we learned that a large oak tree on the edge of the Cohn property was deemed the best tree to attempt to move to replace the old oak that fell on our house four years ago. Several experts said the tree was too big and would not survive a move. Francis was determined. He said he couldn't look at our house without its oak tree. The neighbor's tree was dug up, its enormous root ball wrapped in canvas and set on a pallet. A number of smaller trees in our garden were temporarily removed to clear a path so the oak could be trucked across a dirt road through the vineyard and into our garden. It was set into position in a huge hole in front of our house, breaking a crane in the process. Now the new tree stands just where the old one was. From the shock of the move it lost all its leaves and appeared completely dead but new green foliage has grown in and now it looks as if it has been there all its life. Francis and I both talk to it. I say, "We are so happy to have you here presiding over our house and family. You will stand at the center of many celebrations, birthdays, weddings, harvest parties and more. You'll hear music. Children will hunt for Easter eggs at your feet and swing from your branches. Oh you're so much better off here with us in our garden where you are treasured instead of next to the road with only passing cars for company." Francis admires the tree while he's in the swimming pool. He happily observes birds coming and going from its foliage and considers which branch would be best to use to hang our old wooden swing.

I've been thinking about Joe.

September 10, 1979

Joe Cohn stopped by. He is eighty-six years old with bushy white eyebrows and mischievous, twinkling eyes. He wore white trousers with a navy blue blazer and salmon pink shirt. A silk handkerchief with polka dots peeked out of his breast pocket. He greeted me with a kiss and a firm pat on my behind. I allow him, due to his advanced age, and I hear I am not the only one. He brought a bag of fresh prunes and a jar of almonds from his trees next door.

We went up to the bedroom where Francis lay on a Japanese mat on the floor. His back is bothering him. I got a chair for Joe. He started talking about the old days in Hollywood where he was a producer at MGM for many years. He told us about having dinner with William Randolph Hearst. "You know, Marion Davies gave him her jewels when he was down on his luck." The conversation turned to the Philippines. We were discussing lizards and insects. He said, "You know, once I was playing bridge with Billy Wilder and a moth landed on the table. Just like that I caught it and ate it. It tasted like nothing, no flavor at all, but it had quite an effect on the game." It reminded me of a story Francis once told about playing poker with Billy Friedkin. At one point in the game, Billy took off his pants. For the next four or five hands Francis wondered why he had done it. Then he realized that while he was wondering, Billy was winning.

August 8, 2004 San Diego

For the last four days I've been in San Diego, California, installing Circle of Memory in the Museum of Photographic Arts. The museum is in Balboa Park. I hadn't been in the park since Francis and I brought our small boys to its famous zoo many years ago. Now a cluster of museums occupy the handsome old Spanish baroque buildings interspersed with gardens, a carp pond, and fountains at the park's center. Arthur Ollman, the director of the museum, took us outside and pointed out the intensely ornamented building across the walkway. "Look at that. Orson Welles filmed it to represent Hearst's castle in *Citizen Kane*."

Early Tuesday morning I began shooting video of the trucks of straw bales arriving and being unloaded on pallets. I shot our crew and volunteers using hay hooks to stack bales in a freight elevator and bring them to the gallery level. The heavy bales were moved onto dollies and rolled into the main gallery, then slowly lifted into position, forming the layered construction of our Circle. The aroma of fresh straw came deliciously through the painter's masks we wore as the dust and straw fragments rose in the air.

The work over four days was long and hard. We walked more than a mile to and from the hotel provided by the museum. It is old, with faded carpet in the halls and large rooms with kitchenettes. The cupboard moldings have been painted over so many times the once crisp details are nearly gone. Some cabinets have long been painted shut. I was happy to be with my collaborators, completely focused on our project together. Late in the evening four of us gathered in my room around the Formica dinette table to play Machiavelli. We sent the loser to the 7-Eleven across the street to buy drinks and candy bars.

On Saturday we swept loose straw that had drifted everywhere in the gallery and adjoining hallways, Jean finished hanging her photographs, Alex set the final lighting, and Richard adjusted the sound. At 5:00 p.m. I was upstairs in the museum offices when an assistant told me Francis had arrived. As I came down, I could see him in the lobby behind glass doors, smiling. He brought me a surprise; seventeen-year-old Gia was standing behind him. We hugged, the three of us pressed together like a sandwich.

All during the opening reception, Francis sat at the far side of the room with Gia on his lap, talking with my brothers and a friend who had been my college roommate. Arthur ushered me around the room, introducing me to board members and to a couple who had lost a child and made a major donation to the museum for our installation.

A microphone was switched on and Arthur spoke about the project and introduced me to the several hundred guests. I talked about the inspiration for the project, our collaboration and each artist's contribution. Arthur suggested that in order for all the people attending to see the Circle, we take hands and walk through it in a long chain. I didn't care for the idea; to me the installation is meant to be an individual experience, reflecting the way people remember and grieve which is as unique as a fingerprint. But in order for everyone to pass through the interior of the Circle, it seemed the best solution. I wished I was standing with Francis and Gia but they were across the room. I knew he was trying to stay removed so that he wouldn't draw people away from the focus of the evening.

A robust man clasped my hand and, gathering people in tow, urged me forward as the gallery doors were opened. Encountering the huge shape of the straw-bale cairn and the aroma that filled the room, I heard people gasp. As we walked, hands linked together through the darkened center of the cairn around the thin glowing stream of salt falling, I invited those who cared to, to say the name of a remembered loved one. Most walked in silence but a few spoke. I said, "Gian-Carlo Coppola" and the man next to me said, "My daughter, Jenna Druk." Out in the gallery afterwards I could see that many people were writing messages on slips of paper we'd placed in a stone bowl and then wedging them into the straw walls. I could see Francis take Gia inside the Circle.

When we returned to the hotel I ordered a fold-out bed for Gia and we settled into my one large room, it was similar to camping. Gia has stayed in luxury hotels attending film premieres and award ceremonies for Francis and Sofia. I hoped she wasn't disappointed by the accommodations. She explored the kitchenette, the large closet, she looked out the window at the view over the parking lot to the 7-Eleven, she sat down on the worn green couch, kicked off her shoes, put her feet up and said, "I like this place. It's comfortable."

Circle of Memory broke museum attendance records. The many thousands of notes left in the straw walls at the end of the exhibition were gathered and included in the piece constructed in Santa Fe in April 2005.

Part Eight

August 14, 2004 Bali

Francis and I arrived last night. The sky above our hotel was indigo black, palms and tropical trees were up-lit dramatically in the darkness. The air, scented by blossoms we couldn't see, was mixed with the smell of a mosquito coil burning by the bedroom door. A gecko on the wall near the ceiling cackled sharply. Frogs hopped on the limestone steps. Occasionally a bat swooped in under the terrace roof to catch insects drawn to the lights.

Jet-lagged, we fell asleep early in the dramatic four-poster bed surrounded by sheer curtains. In the gray light of early morning I stepped onto the smooth, wide floor boards and slid back tall shuttered doors. I faced a white stone terrace with deck chairs framing a plunge pool. The water appears to flow over the edge into a small bowl-shaped valley with a river running through at the bottom. In every direction there is lush foliage and landscaping artfully trimmed to look as if it were well groomed by nature. It is a thick tapestry of banana palms, tall coconut palms, enormous flowering trees with red blossoms, plants with huge leaves, yellow-green sword-pointed leaves, purple and black leaves, yellow, orange, and magenta flowers. For 180 degrees nature surrounds us with the exception of a distant wedge of thatched roof. The air is cool and fresh with a faint hint of smoke from burning chaff in a nearby rice terrace. Birdsong emanates from the thousand shades of green fluttering leaves. The river flowing briskly over rocks masks any outside sounds such as vehicles or voices. I feel completely embraced.

Francis gets up from his computer; we swim. The pool water is the same temperature as the air and our skin.

A waiter brings a tray with a small Italian espresso machine which he plugs in and begins to make coffee. I can see Francis's look of displeasure in the way he is going about it. He says, "I'll show you something," and proceeds to teach the young Balinese man how to make a perfect cappuccino. He succeeds and Francis sips with satisfaction. I have Balinese black rice pudding, which is dark and sweet with chunks of candied ginger. We eat from a platter of mango and papaya and watch the morning sunlight move down the sides of "our" valley, illuminating layer after layer of tropical foliage. Or more precisely, I watch the changing light and Francis reads the day-old *International Herald Tribune* which came on our breakfast tray.

We are not on vacation in Bali, we are here on a buying trip for the Belize resorts. We reserved a regular room in the main building of the hotel knowing we wouldn't be in much. When the manager saw Francis he upgraded us to a river-view villa. I knew it sounded banal but I said, "We're so lucky. This is paradise!" Francis looked up from the paper, he looked around and said, "Maybe we're dead."

We dress and call for a golf cart to take us to the hotel entrance to meet Made (pronounced Mahday). Made is a short, muscular man in his mid-twenties wearing a T-shirt, shorts and sunglasses. His black hair stands up in a gelled crew cut above his round smiling face and dark sparkling eyes. Made is a stone carver who Francis met on a previous trip and brought to Belize to work on Turtle Inn.

Made arrived in Belize with four relatives, all carvers, who worked together to install limestone carvings they'd made in Bali and shipped ahead. Made was the only one who spoke English. He told us he learned by watching American movies on TV. His small crew worked tirelessly for many weeks. They taught the Mayan workers how to create Balinese-style walls in a pattern called "crazy stone," which surrounds the private gardens and outdoor showers of the 24 villas at Turtle Inn.

At meal times Made and his men ate by themselves in their cabin, embarrassed by the way they ate in traditional style, sitting on the floor, eating with their fingers. They preferred to have rice and fried chicken every day rather than American food. Although Made admitted that he liked the pizza.

Now Made is guiding us on a shopping trip for our resorts. We drive first to Made's "yard," a long open stall on the main road among many stone carvers' shops. He has twelve carvers but only four are at work: "Because it is festival day. They are at the temple." There is a steady sound of pinging as tools chip stone. Men work sitting on the ground before blocks of limestone. I see a monkey emerging from one stone slab and a frieze of birds and leaves from another. Made guides us around his yard as Francis chooses pieces for Belize, planters carved with tropical foliage, a mermaid and turtles for Turtle Inn, and two stone jaguars for the entrance gate at Blancaneaux, our lodge in the mountains.

One afternoon while Francis met with a builder in his office to go over drawings for a prefabricated tropical lodge, I sat outside on an old chair in the shade of a banana palm. Made joined me. Over the days of driving together I learned he was a big movie fan. He watches movies on cable TV almost every night. "I see *Rambo* six times maybe. *Terminator* a lot a times too." He asked me with excitement, "How feel walk red carpet, Miss Ellie?" I could see by his expression nothing I could say would meet his expectations but I tried to make my answer colorful. He asked, "How Mr. Francis get his movie money?" Fortunately, at that moment Francis emerged from the office with a roll of drawings and Made hurried to open the car.

A highlight for me was an evening when Made invited us to his house for dinner. The Jeep turned off the dusty, noisy main road and in minutes arrived in a quiet village. I would never have known there was such tranquillity so near the traffic-clogged route we took every day. Rice paddies bordered the houses. The sound of dogs barking, children at play and birdsong were woven into the air. Only an occasional motor scooter interrupted the calm. We stopped in a narrow dirt lane at a traditional gate. Made's smiling father opened the latch and greeted us warmly (we'd met in Belize). To enter we stepped up several steps and down around a carved stone guarding the house from evil spirits and found ourselves in a courtyard. Made introduced us to his mother, his sister and brother, an aunt and uncle, niece and nephew and his young wife with their eighteen-month-old daughter, Putu. The family spoke few words of English. His father and uncle were taller than most Balinese men; they were dressed in sarongs with T-shirts. His mother and aunt, small and slim, wore batik sarongs with traditional lace blouses that looked as if they had been washed many times. The sarongs were soft and faded, the colors in the patterns blended into one another. The young adults and children wore T-shirts with shorts.

The family invited us to sit down on red plastic chairs which I imagined were borrowed for the occasion. I was expecting to sit Bali-style on the floor. We brought presents with us and gave them out to the family; a stuffed toy and fancy dress for Putu, coloring books and felt pens for the niece and nephew, fine quality sarongs for Made's mother, his wife and aunt on the advice of our driver Kuming. A new set of carving tools for his father and a DVD player for Made with a stack of movies.

Made's father had roasted a small pig for us, something only done for weddings and festival days. He motioned for us to move our chairs to the table which was a piece of plywood on sawhorse legs with a sarong laid over the top. There were eight chairs. I noticed that Made's wife and I were the only women at the table with the men. The carcass of the pig rested on a board at the end of the table. All the meat had been carved onto a platter. There was also a roast chicken, a bowl of cooked green beans served with peanut chili sauce, a bowl of sliced mango, a plate of fresh pineapple wedges and a large pot of steamed rice. There was a spoon and fork wrapped in a thin paper napkin for each of us and a shallow bowl at each place. I was touched by the efforts the family had gone to, to create a table and provide chairs and silverware for our comfort; and the expense of roasting a pig and a chicken.

Mugs were scattered along the table top; giveaway-type mugs with Bintang Beer and Kmart logos. We brought two bottles of our wine. It hadn't occurred to us that they wouldn't have a wine opener. Francis started to dig out the cork with a screwdriver. Made's brother disappeared and returned with a red Swiss Army knife that contained a small short corkscrew. It was just long enough to get the cork out and Francis poured wine into the mugs. The wine tasted OK but in the warm humid evening I found the local beer more appealing. Made's uncle drank most of the wine.

I was curious about the central raised platform that dominated the courtyard with its gleaming white tile floor, its decoratively carved corner posts, and roof but no walls. At its center there was a canopied bed. Made noticed me looking at it and said, "That's where we marry, where we are born, and we die." I said, "So you were married right here on this platform?" He said, "Yes, everybody came here. First we file the teeth." I must have looked startled. He explained, "We have ceremony to file incisor teeth. Take away our animal nature. No more angry and fighting." Putu toddled over to him and held on to his knee. He said to me, "I have to have son. Take care of me when I'm old. My daughter leave me."

When we finished eating the women began clearing the table. I got up to help but they protested. After a few minutes I thought I really should help and carried several dishes to the kitchen. I startled Made's aunt as she was eating the leftover food from one of the men's plates.

We shopped for ten days straight. As we drove to the airport I said to Francis, "We worked every day and didn't even take one day by the pool. If you're going to work this hard you could be making a movie." He said, "It's the same thing, without the camera."

After the exhausting flight from Denpasar to Singapore to Hong Kong to San Francisco, we stood in the long line, too tired to speak as we waited our turn to present our passports. When we reached the head of the line, I followed Francis in a daze to the immigration officer's desk. The officer looked at the passports, then at Francis. "Are you him?" Francis nodded. "You done some pretty good stuff . . . pretty big money, huh. Say, would you sign an autograph?"

September 6, 2004 Napa

Roman burst into our small guesthouse at 8:15 this morning calling, "Mother, get up, Mother," in a playful, scolding voice as if I were late for school. Hot wind followed him and his girlfriend, Jennifer, in through the open door. While Francis and I put on robes they went into the kitchen. I could hear the espresso machine hissing as milk steamed. We ate breakfast on the narrow side porch and frequently had to stand up and make room for one of us to pass on their way to the kitchen for more jam and cappuccinos. The hot dry air felt as if it were the final efforts of summer, when temperatures reach into the 90s instead of the 100s, and thick sweet scents of overripe fruit roll up the steps from the garden and in from the vineyard. The fig tree is laden and bees hover over sticky fruit squashed on the driveway. Grapes hang dark and heavy on nearby vines. In the distance I hear a picking crew shouting to one another. "*Andale! Andale!*" They are paid by weight and hurry to fill bins that will stop at the scales on their way to the winery. Harvest is in full swing and Sunday is not a day of rest.

On Friday Francis, Roman and Jennifer went out early in the morning to pick with the crew. It is stunningly hard work using a small curved knife, avoiding being stung by bees and selecting only clusters of grapes that are not underripe or overripe. Our winemaker Scott McLeod was there. He said, "The idea is to work fast and come back with all your fingers." They were picking syrah, the grape varietal used in RC Reserve, a proprietary wine Roman created with the winemaking staff.

At 9:00 a.m. we gathered in the Rubicon winery, which is only two years old. It is in the château, where wine was made from 1880 until sometime in the 1960s. The next owners moved winemaking to a warehouse off the premises where they focused on volume. We acquired the winery in 1995, and Francis has always directed Scott to make quality our goal. A new state-of-the-art winemaking facility was completed last year on the second floor of the château in the room where the great wines of Inglenook were created in years past. It combines the best of traditional techniques with the new; wooden fermentors stand next to a stainless steel sorting table.

Scott welcomed the hundred-plus employees to the 2004 harvest. I like gathering together the field workers with the managers, tasting room staff, winemakers, gardeners and accountants all in a stew of vital people who work to make the winery thrive. Scott remarked on this year's vintage. "We had the warmest March to May on record followed by a relatively cool summer. It looks as if this will be a great vintage! . . . Mrs. Coppola has a few words to say."

I talked about the inhabitants of the property long before us. "The Wappo Indians lived on this land. We had an archeological dig in the front vineyard and found artifacts up to 3,000 years old. We are still finding arrowheads and occasionally a grinding stone on the property. This land has nourished people for thousands of years and we farm organically to conserve it into the future. In tribute to our Indian forebears, let's salute the four directions as they may have, to call the great spirit's attention to our blessing of the grapes and give thanks for an abundant harvest." Everyone followed me as I faced the east, raised my arms and spoke loudly:

"*Hail to the East,*
to the rising sun,
to Spring,
to new growth."

We all turned toward the south.

"Hail to the South,
to the noonday sun,
to Summer,
to ripening crops."

Turning in the direction of the western hills:

"Hail to the West,
to the setting sun,
to Autumn,
and an abundant harvest."

And all facing the north corner of the room:

"Hail to the North.
to the north star,
to Winter,
to pruning and reflection before a new dawn."

When I got back to where I'd been standing next to Roman he said, "That was nice." Then he shook my arm and said in a teasing voice, "Oh, Mom, you're such a kook." I winced before I grinned. I had explored untraditional spiritual thought in the '70s and was the brunt of family razzing.

Francis looked terrific in his white linen suit and Hawaiian shirt as he climbed the ladder to the top of the crusher filled with just-picked grapes and said, "In the name of the Father, the Son, and the Holy Ghost" and, with a flourish, poured a bottle of champagne onto the glistening fruit. He climbed down and went to an electrical box containing the black "start" button and pressed. The crusher went into noisy action. Everyone clapped as clusters of grapes sank into the mouth of the machine at the top and stripped bare stems were spit out into a bin at the bottom. The 2004 vintage was under way. A glass of bubbling Sofia Blanc de Blancs was served to everyone.

Francis and I savored the last moments of Roman's visit before he and Jennifer left to drive back to Los Angeles. As their car pulled away, tires crunching on the gravel road, Francis said, "You should have had more kids." When we are alone on Sunday it's hardest. There are no grandchildren to run on the lawns, play in the pool and gather around the dinner table. No children living nearby dropping in with their friends, not even an uncle or nephew or cousin living within 500 miles.

September 7, 2004

Just when I thought my feelings about the main house were perfectly clear and I cared little about it, I spent the morning with Jonathan Barnett, the designer, walking through the renovation construction. Even though the house is only about a hundred yards from the guest cottage where we are staying I never visit it, claiming to be interested only in the new house.

Lots has happened since I was last in the main house. The marble on the kitchen counters is a stunning amber-rose color with striations that look as if they were great brush strokes. Jonathan showed me fabrics he was planning to use in various rooms, pattern on rich pattern and silk for the living room walls. I suggested burgundy carpet in the foyer and stairway instead of the gray-green sample he showed me. There I was, having to admit that part of me is drawn to the rich color, the velvets, patterned silks, thick slabs of marble. I was startled to be reminded that I do have a love of lush baroque beauty even though my deep desire to live in a spare, minimal home grows more insistent each year.

I tried to imagine how I will feel being back in the big house again. Now it looks as if we may be living in it for a year or more before the "Tree House," as we are calling our contemporary concrete and glass home on the mountain, is finished. It will feel to me as if I am living in a beautiful boutique hotel with its five elegant guest suites each with a large marble bathroom. Familiar family pictures and objects will be set among the fine furnishings. I imagine the house speaking to me, asking me why I didn't get involved with the design when I notice aspects that I could have liked more. I have always done our homes. This is the first time a professional designer has done it all. And I think about the many guests who will be in the huge new kitchen, refurbished dining room and wine cellar. There is no longer my small private room on the third floor with its simple table facing the windows looking out into the giant oak tree, across the lawn and vineyards to the hills on the other side of the valley where I could watch the moonrise; it is now a charming guest bedroom. And how can I come downstairs in my favorite old sweatpants? I won't look fine enough to be in this elegant house.

September 11, 2004 Deauville, France

The breeze coming in the tall open window is cool and damp. From my fifth-floor room I can see the English Channel perhaps a quarter mile away. To the right is a line of colorful flags snapping in the wind in front of modern white buildings where the Deauville Film Festival is taking place. Francis is there somewhere doing a press conference.

I am in our hotel waiting for room service to bring me strong tea to fend off a bout of late morning jet lag. I face the open window rather than into our room in this grand old seaside resort built early in the last century. The room smells faintly of musty cupboards and damp wallpaper paste. The high walls are covered with patterns of stripes overlaid with large red, pink and blue roses. The same pattern is on the massive upholstered furniture.

A plaque on the door says, "Johnny Hallyday Suite." He is a famous French rock star; we saw him perform in a stadium near Paris years ago. He was a slick, tan singer with a lot of style. I remember his silver jumpsuit with open neck and silk scarf. His show was very avant-garde in its early use of laser lights. I can't picture him sitting in his namesake suite.

Sofia e-mailed me photos of the apartment she rented in an old building in Paris where she is living while she makes her next film. The walls are paper white, hung with a few fine art photographs. I could see a large bouquet in a clear vase reflected in a mirror. Her e-mail said, "They have such nice roses here that smell!"

Four days ago we were in Napa treasuring the beloved signs of fall. The harvest began and the aroma of ripe grapes filled the air. Wednesday Francis and I departed from Oakland in a private jet bound for New York City with George, his companion, and Walter and Aggie Murch.

Thursday evening we all went to the Guggenheim Museum of Art for a screening of *THX 1138*, followed by a tribute to George. The film was released in 1971. Warner Brothers had no idea what to do with this artistic work of science fiction, no idea how to promote and distribute it, and it quickly disappeared.

The tribute focused on the serious artist aspect of George. *THX 1138* shows that. Each frame is a visual composition, a white canvas with images sparingly added. It has the most overtly sexual scenes in any of George's films, scenes between Robert Duvall and Maggie McOmie. Curiously, Maggie never made another film. The message of the piece is powerful and dark and concerns the future of humankind. It is an amazingly thought-provoking work by a filmmaker in his mid-twenties. I saw it at the time of its first release and hadn't seen it since. I saw so much more in the film from my vantage point of age and now was struck by the many echoes reverberating through George's later work.

A documentary was also shown of the early years of American Zoetrope with images of all the young filmmakers who were involved. The film traced their dreams and adventures those first years in the late '60s as they struck out to form a company and make films outside of Hollywood. George and Francis were thin with black beards. In one shot I saw a glimpse of six-year-old Gio pounding nails in the wall of the new mixing studio as it was being built. There were shots in rooms and offices I had decorated with walls painted in bands of orange or purple and banners of bright Marimekko textiles.

George stood onstage with Francis, Walter, Martin Scorsese, cinematographer Caleb Deschanel, writer Matthew Robbins and others who had worked together and been friends for thirty-five years. The stars of *THX*, Maggie and Bobby, were at George's side. The room felt layered with memories and emotions, the dreams and expectations of those early years measured against the realities of the paths each one had taken, their defeats and their triumphs now evident.

Aggie and I walked through Deauville. A charming town with the traditional architecture of Normandy being kept in good repair as a valued tourist attraction. We walked briskly around the yacht harbor trying to dissolve the memory in our bodies of the many hours we had sat on the plane flying from California to New York, and from New York to France in the last three days. Aggie said, "The best part was seeing our husbands enjoying each other's company. I don't think they've ever had that much time together when they weren't working." We had sat around a table in the rear of the plane playing cards and occasionally could hear bits of the men's conversation as they discussed world affairs, good and evil, the nature of galaxies, experiences building, systems of education, the state of the movie business and the environment. As we passed over Greenland, Walter called us to the window. "See those brown spots?" We looked down on expanses of white snow-covered earth below and could see several large brown ovals. "That's where the ice cap is melting from global warming."

⚘

Saturday evening we all went to the film festival theater. We walked in on a red carpet. A publicity person asked me to stand aside so they could get photos of George, Francis and Walter together. Aggie and I stood on the sidelines and mused on our mutual experiences of being asked to get out of the way. When the photos were finished we entered a private side balcony where we could see out into the 1,500-seat theater which was nearly full with a waiting audience. A festival official led Francis, George and Walter to the back of the huge auditorium and after a lengthy tribute to George in French and translation in English, the official asked him to walk down the long aisle in the glare of the following spotlights to the stage. George received a standing ovation and a shiny award in a green velvet box, then the festival director asked him to stand at the center edge of the stage before a crowd of photographers. The flash bulbs going off from all directions created George's silhouette shadow popping across the movie screen behind him. Finally Francis and then Walter was called to the stage. Each told a short anecdote about George. Francis said, "I got to know George when he won an internship at Warner Brothers. The only production on the lot was a film I was directing so pretty soon I saw this skinny kid hanging around the set. I told him to come up with one good idea a day, and he did!"

We didn't stay for the screening of *THX 1138*. Our group was taken to the home of Deauville's mayor for dinner. A festival attendant gave us each a typed sheet to read about him before we arrived. It said he had received a Legion of Honor award for his work in tourism, he had five children and an extensive art collection. The mayor lived in a large rambling apartment on several floors above a store. He was a handsome man in his early fifties; his wife was a vivacious woman with long frizzy auburn hair and there were three children at home, teenagers to early twenties. We were all invited out onto a deck overlooking a lovely small garden where a waiter in formal uniform served champagne and appetizers. A photographer appeared and took pictures of Francis and George with the mayor and his family. Francis talked to the children and I thought about him being envious that the mayor had many. As we went in to dinner I said to Francis, "I could see you were enjoying the mayor's children. I hear he has five." He said, "Yeah, but each one has a different mother. He's had four wives, you know."

In the dining room the mayor's wife sat at one end of the big oval table between Francis and George, and at the opposite end the mayor was seated between a film distributor's wife and me. At a moment when the conversation lagged I said to the mayor, "I see you have quite an art collection." He said, "Oh no, that's my wife's," and looked longingly to the other end of the table, straining to hear the conversation with Francis and George.

The dinner was hurried along to get through the many courses in time for us to go back to the theater, where Francis was to introduce a screening of *The Godfather* as part of a tribute to Marlon Brando. We arrived just in time and watched from the balcony as the president of the festival made a long rambling introduction of Francis, pausing every few sentences for the translation into English. Finally a festival attendant gave Francis the signal to walk down the long aisle to the stage. He received a wonderful ovation and told several anecdotes about his experiences working with Marlon, concluding with "On *Godfather* I was working with Marlon and he had all his lines on cards taped to the furniture and all around and I said, 'Marlon, come on, you don't really need those, you've done great stuff without having your lines on cards,' and he said, 'Remember that scene you said you liked in *On the Waterfront* when I'm in the back of the car?' 'Yeah.' 'Well, I had my lines on the seat.' Of course, he was lying."

September 29, 2004

The air is cooling, mornings have been gray, the leaves in the vineyard are beginning to turn yellow, the winemaker tells me our harvest will finish this week. Still the distinctive rich aroma of sticky ripe fruit drifts through the valley, a wave catching me at the edge of the steps or through the open car window along the highway.

Perhaps the weather is affecting my mood. It was the autumnal equinox a few days ago; halfway between summer and winter, with an undertow of forces from each. This afternoon is sunny but there is a chill in the air. I have walked to my studio up the steep deer path winding through the tall dry grass, burrs collecting on my socks; translucent blue dragonflies darting next to me along the tree line.

The barn-style doors of my studio are open. Sunlight defines a long arc stretching across the floor. I hear sharp intermittent pops as ripe acorns fall and hit the metal roof. This year's crop has been the biggest we've ever seen. Francis has gathered a bucketful; he wants to try making flour as the Indians did.

I can feel the pull at my throat of all the things I might be doing. At the same time I can feel forms occupying my heart, my mind, and even though not fully defined, they urge me to take time to discover them and commit them to paper, the page, a video, an installation.

A few days later . . .

Today there was an interview with Tom Waits in the newspaper. He lives about an hour's drive away from us in the country with his wife and three children. Reading the article felt as if we'd had a visit, his distinctive voice growling off the page. "Family and career don't like each other," he says. "One is always trying to eat the other. You're always trying to find balance. But one is really useless without the other. What you really want is a sink and a faucet. That's the ideal."

October 11, 2004

I am reading an article in *Art in America* about Manny Farber, the painter and art critic. There is a photograph of one of his paintings, a view down on a table top; on it are scattered asparagus, a bowl of eggs, assorted notebooks, a piece of string, a red place mat under a colander of turnips and potatoes, an eggplant resting on a spiral notepad and several scraps of paper with handwriting. One says, "This is not debris, each of the items means something." It feels more and more as if objects around me and incidents in my life are calling out to me with memories from the past. A little sake jar on my window sill with a dry vine scrolling out of it reminds me of purchasing it on a stopover in Tokyo on our way back from the Philippines in 1977. A small pair of scissors on my desk are the ones I used to take backstage when I was designing costumes for the ODC Dance Company. The yellow polar fleece jacket I am wearing warmed me on a trek to mountain villages in Peru.

Tonight at dusk, a dry wind is blowing, the scent of smoke is in the air. I have heard there is a forest fire in Yolo County many miles away. The sky is a particular orange-gray behind black silhouettes of pine trees in the west. It looks the same as an illustration in my childhood storybook of Bambi when his mother sees impending danger in an approaching forest fire and instructs Bambi to run and we know he never sees her again. A surge of sadness has overtaken me and I am slumped down in a chair on the porch, relieved that I am alone.

A few minutes later Francis arrived from work and came in

through the back door. He opened a bottle of wine in the kitchen and came to the porch with two filled glasses. As he approached he looked at me. "What's the matter?"

NOVEMBER 19, 2004

The soft flesh of a ripe persimmon I picked from our garden is lying on a dark blue glass plate. I am sitting outside on the apron of my studio eating late lunch in the last of the warm light before the winter sun slips early behind the ridge of Mount St. John. My feet in hiking boots rest in a new crop of crisp oak leaves that fell in last night's wind. I am utterly content. The family is well. Francis has just returned from an extensive physical exam in Southern California where he was found in good health. He continues to be passionate about projects he is working on. Roman is here for this week with a group of animators creating an experimental film. When Sofia calls from Paris she sounds both excited and overwhelmed, which seems normal for a director preparing a big production. She starts shooting *Marie Antoinette* in two and a half months. Gia is nearly eighteen. She is going to junior college and is particularly enjoying her classes in journalism and cinema history.

I am treasuring a few days in my studio before the holiday activity and we begin our move back into the big house, where we will live temporarily until our Tree House is finished. Last June, Jonathan told me, "Plan your party! Get a great costume, you'll be having Halloween in the main house." In September he said, "Looks as if it will be Thanksgiving dinner." Now they're trying to finish for Christmas. Workmen are here Saturdays and Sundays. I've heard whispers that some think it won't be done till Easter.

Yesterday Francis and I walked through the big house to see the progress. Oak paneling made from the tree that fell on the house was being applied to the large refrigerator doors. The casings of the new elevator were being clad in mahogany. Two craftsmen were applying panels of silk to the living room walls. Painters hand-rubbed a decorative finish on the foyer walls. Workmen were rehanging our Murano glass chandelier in the dining room. Francis found the fixture in Trieste, Italy, while he was shooting *Godfather II* years ago. I disliked it and was very discouraging, saying, "We really have no place it would look right." He bought it anyway. Years later when we moved to Napa it fit the dining room perfectly, as if it had been custom-made.

I stepped into my bathroom. It had originally been a large bedroom and now looked particularly enormous. There were two sections of wall with new details I hadn't seen before. There was a marble floor, a differently toned marble wainscoting, a large marble shower and a marble fireplace. Our Victorian tub sat out in the room facing toward the view out the tall windows. I'd never been in such a big elegant bathroom and I've traveled the world. I felt I would appear out of place if I wasn't wearing a silk dressing gown trimmed with flowing marabou feathers.

This morning over breakfast Francis talked about how he is searching for a new language of cinema ". . . to express time and consciousness. Film is a young art. Do you think everything has already been discovered? No." As I sipped my green tea and he talked about his ideas, I knew how fortunate I was to be part of such a conversation.

Part Nine

December 30, 2004 St. Bart's

I've put two extra pillows on my chair and still I can barely reach my teacup and plate of tropical fruit on the dining table. We are on a chartered yacht whose owner we're told is a six-foot-nine-inch ex-kickboxing champion of Russia. The furniture is of gigantic proportions. Francis and I, Gia, Jacqui, and her husband, Peter, are guests of George Lucas. With George are his three children and two guests. We are having a holiday vacation together in the Caribbean.

The yacht has a Las Vegas flavor. It is spacious and luxurious, featuring a gym with glass walls facing the sea. A crew member told me, "The owner works out three hours a day in that gym." There is an outdoor hot tub and expansive lounge area on the top deck and two decks with large salons, each with huge sofas, accordion-folded cashmere throws and big-screen TVs. The aft decks are furnished for dining and sunbathing. The master suite is on two levels and has a discreet unmarked door to an adjoining small bedroom that exits into the hall "for a massage therapist." The level below has four guest cabins and a deck where the tenders come and go, tethered Jet Skis float at the ready and an open storage area is filled with snorkeling gear, water skis and water toys. Ice clinks as it falls in the icemaker behind the bar where Brendan stands, one of the sixteen crew members who attend the eleven of us day and night.

The yacht is at anchor in the bay off St. Bart's. Tonight we are invited on board Paul Allen's yacht, *Octopus*. I admit I am curious. It is a huge beautiful new boat anchored next to Larry Ellison's. We can see both from our aft deck. It is rumored that Larry Ellison insisted on having the bigger yacht so built his three or four meters longer. Both are too big to go into the dock so rest at anchor in the harbor. The grand boat we are on is a midget by comparison.

We went ashore and walked along the town's small streets past a mixture of funky shops, chic restaurants and exclusive stores. The sidewalks were crowded with guests and crew members from the many boats in the harbor. Gossip about celebrities seemed to swirl in the air. "John Travolta is here, which boat is he on?" "I heard Oprah is here." "Puff Daddy is definitely here." "I saw Ron Perelman and Ellen Barkin's yacht *Ultima* docked in the same place as last year." I overheard conversations about shopping. "I'm going to get another pair of these sandals at Louis Vuitton." "He got me this bracelet at Cartier." "Hermès has the best men's shirts."

In my mind's eye I see my version of a tropical island paradise. There are a few shacks at the edge of the beach and some small fishing boats pulled up on the sand. A local man is cooking fresh fish over a fire of coconut husks on a grill made from an oil drum. He puts grilled fish on a banana leaf with lemon and chilies and serves it on a board. There are fresh fruits in a basket and a cooler with cold beer.

Here the cast of characters doesn't seem quite real and the dramatic sunsets through the masts of yachts look as if they are special effects. Yet there are moments when the show is familiar. Today, for instance, we were driven to the other side of the island for lunch at a restaurant on the beach. The owner rushed out from behind the hot grill of the open-air kitchen when he saw Francis. We had come to this restaurant 25 years ago with Gio, Roman and Sofia when the island was virtually unknown and the restaurant was a small place on the beach, the only oasis of good food.

At our table now there were Francis, George, Steven Spielberg and six children ages eleven to twenty-three. The men, old friends, talked as if they were aging generals recalling their various campaigns. "Remember that time in the desert on *Indie* [*Indiana Jones*], the sand was blowing so hard we . . ." Or speaking about their work processes, such as how to prevent a cinematographer from slowing down the pace of shooting: "I tell 'em, good is good enough. If the sound and story can't carry the scene, no amount of fancy lighting is gonna do it." "Yeah, 'better' is enemy of the 'good.' " Or regarding choosing films to direct: "Sometimes I want to work so I take a project that I'm not in love with. It's like an arranged marriage—slowly I find ways to care about it."

I sat with Francis on my left, Steven and George across from me, and four of the children to my right. I appreciated seeing the affection these fathers expressed for their families, how they planned their work around them. "I'm shooting my next film in Berlin during the summer so the whole family can come." "Yeah, I only shoot in the summer so the kids are with me, although I usually run over schedule three or four weeks."

At the table were two of Steven's seven children, George's three and our granddaughter. Gia and Steven's son discovered their colleges were near each other. George's daughter and Steven's other son realized they shared being adopted children, and stuck out their hands and high-fived. Steven said with a grin, "Yeah, we had to fight for three years to legally adopt him. He was our foster child since infancy but the black adoption agency didn't want to release him to a non-black family." The kids talked about driving. One of the boys confessed that he'd gotten in trouble because he rode to school with a classmate who didn't have his license yet but told his mother he went to school on the bus. "My mom found out and now I can't drive for six months." He said it without rancor. I was glad these children had discipline in their lives.

When the main course was finished the kids got up from the table and went out on the beach. I could see Gia walking along the sand where Gio had walked, her skin and hair the same color, her hand gesturing in his distinctive way. Even all these years after Gio's death I can be surprised by deep volcanoes of searing emotion erupting without warning. I accept this. It reminds me that I had a son whom I treasured and lost and won't forget.

In Napa, nature is in full focus and fame and wealth are in the background. Here I learned on my first day aboard that Bill Gates is the wealthiest American, Warren Buffett is second, Paul Allen is third, Larry Ellison is fourth and he resents it. I can see the yachts of two of these four men a short distance away.

This afternoon, while the others went shopping in town, Francis and I stayed on the boat. He is reading and I am sitting in a comfortable deck chair making sketches in my notebook. In my mind's eye I see the knoll in front of my studio where I am imagining making a line of gray wood fence posts with pointed crowns marching across the meadow about 8 feet apart. I've painted the crowns silver, catching light in the winter sun. I'm imagining installing a large burgundy theater curtain on a big overhanging curved branch of an oak tree on the north side of my studio, forming a proscenium arch. The curtains would be open and frame the deer and wild turkeys that pass by.

We were invited to a party for "light snacks" at 9:00 p.m. aboard Paul Allen's boat. After dinner our tender took us a few hundred yards across the bay to the *Octopus*, which was lit dramatically. As we stepped on board we were directed to take off our shoes; a yacht etiquette I enjoy. As we walked up the long stairway toward party sounds, we passed a helicopter parked on a basketball court and an area which could open into a stage with stadium lighting and equipment for bands to perform.

The party was on perhaps the seventh level, a deck with an outdoor pool. The pool was covered with a translucent dance floor. We had arrived at 9:30 thinking we were slightly late, but only a few guests were there moving between the bar and tables of hors d'oeuvres. Waiters stood with trays balancing glasses of champagne. I noticed that people were being invited to tour the boat so Gia and I joined a group. The first stop was at the end of the pool area where we were shown a full-size professional music studio with mixing consoles, instruments and soundproof recording booths.

We visited the bridge where we learned that the yacht didn't have anchors out; it was kept in place by an electronic positioning device. The huge boat didn't move more than three feet in any direction without self-correcting. There were large leather sofas in the bridge area where guests could watch the captain and crew at work while they sailed. We saw a luxurious screening room with big comfortable chairs, footrests and cozy throws. Each sleek stateroom had two bathrooms. On the lower deck where the tenders launched there was a twelve-passenger submarine. A full dive shop had state-of-the-art equipment including a variety of oxygen mixes for filling divers' air tanks. Six Jet Skis were stored within easy access.

My favorite amenity was a small viewing room at the bottom of the boat which had a glass floor. Spotlights lit up the water below and we sat and watched fish swimming under the boat. There were lots of small silvery fish near the surface while several sand sharks came in and out of view on the sea bottom. Occasionally a large fish such as a barracuda or tarpon would cross the viewing window.

An excellent collection of contemporary art hung in the hallways. I noticed an early lead-color Jasper Johns number painting hung next to an elevator and Chihuly glass pieces beautifully lit and artfully displayed. A series of photographs of the surface of ocean water in various weathers and photos of undersea life hung handsomely in the hallways. On each floor there was an electronic touch screen which provided directions to guide guests to destinations on the nine decks. We learned there was a crew of sixty on board.

When we returned to the deck where the party was taking place it was crowded. A full buffet dinner was set out but no one was eating. I talked with the few people I knew but mostly I found myself looking at the guests. A tanned, silver-haired art dealer arrived with seven scantily dressed young women. One wore a very short black, nearly transparent dress with only the tiniest thong underneath. Another wore a turquoise minidress with no underwear. Her nipples protruded through the holes in the crocheted design and her bottom was completely visible. A woman with an extremely plunging neckline and hard-looking enhanced breasts moved into position to chat up George's son, who is nearly six feet tall. He retreated behind Peter whimpering, "I'm only eleven."

He was telling the truth.

Our host appeared, an almost invisible personage in gray slacks and a gray-green long-sleeved shirt. Everyone was overly smiley to him. He seemed quite shy and yet I assumed he must be enjoying the whole scene or he wouldn't have created it. An attendant approached Francis and said, "Mr. Allen is ready to have dinner now, would you please begin by serving yourself at the buffet." We had already eaten dinner before we arrived. Francis dutifully got up and filled a plate and others followed.

After Paul had eaten, he and several of his friends went into the recording studio opposite the pool. The studio's glass walls retracted and they began to play rock and roll. We sat in deck chairs listening. I don't trust my musical judgment but Francis said they were good. Paul seemed to be happy inside his music studio, jamming with friends, removed from his guests.

January 1, 2005

Today is Gia's eighteenth birthday. Last night we celebrated on the Perelmans' boat just after midnight. It is Ron's birthday too. Ellen brought out a chocolate cake with Ron and Gia's names written on it in scrolling white icing. Everyone sang "Happy Birthday," then Gia and Ron's precocious nine-year-old daughter cut the cake, added large strawberries to each plate and served everyone.

Today I find myself looking at Gia. She is a bit taller than I am, thin and has her own sense of style, such as the unique way she is wearing a dress she chose in a thrift shop. Her legs are thrown over the arm of a deck chair, she is holding a cup of tea in her long fingers. She looks like her mom but has Gio's distinctive dark eyes and many of his mannerisms. She has his personality: thoughtful and observant with his "old soul" quality (which I interpret as a developed inner life) and also his spirit of mischievous fun. She asked for birthday gifts that had sentiment. I gave her a book of Eisenstaedt's photography that Gio had given to me as a birthday present when he was her age. At the time I wondered why he had given me that book as I wasn't especially a fan of Eisenstaedt. Years later I realized Gio had given me a book he was interested in, given me a way to know more about him after he was gone. Now Gia is taking photography classes and will have a book of work by a photographer her father admired.

Several times today I've thought about Gia's birth.

January 1, 1987 Los Angeles

I am at Cedars hospital in a labor room with Jacqui. The large clock on the wall says 5:07 a.m. She has been given a painkiller and is dozing. She hasn't had any notable contractions for twenty minutes or so. Roman is asleep on a couch in the lobby; he is curled up in a ball, snoring softly. I covered him with Gio's navy blue blazer which Jacqui wore to the hospital. I can hear the heart monitor attached to Jacqui's bulging abdomen producing a rhythmic beat. It sounds as if it were a fast-paced old-fashioned washing machine. A long strip of graph paper is sliding slowly out of a slot in the front. The lights are off except one turned toward the pale blue wall. An IV hanging over the bed is feeding into Jacqui's left wrist. I haven't fallen asleep, I'm too excited. Jacqui's contractions started almost exactly at midnight; just a few minutes after twelve while we were still making our way around Dean's crowded house kissing friends and saying, "Happy New Year," Jacqui felt the first pains. It looks as if the baby will be born on this first day of the new year.

I dozed off and woke up when the resident doctor came in at 6:30. He looked at the graph monitoring the contractions and noticed there were none. Apparently the medicine in the IV had stopped labor. He recommended we walk in the halls for an hour or so. A nurse helped Jacqui up and put her IV on a rolling fixture.

We went out in the lobby and woke Roman up. The three of us toured the halls. We started at the nursery, hoping to see the new babies behind the glass but Venetian blinds had been lowered and we couldn't see much through the cracks. We went down to the main lobby. On the wall near the gift shop, there was a wonderful set of Andy Warhol prints of flowers in vases. I'd always wanted to see that set of prints. I have a gallery announcement with each reproduced in miniature that I've saved over the years. Near the entrance was a whole group of Claes Oldenburg prints and a four-foot-high sculpture of an ice bag in a glass case. Roman pushed a button and the ice bag slowly rose up, puffed out and then sank back down in a squashed position. I found myself giving Jacqui a mini lecture about Oldenburg and his giant baked potato before I realized she was slumped against the wall having a strong contraction.

Roman pulled Jacqui's IV stand along and I shot the video camera as we walked. The sun came up and bright light streamed in from the outside windows. The inner courtyards were still in shadow. We walked and then stopped every time Jacqui had a contraction. I was enthralled by a hall with Rauschenberg prints, one with Ellsworth Kellys, and another with Diebenkorns. There I was walking along with Roman and with Jacqui carrying Gio's child, in a hospital similar to an art museum. I tried to assimilate all my emotions and felt dizzy.

We returned to the labor room at 7:30. Jacqui got into bed and the nurse attached the monitors again. The contractions were about seven minutes apart. Tally arrived with toothbrushes, sandwiches and fruit for Roman and me. Roman went back to sleep in the waiting room and Tally and I stayed with Jacqui. When the doctor came in around eight, Tally and I went out into the hallway. In a few minutes the doctor joined us. He said, "I broke her water, so now the labor will get more intense. I've prescribed a light epidural to be given during the next hour and I expect the baby will be born around three or four this afternoon."

At 9:30 Sofia and Stephanie arrived. The doctor had gone home after the anesthetic took effect and Jacqui was chatting with Sofia right through heavy contractions registering on the monitor. We talked about calling Jacqui's mom and calling Francis and the rest of the family but decided to wait awhile and let everyone sleep in after New Year celebrating.

About 10:30 a resident doctor gave Jacqui a routine examination. The resident said there had been a dramatic change, the baby would be born in about an hour. We went to the phones in the hall and called Jacqui's mother, Francis and Tally's husband, Jack. A nurse gave Tally and me blue scrubs to change into so that we could enter the delivery room. My street clothes were tossed in a plastic bag and my feet and hair were covered with what appeared to be paper shower caps. The nurse handed me a surgical mask, then I stepped into the hall and asked Roman to give me instructions on how to use the bigger video camera. Suddenly Jacqui was being wheeled out of the labor room, rapidly down the hall and into delivery. I was hurriedly trying to shoot video and tie on my surgical mask. We got into the delivery room and there was a flurry of activity. I was shooting and Tally was moving me over cords and around equipment to better positions and at the same time holding Jacqui's hand or stroking her forehead. As Jacqui settled into the stirrups, I could see the top of the baby's head in the mirror. The doctor arrived, breathless. Only moments passed and I could see the baby's head and shoulders emerge. Then the doctor said, "You have a baby girl!" The baby gave a little cry, opened her eyes and looked around in the most alert manner. A few minutes later she was in the tiny bed at Jacqui's side, calmly looking while the nurse examined her. Jacqui was ecstatic! "Oh, please let me have my baby." The nurse laid her on Jacqui's chest. We looked with amazement at the baby's alert little face. She stuck out her lower lip in a pout to cry. The expression stunned me, it looked so much like Gio and Sofia. Tally asked what time the baby was born. "Eleven twenty-two," the doctor said. "This is only the second time in my career that I've delivered a baby with my bare hands."

I thought about the numbers in Gia's birth time. In numerology 11 and 22 are master numbers. "Eleven is called the Inspirer and stands for bringing a message. Twenty-two is referred to as the Master Builder because someone who has the number is usually a visionary." After Gio's death we found a short video he shot on his twenty-second birthday. He shot in front of our house, aiming the camera at himself and objects around him while he narrated: "Most people think 21 is an important birthday but I think it's 22. See, everywhere there are 2's; two wheels on my motorcycle, the car has two headlights. I think when you look back you'll see that 22 is a very significant year." The year he died.

The nurse put the baby back in the plastic bassinet. She said, "Who is going to cut the cord?" Tally indicated me. An inch or so from the baby's navel there was a clamp on the umbilical cord and four inches of cord extended beyond. The nurse gave me surgical scissors and told me, "Cut just beyond the clamp." I was surprised how tough the cord was. In photographs of fetuses the cord always appears to be soft floating spirals. It took me three hard snips to sever it. A little spurt of blood erupted from the end.

My body felt lighter than usual, as if I could jump ever so easily and touch the ceiling. I felt utter happiness in that moment, then a jolt. Involuntarily my head bowed, acknowledging the mysteries of birth and death.

I ran hard down the hall, into the waiting room to tell Francis, Roman, Sofia and others, "It's a girl! A healthy girl! Gia is here."

MARCH 16, 2005 FLYING FROM PARIS TO SAN FRANCISCO A package of Kleenex is in my lap. I have a miserable cold from overdoing it in France, working on Sofia's set, shooting a documentary of her directing her third feature film, *Marie Antoinette*.

The film, about the young, eighteenth-century queen of France, was supposed to be her second film but after optioning the biography by Antonia Fraser and writing for many months she was not satisfied with her script and set it aside. Sofia wrote *Lost in Translation* quickly as a little project to do while she gave herself time before tackling *Marie Antoinette* anew. *Lost in Translation* was a surprising success, taking her to film festivals and awards ceremonies and delaying her return to *Marie Antoinette*, resolving the script and preparing for production.

This is the fifth documentary I've made of my filmmaking family. After *Hearts of Darkness*, I shot a "making of" for Francis's film *The Rainmaker*, Sofia's film *The Virgin Suicides*, and Roman's film *CQ*. Over the last two weeks I've been shooting long hours, hand-holding my new heavier camera, going outside into the snowy cold surrounding the location château for a cup of tea and back into the set overly warmed by the lighting, getting up very early and home very late. I found it exhausting. One of the hardest lessons for me to learn about growing older is setting a pace that is right for me, not just expecting to keep up with a production where everyone is in their twenties and thirties. Sofia was coughing all the first week of shooting, she tried alternative therapies and finally on Friday, without telling her, I asked the producer to bring in a doctor. She had bronchitis and was given antibiotics.

The first day of shooting took place in Millemont, a crumbling eighteenth-century château 45 minutes from Paris in the countryside. As we approached, I saw the handsome old building surrounded by equipment trucks and trailers for makeup, props, costumes, production offices and actors, catering trucks and portable toilets, scaffolding towers for the big lights, and lines of thick black electrical cables running along the ground. I felt as if my cells were responding with recognition and excitement to the adventure ahead.

I arrived with Fiona, each of us carrying our equipment. She is an attractive woman in her early thirties with light brown curly hair and a mischievous grin, hired by the production to work with me and record sound as I shoot. She lives in London, has a charming English accent and speaks French. First thing, I sent her to find a place for us to have as a base for our equipment in the rooms adjoining the set, where the camera and lighting crews were already at work. I knew she could persuade a young crewman to let us use part of one of their carts or designate a small area where we could set up our equipment and be sure it wouldn't be blocked by production supplies or moved during the day.

On the set the production designer, K. K. Barrett, was moving around the room directing his crew to place the final props, porcelain figurines, vases of flowers, candelabra, plates of sweets. He had built a replica of Marie Antoinette's bedroom and furnished it in fresh, bright, rich fabrics as they would have been when they were new in Versailles, although perhaps his is a stylistic exaggeration using textiles that are more vivid, bubble-gummy colors than the originals were.

I was enthralled with every detail of the thick embroidery on the massive headboard and canopied bed; fat tassels, flower-patterned silk draperies, upholstered furniture and the decorative gold details of the woodwork. Huge fresh arrangements of exotic flower combinations in large chinoiserie vases complemented the colors in the room like masterful works of art. Usually fake flowers are used on sets and the illusion of embroidery is created by printing stitches with shadows to look as if they are raised surfaces. I noticed I was breathing in short gasps, an involuntary response to being in a room so visually dense with exquisitely beautiful detail, a room I could actually walk around in and look at things closely, not just stand at a distance behind a cord in a museum.

I found Fiona. She whispered, "I chatted up Benoît and we're set." A young man preparing a slate smiled. I could see our equipment nicely arrayed on a shelf on one of the camera department's metal carts. "So let's saddle up," I said, and put tape number one in my camera, cleaned the lens, loaded my belt pack with sound equipment and put on my earphones. I caught a glimpse of myself in a dusty mirror across the room. I'd forgotten how I actually look in my gear. I was wearing a black shirt and black pants and I'd asked Fiona to not wear any bright colors. I want us to look similar to the stagehands in Noh theater who wear all black and come out onstage in the middle of scenes to move set pieces. I want to be as invisible as possible on the set. Fiona had her earphones around her neck, was carrying the boom and had a mixer at hip height slung from a shoulder strap. We tested the sound levels to make sure the small radio microphone which would be worn by Sofia and the sound boom were balanced and functioning properly.

We were on set and ready when Sofia arrived at 8:00 a.m. wearing jeans, Vans, a cotton shirt and thick sweater. She looked too small and unprepossessing to be the director of a $40 million movie. She had a bad cough but an excited smile lit her face. "Hi, Mom. Can you believe it? After all these months we're really here and it's the first day of shooting!" She was accompanied by Ross Katz, her jovial thirty-two-year-old producer, and her cinematographer, Lance Acord, who had both done *Lost in Translation* with her. Sofia and Lance began blocking out the movement of the actors and the position of the camera; Sofia was collaboratively open to suggestions, but focused and made the final decisions. Fiona had slipped the radio microphone under Sofia's sweater, clipped it to her shirt collar, and put the transmitter into the pocket of her jeans. I had the receivers for her microphone and the boom in my belt pack with their cables connected to my camera. I could hear both in my earphones. The documentary began.

The first scene consisted of shots of Marie Antoinette entering her suite of rooms for the first time on her arrival at Versailles. Marie is played by Kirsten Dunst, who was in Sofia's film *The Virgin Suicides*. Kirsten arrived on set for rehearsal in her robe over the stiff-boned undergarments of her costume, her hair still in rollers and no makeup. When she saw me she gave me a sweet little hug, as if to say, "Oh, I see, you again, shooting a documentary." It was a friendly resigned acceptance that I was going to be an annoying presence on the set, always possibly photographing her in between shots when she would prefer to feel relaxed with no camera pointing at her. In fact this is my role, to shoot during the in-between times catching the cast and crew at unguarded moments. I am basically a shy person and hate to intrude. It is counter to my personality to shoot a documentary, yet over and over I do it. I can understand actors who say they have stage fright and yet have chosen a profession that requires them to perform as if it were a kind of antidote to their problem. I am fascinated to be an observer of the creative process. I am curious to see how Sofia will shoot the script she wrote about Marie Antoinette and Louis XVI, her interpretation of historical figures who lived in eighteenth-century France. During the course of making the documentary I will constantly be in people's way, be somewhat of an irritant to the production when the last thing in the world I want to do is be annoying, especially to Sofia. As much as I'll try not to, I know I will be, and she'll ask me to get off the set and turn off the microphone numerous times before the film is finished. I'm the lesser evil. If I don't shoot, someone hired by the studio publicity department will, which would be even more irritating. Sofia knows she has control if I shoot. She can edit out anything she doesn't want seen. For me it is a rare opportunity to see my child at work, be included in her world, even listen in on her conversations. Of course she can turn off the microphone she is wearing anytime but there will be moments she'll forget and I'll hear personal thoughts.

Francis told me, "Being a film director is one of the last dictatorial posts." Sofia doesn't work in that mode; she works quietly, collaboratively and appears calm and composed, although I know her well enough to see the tension in the set of her shoulders. She doesn't yell at anybody, yet she seems to get what she wants and is clearly in control. She is often amused by the performances of her cast and stifles giggles while the camera is rolling.

Kirsten, who is twenty-two, looks so fresh and lovely. She maintains an amazingly patient good humor about the discomfort of the extremely tight, boned bodices of her luscious macaroon-colored silk dresses and the hair and makeup that takes two to three hours every day to complete and sometimes requires a second or third change in a day. She is constantly being fussed over after every take, crew members are there to straighten an imperceptible wrinkle in a ruffle on her bodice, or adjust a strand of hair, or spray a little more powder on her wig, or apply a little more blush to her cheeks, and the sound man adjusts the small microphone hidden in the cleavage of her breasts all too frequently.

So many emotions, so many worries are running through my heart and mind; worry for Sofia's stamina with twelve long weeks of shooting ahead, more than twice as long as her previous films, at the end of which she was exhausted, had lost weight, was pale and gaunt. I wondered why she had chosen this difficult project requiring 56 days of shooting in complicated, far-flung locations. Why she had chosen as her subject an historical figure in a foreign culture. I wondered why she had chosen a production designer who was known for his hip contemporary films and had never done an historical piece. How could he be up to speed on the visual details of the eighteenth century? How would Ross control a $40 million budget in a foreign country when he had only done low-budget films?

April 3, 2005 Paris

Much has intervened. After shooting nine days I went back to California for several weeks before traveling to Santa Fe, New Mexico, to install Circle of Memory at the Santa Fe Art Institute, our third location for this project. After working on the installation, doing press, a symposium, the opening and afterparty, I left early on a Sunday morning, to fly back to Paris where I arrived at 8:00 a.m. on Monday and was driven directly to the set to resume shooting the documentary. The production is on location at Versailles every Monday, the only day of the week it is closed to the public and filming is permitted.

I had my eyes closed, dozing in the back seat, when the driver said, "There it is just in front of us." I looked up to see the huge palace in silhouette against the gray morning sky. I'd forgotten how truly enormous it is. It seems more real to me in books and my memories of arriving in a bus as a high school student. The production trucks were parked at one side of the vast cobblestoned courtyard. I could see scaffolding towers around the chapel walls with huge lights high up focused on the tall leaded glass windows.

I put on my identification tag. An on-set documentary is usually referred to as the "making of." The tags Fiona and I received for access to locations have a typo: below our names our department is listed as "Making Off." I followed the lines of cables through a side door into a cavernous marble hallway where there were rows of makeup tables and stylists hurrying to complete every detail of the extras' eighteenth-century appearance. Three women inspected each person before they were sent on set. One had a box of jewelry and selected pieces, one added hair ornaments, one was inspecting wigs and removing some people from the line and sending them to a booth to have more white powder sprayed in their hair. I hurried to find Fiona.

The scene was set in the chapel, the wedding of Marie and Louis. Hundreds of costumed extras were already in place in the breathtaking vaulted chapel. Outside it was a gray morning, but in the chapel with Lance's lighting it appeared to be a golden afternoon with rays of light slanting through the high arched windows. Fiona whispered, "Kirsten is due on set any moment." As I looked around the room I could see that Milena, the costume designer, had outdone herself! She, with the help of her staff of the best tailors, seamstresses, milliners, makeup artists and wigmakers gathered from Italy, France and England had created the most extraordinary array of eighteenth-century nobility. I could clearly see Sofia's concept for the colors of her costumes. Usually in period films royalty are dressed in shades of rich burgundy red, dark blues, purple velvets and deep golds. Sofia had chosen a pale palette, colors inspired by macaroons from a famous Paris pastry shop, Ladurée, that has served discriminating Parisians since 1862. The colors were soft pinks and yellows, apricots, pale lime greens, vanilla, lavenders and light aqua blues. I could see Sofia's vision executed to perfection.

As Sofia and I hugged, she said, "Have you seen Jason?" [Sofia's cousin Jason Schwartzman was playing Louis XVI.] I found him nearby. In his costume he looked more like Louis than I expected, as if Louis XVI was impersonating Jason. Germanel, his dresser, was adjusting the brocade vest under his silk coat. We stood carefully apart and kissed lightly on both cheeks taking care not to bruise his makeup or disturb the perfect ruffles at his collar. "What do you think?" he said, doing an elegant royal bow.

In my mind's eye I could see Sofia and Jason working together as teenagers staging a play in our barn in Napa, Sofia directing Jason in a leading role in *Bernice Bobs Her Hair*.

APRIL 14, 2005

I was watching Roman directing his crew, speaking quietly in French, instructing them to adjust his camera position. Sofia saw me. She came over and said with relief and the deepest appreciation, "Mom, I'm so glad Roman is here." He came to direct the second unit and shoot the second camera for her. She is so completely at ease with him, trusts his taste without question, knows he will help her in any way and truly be on her side. There was so much emotion in my throat I just murmured, "Uh hum." Their relationship is one of the most profound treasures in my life.

APRIL 18, 2005

I am tired; when I look at Sofia during a moment she is not engaged in conversation, I see her deep exhaustion; Roman looks worn. Today the location is at Versailles in the Hall of Mirrors. Francis is sitting in a folding chair to one side. "Imagine, this is where Marie Antoinette actually walked." He is the executive producer but is trying to stay out of Sofia and the actors' eye line. Roman is instructing his assistant to change lenses on the second camera. I have put my video camera down for a few minutes to rest my sore arms while Fiona has gone to get fresh batteries. Sofia is talking to Kirsten, who is wearing the most stunning dress, one of Milena's best. Marshall, Milena's husband, came to the set today to see it. He's been visiting her in Paris the past three weeks. He told me, "She literally works night and day, we've only had dinner together once."

Sofia is preparing to rehearse a scene between Marie Antoinette and Madame du Barry where Madame du Barry walks past Marie Antoinette and bumps her slightly in a bullying way in front of the members of court in the Hall of Mirrors. Over my headset I can hear the microphone on Sofia, she is saying to Kirsten, "This is like the high school quad. It's the first time you've seen du Barry since the dinner, it's where the haughtiness starts. She's not going to get out of your way. It's very high school, like the Socs and the Greasers. Du Barry is definitely a Greaser." I smile when I hear that reference. The family was on location with Francis while he was making *The Outsiders*. Sofia was ten.

After the first take of the shot Sofia walked out in front of the camera and said laughingly to Asia Argento playing Madame du Barry, "That looked like a mosh pit slam. You need to bully, but not like you're going for her . . . More of a brush."

May 31, 2005

The last week of shooting was "split days," with work beginning at 3:00 in the afternoon and ending around 3:00 in the morning with lunch served about 10:00 p.m. I hate split days. I always feel disoriented working those hours and know from experience that they often go into overtime and the work day doesn't end until 4:00 or 5:00 a.m. The first day was Monday so we were at Versailles outside in the gardens. It was nearly the end of May and I'd taken my winter coat and heavy sweaters back to California. The script said "sunny day." The scene was on a terrace at Petit Trianon, Marie's private playhouse castle in the gardens a distance from the main palace of Versailles. The scene is Marie having breakfast with her friends. While the women gossiped, Marie and her lover, Count Fersen, exchanged flirtatious glances. Because it had been such a cold spring the gardens hadn't bloomed so the art department planted thousands of pots of flowers in the flower beds. It was cloudy and the gaffer looked anxiously at the sky every few minutes, finally saying, "We should have sun briefly in about fifteen minutes." He was usually right, so at the appointed moment the wardrobe assistants took the polar fleece blankets off the actors and makeup artists touched up their wigs. The full sun never broke through and after another hour of waiting Sofia and Lance consulted and decided to shoot the scene in overcast light which meant that if the sun did come out, it would take costly time to build a shade over the area to create consistent light during the various camera setups needed to shoot the actors from both sides of the table and their close-ups.

I tried not to let my stomach crunch up with anxiety as I saw the last day Sofia had to shoot at Versailles devoured by fickle weather. I was shivering in my summer blouse and thin raincoat. I settled on a little stone ledge out of the wind and found myself thinking about why Sofia was making this film. It had become more clear to me over the weeks. Sofia's three films have been about a girl who is different from the culture she finds herself in. In *The Virgin Suicides* Kirsten plays an aware sixteen-year-old, trapped in a suburban family that doesn't understand her. She has a rich inner life and her parents, the boys and her school don't see who she really is, don't recognize what it feels like to be her. In *Lost in Translation* the girl Charlotte is in a foreign land, a foreign culture, and her workaholic husband doesn't understand her, doesn't recognize her isolation and what she is feeling. Marie Antoinette is a princess in a foreign country not understood by the court surrounding her, yet all eyes are upon her.

Perhaps Sofia is part of all of these women. Growing up she was in a way a princess in Francis's kingdom. On his sets she was treated as the adored daughter of the boss, a child of a celebrity. She was not seen as a thinking, feeling person with her own identity and acute perceptions. As a child she attended many different schools in the locations where Francis worked. She went to private schools in the Philippines, Los Angeles, Tulsa and New York. In between she went to public school in what was then a small farming community, the Napa Valley. She was perceived as a special person, a rich celebrity kid (even though we were in and out of bankruptcy court more than once). In high school in St. Helena she was the only child who had traveled so extensively, was so intensely interested in fashion—she interned a summer at the studio of Chanel in Paris—had strong interests and opinions about music, art, literature. Then her oldest brother died and indelibly set her apart. Sorrow and isolation can be crippling. Sofia worked hard to survive and to develop herself, and has grown to weave reflections of her experience into her films.

The lunch break was called at 10:00 p.m. A meal lifts everyone's spirits. The food is a vast array, as only the French provide on location, freshly prepared in a portable kitchen. It is set in a large dining tent furnished with a wood floor and picnic tables. There are always four hot entrées. There is a buffet table 30 feet long filled with salads of every kind, there are platters of pickled herring, cold shrimp, steamed salmon, periwinkles, pâtés, then a huge selection of cheeses and finally at least a dozen different desserts and a selection of fresh fruits. On each picnic dining table there is a bottle of red wine. When I noticed it on the first day of shooting I was startled and asked about it. The answer: "It is part of the union contract. It is required by law to have wine on the table." And it's quite good quality. There is also white wine and beer available next to the espresso machine. Of course in the U.S. it would be illegal to serve alcoholic beverages at a meal for a film crew.

After dinner we walked to a new location for a night scene, an outdoor summer evening party. A long table was set in the grass under a fancy canopy. The theme was all white, white flowers, white food such as white asparagus, cauliflower, meringues on white china with white damask table linens, champagne and white candles. When Sofia saw it she said, "I know that's what I said in the script but it's too much." Subtle colors in flowers and food were added. I am always amazed by the way the various departments come up with changes when they are needed at the last minute.

I could see electrical cords swarming around the set, powering heaters hidden under the table to warm the actors on this chilly night and power the lights. The cables were connected to a generator in the distance. A huge white balloon, illuminated from within, was raised into the air to create the appearance of moonlight.

The actors took their places and the work began. The scene was illustrating Marie's penchant for extravagant partying. Everyone was cold and tired but when Sofia said, "Action" the actors sprang to life having a riotous time, eating and drinking, playing games and finally dancing on the table top. All the electric lighting cables in the wet grass made the sound system for my camera hiss and I was unable to shoot. I had to stop working but I somehow couldn't leave my child out there in the cold and drive home to my warm apartment. I borrowed a jacket and stayed, shivering, until she wrapped.

The film finished on May 28th at 5:35 a.m. on location at Château de Pontchartrain, outside of Paris. Kirsten was the last cast member shooting, all the rest had finished in previous days. She said, "When I read the script I never really realized that I'd be working every day!" My camera caught her with Sofia, Lance, Ross and the crew through popping champagne corks. Sofia and I hugged. She said excitedly, "Mom, can you believe we finished on time and on budget!"

Fiona and I were driven home as light spread up from the horizon and over the countryside. When we reached Paris the sky was turning pale blue. In the apartment I sat on the sofa looking out across the river watching turrets on the roof of the police building turn from silhouettes to slate gray. I could feel my body releasing tension coiled in my flesh for these months, worried for Sofia, for the huge project she had undertaken. I wondered if Sofia's film and the emotions that went with it had been providing a shield for me to hide from facing myself, my fears about doing my own work. I couldn't sleep for several hours.

The phone rang waking me in the late afternoon. I ate a leisurely breakfast around 5:00 p.m., had a long bath and got dressed for the wrap party. The invitation said, "... have the great pleasure to invite you to celebrate the completion of principal photography of

‹‹Marie Antoinette››
Saturday, May 28, 2005
From 8:30 p.m. to 5:00 a.m.
At the Orangerie of Château de Versailles.

June 26, 2005 Napa

The tall barn doors of my studio are open. I can smell warm wild grasses and hear a woodpecker tapping industriously nearby. A small lizard has just ventured over the threshold and I've sent it scurrying back outside with nudges from my dust mop, concerned that the approaching gigantic yellow fringe would terrify it. I hate to find lizards that have starved to death under my rolling cart of pencils and paints or encounter one under a drawing I've left on the floor. I told the architect I wanted my door at ground level so I could walk straight out into nature; I didn't realize what would walk in.

Francis e-mails me several times a day from Romania, excited about a film he is preparing to shoot there in the fall. The film is called *Youth Without Youth*, from a novella by Romanian author Mircea Eliade. He is passionate about his independent production and the script he wrote which is both innovative and intellectually challenging. I am deeply thrilled that he hasn't taken a typical Hollywood studio assignment and instead is going back to his roots, making an independent film on his own terms that explores the outer reaches of his imagination.

Francis has asked me to shoot a "making of" documentary. I thought shooting on Sofia's set was my last for the family. My camera feels heavy now but he has persuaded me to pick it up again. A documentary about Francis's new film could form a bookend with *Hearts of Darkness*, show his creative process now, thirty years later. I will be with him, looking through my camera as he works, observing his adventure. And I've done something for the first time: I've asked the production manager to find a room for me with white walls and good light where I can go to draw on the days I'm not on set.

Sofia is in New York City, editing *Marie Antoinette*. We talked on the phone yesterday. "Mom, I shot so much. What if it doesn't all cut together?" I could hear the self-doubt in her voice and also the strength of her determination to continue into the unknown ahead. Roman is in Los Angeles. His partner is leaving his company, the Directors Bureau, and he is taking over. Next week a retrospective of Roman's work is being shown at the Egyptian Theater in Hollywood. Gia is working as an intern on a magazine this summer and preparing for a study abroad program in the fall. The family is well.

I returned home alone. Most of our possessions are moved back into the main house. I am getting used to living there, although half asleep the other morning I headed for the bathroom and went in the wrong direction. Familiar things are in different places. I am enjoying the fine craftsmanship although the kitchen looks too much as if it's a set for *House Beautiful;* it needs Francis to make gnocchi on the marble counter, scattering flour, spilling crushed tomatoes on the floor, roasting peppers from the garden on the burners, blackened skins sticking and crumbling across the stove top. I am trying to adjust to new technology, such as the house locking and unlocking electronically and several times locking me out. I am learning to use the state-of-the-art lighting system which turns on a "scene," a group of lights set at different levels, rather than an individual fixture. Yesterday I drove up to the site where our Tree House is being built. I watched a huge crane lift a wood form off a recently poured concrete wall. The contractor approached me with a grin: "You'll be moving in next summer."

Now I've enjoyed an hour of solitude and it's time to walk back to the house and interview a landscape gardener to replace plantings destroyed by construction surrounding the main house and meet picture-hangers to continue putting artwork back on the walls. There is a lot to do before I join Francis on location.

I'm quietly smiling about my life. The whole of it.

ACKNOWLEDGMENTS

I am fortunate to have a number of generous friends who have provided me with wisdom and insight as I've been writing over the years, but this book would not have come to completion without the essential contributions of Jean McMann, Nancy Nicholas, and Nan Talese. To them I extend my deepest gratitude.

A Note About the Author

Eleanor Coppola is an artist, documentary filmmaker, and the author of *Notes on the Making of* Apocalypse Now. She lives in Napa Valley, California.

A Note About the Type

The text of this book is set in LTC Kennerley, designed by Frederic W. Goudy in 1911 for the publisher Mitchell Kennerley. Today it is owned by the Lanston Type Company.

Goudy described the font as a "book letter with strong serifs and firm hairlines." Kennerley is one of the famed designer's best text typefaces. It was not based on historical type designs, and thus is considered an original American Classic.